Camp free in B.C.

VOLUME TWO:CENTRAL BRITISH COLUMBIA
From Trans-Canada Hwy 1, north past Hwy 16.
From the Coast Range to the Rocky Mountains.

Explored and written by Kathy & Craig Copeland
Voice in the Wilderness Press, Inc. Riondel, British Columbia

First Edition

First edition, April 1999

Published by Voice in the Wilderness Press, Inc.
P.O. Box 71, Riondel, British Columbia
Canada V0B 2B0

Typesetting / Production / Maps by C.J. Chiarizia

Cover design by Matthew Clark

Photos by Kathy and Craig Copeland

Canadian Cataloguing in Publication Data

Copeland, Craig, 1955-
Camp free in B.C.

Partial contents: v. 1, British Columbia from Trans-Canada Hwy 1 to the U.S. border, Vancouver Island to the Rocky Mountains — v. 2, Central British Columbia from Trans-Canada Hwy 1, north past Hwy 16, from the Coast Range to the Rocky Mountains.
Includes index.
ISBN 0-9698016-2-9 (v. 1) — ISBN 0-9698016-6-1 (v. 2)

1. Camping—British Columbia—Guidebooks. 2. British Columbia—Guidebooks. I. Copeland, Kathy, 1959- II. Title.
GV191.46.B7C66 1995   796.54'09711   C95-910165-9

Printed and Bound in Canada by Transcontinental Printing

Over 50% recycled paper
including 100% post
consumer fibre

ACKNOWLEDGEMENTS

First, we thank you. We appreciate anyone who's adventurous enough to buy this book and get out in the wilds and use it.

We also thank both our parents. They continue to be understanding about our love of exploration, even though it keeps us from visiting them often.

And we thank each other. To create *Camp Free*, we endured arduously long drives on rough roads; days without exercise, showers or proper meals; arguments incited by discomfort and close quarters; the endless recording of niggling details, when we just wanted to cut loose; then months of sitting indoors, writing, while we ached to be outside. Each of us is deeply grateful for the other's extreme perseverance.

CONTENTS

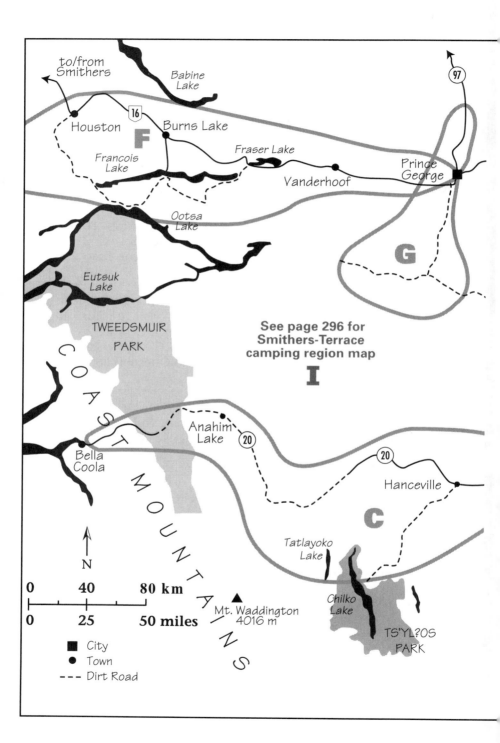

to/from
Smithers

Babine
Lake

16

Houston

F

Burns Lake

Fraser Lake

97

Francois
Lake

Vanderhoof

Prince
George

Ootsa
Lake

G

Eutsuk
Lake

TWEEDSMUIR
PARK

**See page 296 for
Smithers-Terrace
camping region map**

I

C
O
A
S
T

Anahim
Lake

20

Bella
Coola

20

Hanceville

C

M
O
U
N
T
A
I
N
S

Tatlayoko
Lake

N

0   40   80 km

0   25   50 miles

▲
Mt. Waddington
4016 m

Chilko
Lake

TS'YL?OS
PARK

■ City
● Town
- - - Dirt Road

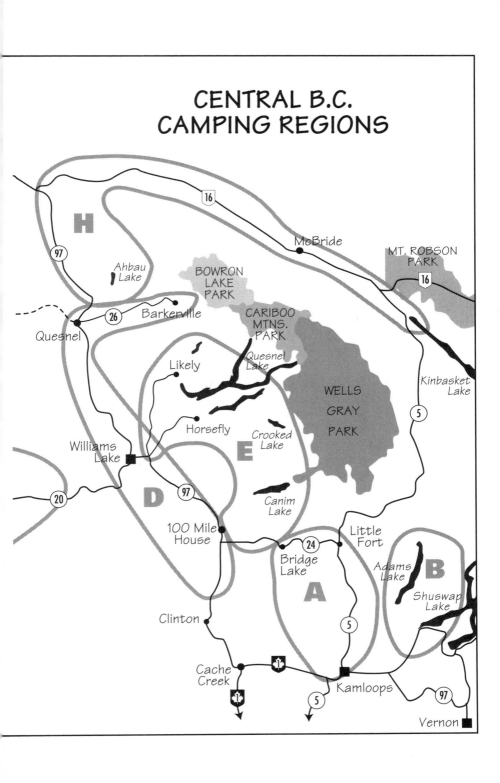

CENTRAL B.C.
CAMPING REGIONS

Philosophy, Strategies and Joys of Camping Free

British Columbia has more than 1,400 free campgrounds.

THE ANTIDOTE FOR CIVILIZATION

British Columbia has more than 1,400 free campgrounds—tucked into immense forests, in the shadows of noble mountains, beside dancing rivers, snuggled up to lakes grand and petite.

A few of these campgrounds are big, organized, groomed, much like provincial parks and nearly as popular. Others are tiny, rough hewn, seldom visited, almost certain to offer you solitude. Many are hidden just a short distance off paved roads. Some are deep in the woods. And most are free. Open year-round. No reservations required. They're provided by the B.C. Forest Service. Once you buy a low-cost, annual Camping Pass, you can pull into any of these campgrounds whenever you like. Just pick your site and camp. Only a handful of the most heavily-used campgrounds require a minimal per-night fee to help cover higher maintenance costs.

En route to any of these campgrounds, you'll savour a fresh perspective on the stunning geography of our glorious province. You'll be astonished at where B.C.'s seemingly endless network of backroads can take you. Just getting your tires off the pavement is fun. Though there's a lot to see from the highways, there's much more beyond. Even with *Camp Free's* detailed directions, you'll feel the excitement of discovery.

Nearly all these campgrounds are away from towns and highways, so you'll likely glimpse one of the locals: perhaps an owl or a coyote; maybe a bear or a moose. Even the common sight of a deer or a salmon can thrill and comfort, reminding you that despite the damage done, wilderness still exists and nature is alive and well. That's the joy of free-camping. Not just what you keep in your wallet, but what you take away in your heart.

Camping is CPR for your senses. It opens your eyes to the night sky, with stars so thick they look like clouds. It opens your ears to the music of wind in the trees, water rushing over rocks, or maybe absolute silence. It reacquaints you with the simple, sweet pleasure of not feeling cement under foot, not being confined by fences or walls, not complying with rules, and sometimes not having to look at another human being. It's the antidote for civilization.

Taltzen Lake, near Smithers

And *free* camping is *real* camping. It's an adventure—something sadly missing from most people's lives and impossible to find at commercial campgrounds. Neon signs? Reception offices? Pop machines? Hook-ups? TV antennas? Where's the adventure in that? It's hard to tell many campgrounds from RV dealerships these days. They're just parking lots. Even provincial-park campgrounds are often within earshot of a roaring highway.

You'll forgo conveniences at the campgrounds described in *Camp Free*. None have showers, flush toilets, or even running water. But what most people consider necessities are actually luxuries. Doing without can make you feel more complete. And camping, by definition, means contending with the elements— bugs, wind, rain, cold, heat. But if you're prepared and can shrug off minor discomfort, the elements can make you feel more alive.

If you go with an open mind and soft heart, *Camp Free* will guide you to a rousing experience. You'll be revitalized, able to calmly slip back into the shackles of civilization with renewed vigor. Your memory, your mental gallery, will be filled with vivid images—sustenance for the soul until your next outing. At the very least, you'll have a story to tell neighbours and co-workers who've never sought adventure beyond the nearest video store.

GET OUT WHILE YOU CAN

Twenty-five years ago, free-camping was so easy that a guidebook was unnecessary. A short drive from any city would reward you with lots of beautiful places to park where nobody would bother you. But rampant development and population growth have overtaken those of us who would flee. Now you have to drive hours, and still you'll be contending with country homes, resorts, farms and ranches that make it almost impossible to free-camp—unless you know where to go.

That's why we wrote this book: to tell you about B.C.'s extensive network of free Forest Service (FS) campgrounds, explain exactly where they are and how to get there, and encourage you to enjoy and protect them.

The need for a guidebook on free B.C. campgrounds became apparent to us in 1994. Although we'd traveled throughout the province for years, not until then did we stumble upon a free campground on the Nahatlatch River, west of Fraser Canyon. A few months later we found more free campgrounds along the Chilliwack River, in the Lower Mainland. We gave thanks to the Camping God. Then it struck us. During all our explorations, we were unaware of these free campgrounds; other people must be too. Our journey to create *Camp Free* had begun.

Too many people struggle to find places to pitch their tent or park their RV for a night without having to pay excessively for the privilege. Having camped in all kinds of weird, noisy, uncomfortable spots, we know the frustration. Many of those nights, we now realize, could have been far more pleasant, because established, free campgrounds were only minutes away. Today, we still see others repeating our mistakes. Near Sugar Lake, for example, we met a young European couple vacationing with their two kids, traveling across B.C. in a rented motorhome. They parked overnight at a pullout, just off the pavement, next to an ugly gravel pit. They settled for such a dismal spot because it was late, they were tired, and no other option was obvious. Too bad. Just across the highway, an unsigned, dirt road led to an official, free campground. Surrounded by trees, next to the Shuswap River, it was only a kilometer away. Had they known, they would have been safer and enjoyed their stay infinitely more.

With *Camp Free* in hand, you're now a fully-informed camper. This is the most comprehensive guide available to B.C.'s free campgrounds. But get out while you can. Camping is increasingly popular. Most campgrounds are being visited more frequently. Economic pressures have decreased FS budgets. The result: camping in B.C. is not as free as it once was, and that trend could continue.

At a few of the busiest campgrounds, the FS now charges a minimal per-night fee. It supplements the cost of garbage removal, pit-toilet pumping, and access improvement. Occasionally it helps pay for a patrol to keep the peace, or a repair necessitated by vandalism. And while the vast majority of free campgrounds remain free—no toll-boxes, no money-collecting hosts—the *right* to camp free is no longer gratis. The provincial government now asks that you buy a Camping Pass. All funds raised by Camping Pass sales go directly to campground maintenance. The annual Camping Pass costs $27 (1999) and is valid for an entire year beginning in spring. It allows you and your family (or a group of up to six friends) unlimited, free use of more than 1,400 FS campgrounds throughout the province. At the 30 or so campgrounds that charge per night, the annual Camping Pass entitles you to a 50% discount. Camping Passes are available at sporting goods stores and government agent offices. Or you can use the form in the back of this book to receive your Camping Pass by mail. It's a bargain even if you camp only a few times each summer. And it will help ensure that the campgrounds themselves remain forever free.

THE MAP IS NOT THE TERRITORY

Free campgrounds are rarely on paved roads. Signs announcing free campgrounds are never on paved roads. Only after you drive onto a backroad will you encounter a sign, typically *way* after. You might see signposts at the campgrounds. Even some campgrounds are unsigned. For these reasons, *Camp Free* is invaluable.

A highway sign like this could indicate the Forest Service road you're looking for is just ahead.

Researching *Camp Free*, we relied on FS Recreation Maps. Though helpful, they lack detail. They don't indicate the numerous switchbacks and junctions you'll encounter. They rarely label the roads that lead to campgrounds and don't specify where to turn off the highway. Using FS maps, we were reminded: the map is not the territory. And commercially published map books are little better. They too require the skills of an explorer and the instincts of a detective.

A sign or signpost marks the entry to many Forest Service campgrounds.

So, during field trips, we were often on edge. "How much farther?" "This can't be the right road." "Think we'll make it?" "No way there's a campground up here." Sometimes we felt like rats in a maze. But you won't. Following *Camp Free's* precise directions, you can relax and enjoy the drive knowing you *are* on the right road, your vehicle *can* make it, and there *is* a campground up there.

Camp Free is the only resource you need to find most of B.C.'s free campgrounds. FS Recreation Maps, however, can broaden your perspective. Call or visit the FS offices for the districts you'll be exploring. Ask if maps are available. The phone numbers and addresses are in the back of this book.

YOU'LL KNOW BEFORE YOU GO

Camp Free not only gives you directions to the campgrounds, it tells you what to expect when you arrive. How's the scenery? Is the area quiet or noisy? What outdoor activities are possible? Now you'll know before you go.

Example of the excellent Forest Service campgrounds throughout B.C.

Camp Free even rates each campground. Is it a worthwhile **destination** for an extended stay? Good enough for a **weekend** visit? Or useful only as an **overnight** pullout on your way to someplace else? *Camp Free* goes beyond the facts, offering opinions based on widely-accepted, common-sense criteria.

To help you confidently turn off major highways and forge onto dirt backroads, *Camp Free* states the distance to each campground and the quality of the road. **Easy** means it's a short way and the road is good. **Moderate** means it's 15 to 20 minutes from pavement, or the road is only fair. **Difficult** means it's a long way or the road is poor. Road surfaces, however, change over time—usually for the worse—so make your own assessment before proceeding.

Every campground in this book should be accessible in a two-wheel-drive (2WD) low-clearance car. *Camp Free* warns you where conditions could necessitate four-wheel-drive (4WD) or a high-clearance vehicle. *Camp Free* also advises big-rig pilots (motorhomes, 5th-wheels, trailers) if the access road might be troublesome, or the campground too small.

TURN LEFT AT THE BOULDER

"Any chance I'll get lost?" you ask.

Very little. *Camp Free* gives explicit directions that should make sense to you now, and will become perfectly clear en route. "Turn left at the boulder" will be a no-brainer once you're out there, in the shadow of a looming boulder the size of a house.

The forests and ex-forests of B.C. conceal a bird's nest of inter-laced dirt roads totaling more than 32,000 kilometers (20,000 miles). With only rudimentary FS maps to work with, the task of unsnarling all the details severely challenged our endurance and sanity. We believe we calculated all our meanderings accurately. We certainly gave it a supreme effort. But it's possible we goofed without knowing.

On the road, if the book seems unclear or you feel uncertain, try to bear with the directions. The description should be adequate to steer you to the campground regardless of a minor error. Look for the stated landmarks. Be intuitive. Poke your nose around the next corner. You'll find it. Remember: free-camping is an adventure. And when you get home, please mail, e-mail, or fax us your suggested corrections.

Find out what's happening. Do something about it.

YOU CAN MAKE A DIFFERENCE

The roads to most free campgrounds in B.C. are logging roads. Though logging practices have been irresponsible in the past, keep in mind these campgrounds wouldn't be there, so you probably wouldn't either, if logging companies hadn't built the roads. Ideally, the great wild lands of B.C. would be unscarred, preserved in their original majesty forever. Now the best we can do is get out there and look after what's left. It's a lazy king who never leaves the castle to survey his domain. Just be prepared for disappointment: your forests have been logged rapaciously.

Environmental integrity. Scenic value. Future viability. When you see a clearcut, it's hard to believe any of these were considerations. The good news is that improved forestry practices are helping to sustain our forests and save forestry jobs. But we all need to stand guard. An informed public is an empowered public. If you don't know or care enough to hold logging companies and the Ministry of Forests responsible for their actions, who will? Just by exploring the backroads, you can make a difference.

GO GIRL!

Many single women are afraid to camp alone. Perhaps you're among them. If so, your fear is understandable. But the following observations and suggestions should help ratchet your fear down to a reasonable level of concern. Because the reality is that you *can* safely enjoy solo camping at FS campgrounds. If you're drawn to the wilds, go girl! Don't limit yourself to walks in the city park. You'll probably find camping is actually safer. The worst that's likely to befall you is an onslaught of mosquitoes, or a cookie-coveting squirrel.

FS campgrounds are frequented primarily by couples and families. More travellers from across Canada and even from Europe are also now camping in B.C. They'll all be your neighbours while you're out there. Campers are generally kind, trustworthy, peaceful and likable. They're nature lovers, just like you. Most are happy to converse if you approach them but will otherwise respect your privacy. If you've never camped alone, on your first trip you'll probably make a comforting discovery: you're *not* alone.

When they notice you don't have a companion, other campers—usually a chivalrous, older gentleman—might approach and offer to be of service. "Need help starting that fire?" "Want a hand stringing up your tarp?" Don't assume they're chauvinists who doubt your competence. Such acts are almost always genuinely benevolent. If you welcome assistance, accept the offer. If you decline, be tactful and appreciative.

Common sense dictates that a single woman be cautious and vigilant. But that's true anywhere, not just camping. We all have to be somewhat on guard until we've assessed whatever situation we're entering. Here's how single women can do that at campgrounds:

• When reading *Camp Free* and choosing a campground, note what other campgrounds and towns are nearby and how to reach them. That way you'll already have a plan in case you're later unnerved and decide to move.

• Arrive before nightfall so you can see the campground and other campers. Drive slowly through before picking a campsite. The presence of other women, even in a mixed group, is heartening, because they tend to be a calming influence. Try to camp near them.

• If the campground is empty, and you like solitude, stay. If others arrive after dark, listen and observe intently. Get a sense for who they are and how you feel about them. Trust your instincts. If the newcomers seem rude or belligerent, if their behaviour puts you on edge, quickly and quietly pack and leave.

• While settling in, talk to your fellow campers. Ask them questions about the lake, the stream, other campgrounds they recommend, anything to get them talking and revealing themselves. Establish a bond with just one couple and you'll relax. They'll probably comment on your solo status. If not, tell them you're on your own. It will heighten their awareness on your behalf.

After thoroughly assessing the situation, even if you feel at ease about camping alone, take these precautions:

• Sleep in your vehicle. It's safer than a tent. It will reduce your anxiety and allow you a better night's rest. A van is ideal, because you can move from bed to the driver's seat without exiting. A truck and camper (or shell) is good too. Some cars, particularly wagons, have enough space for a bed if you fold down the rear seat.

• Keep a canister of pepper spray handy but concealed. Its intended use is stopping a charging bear, so you can imagine how effective it would be against a mere human. Cayenne pepper, highly irritating to the nose and eyes, is the active ingredient. Without causing permanent injury, it disables the aggressor long enough to let you escape. Obviously, it's a last-resort defense. Use it only if you believe you're at serious risk. You can buy pepper spray—possibly labeled Bearguard, Counter Assault, OC-10, or Phazer—at outdoor stores.

During all our years camping in B.C., we've never met anyone scary or suspicious. We've never felt threatened or perceived any danger. That should reassure you. It's inevitable that you'll

After a long backroad tour, you'll appreciate that you can wash your vehicle in most central B.C. towns.

react negatively to someone. Shabby clothes, a gruff voice, questionable hygiene—something will put you off. But our initial harsh judgments have repeatedly been shattered after a brief conversation reveals a gentle, caring soul beneath the stereotype. We hope your encounters will be equally positive.

HITTING THE DIRT

Inexperienced on backroads? Consider these suggestions before you hit the dirt. A little preparation can increase your confidence and safety.

• Carry more food and water than you think you'll need for your camping trip, in case of emergency. A first-aid kit is also a wise addition.

• Check your vehicle's fuel supply and engine fluid levels before leaving the highway.

• Always drive with your headlights on—even during daylight hours.

Drive defensively. You can encounter a speeding logging truck anytime, anywhere.

• Drive cautiously. You never know who's coming or what's up ahead. It's possible the road has been damaged recently by severe weather or other natural hazards.

• Be patient. Keep your speed moderate, unless the road is clearly flat and straight for a long way. Even then, holes or rocks might surprise you.

• Slow down on washboard roads. Go too fast and your dashboard will clack like a player piano. Worse, you could lose traction and slide out of control as your vehicle hops from one ripple to the next.

• Avoid the middle of the road. Always cling to the right side. Even if you haven't seen another vehicle for hours, one could appear at the worst possible moment. On dirt, reduced traction makes vehicles less responsive.

• Never block the road. If you stop, pull far enough off to allow industrial vehicles to pass at high speed.

• Yield to logging trucks or other industrial vehicles. As soon as you see one (a cloud of dust is a sure indicator) pull as far over as possible and let it proceed.

• Obey all posted restrictions. Some active logging roads are closed to the public from 5 a.m. Monday until 8 p.m. Friday. Don't be tempted to sneak in. The closure is for your own safety. Monster logging trucks are belting down those roads.

• Don't let the logging companies' warning signs scare you off the roads. Except when the

Don't let the signs scare you away. Just drive safely.

area is specifically closed to the public between certain hours, they're just telling you to be aware and drive safely. Sometimes you'll see lots of signs. It can be intimidating. But it doesn't mean you'll be fighting your way upstream against a constant flow of industrial traffic.

TWO-WHEELING IT

Driving a low-clearance 2WD car or RV? Don't worry. The roads in this book shouldn't present any serious obstacles. But if you encounter a stretch of rough, challenging road, these suggestions might help.

• Before leaving home, look at your vehicle's underbelly. Get on your knees and really see what's down there. Make note of where you have the least clearance and where you have the most, so you'll know how to straddle rocks.

• When the road looks questionable, it's often the grit of the driver, not the vehicle itself, that determines whether you'll make it. That's not to say you should be bull-headed and plow through come what may. When you assess the road, just be aware of your level of confidence and your capacity for patience.

No need to check this one with a stick.

• Faced with deeply worn tracks on the sides of the road, and a high ridge in the middle that might scrape your underbelly, drive with one tire on the ridge and the other outside the track.

• When there's a deep rut across the road, don't approach it straight on. You might bottom-out. Instead, slice across at an angle, from one side of the road toward the other. That way your tires drop into the rut one at a time, instead of both at once.

• Before you splash through a big mud hole, get out and check how deep it is. Feel with a stick, or drop a large stone in and see what happens. That's a lot easier than getting stuck.

• In mud or sand, don't slow to a crawl. You need momentum. To avoid getting stuck, it's often best to proceed and hope the road surface improves. If you're not stuck yet, but it appears you will be, reverse out immediately. Trying to turn around can land you in a bigger mess. When fishtailing, straighten your vehicle by turning the front wheels in the direction your rear wheels are sliding.

• Know what you're risking. Ask yourself: "How many vehicles have been on the road today? What's the likelihood of seeing another? How far back is the highway? The last possible telephone? The nearest lived-in-looking house?" Consider your worst-case options before you plunge in. It might sway your decision.

HELP IS ON THE WAY

Concerned about being stranded in the outback? Don't be. Help is probably on the way. Though some roads in this book might seem desolate, they're not. You can usually expect someone to come along within an hour. A few locals and outdoorspeople are always wandering the backcountry. You'll often encounter logging company employees in pickup trucks. If necessary, signal them to stop; you'll find they're friendly and glad to assist. If your vehicle konks out, wave down a logging truck; they all have radios and can call for help.

MEN IN TRUCKS KNOW

Reading *Camp Free* should relieve you of asking anyone for directions. But when you explore backroads other than those described here, you'll probably want to check your bearings with someone. Before you do, a word of caution: assume nothing.

Be very specific when asking for directions. State the names of roads, geographic features, or other landmarks. Be certain you're both talking about the same thing. Rely on your intuition as much as anyone else's opinion—even a local who should know the area. It's alarming how many people are unaware of what's beyond their backyard.

Many rough access roads like this one are passable in a 2WD car, if the driver is careful and patient.

Look for men in trucks. That's not a chauvinistic stereotype, that's reality. Men in trucks usually dispense reliable information. They tend to ply the backroads to earn their living, or at least to hunt and fish. So if you're a man, you're in a truck, and you don't know, you better find out, because here they come.

HOW'S THE ROAD?

Stop four drivers on the same road and you'll get four different impressions of what it's like. Ask "How's the road?" and you'll often hear "It's gravel." Unless you're driving a rugged truck, a 4WD vehicle, or an old beater you don't care about, that's too vague. If you want a detailed road report, ask specific questions. How rough is the road? How steep? How narrow? How muddy? How rocky?

Locals who frequent the backroads are generally quick and direct with their answers. But before you heed anyone's advice, consider the source. Do they seem sensible and mature? Inexperienced and timid? Wild and reckless?

Some four-wheelers are determined to uphold the macho mystique of their off-road rigs. They consider cars an inferior subspecies, little more than go-carts. They would eye ours with disdain and say, "I wouldn't try it in *that*." Then they'd leave us in a cloud of dust, and we'd slowly pick our way through the rocks and potholes until we reached our destination.

Others tried to be open-minded. After scrutinizing our car, one fellow said, "Well, if you go slow, you'll probably make it. But there's a lot of sharp rocks. You better have a good set of spare tires." That sounded like an accurate road-condition summary. And it was. Our car survived, but we hated it and decided you would too, so it's not in the book.

Even when the road looked questionable to us, people were usually encouraging. "Aw, you'll be fine," they said. "Just take 'er easy. Lots of people make it. There's big RVs in there." They were right.

Listen to opinions, then decide for yourself. The power to propel you through a difficult patch is probably in your head, regardless of what's under your hood. Technique and determination will take you surprisingly far. And if the road gets too hairy, just turn around. There's always someplace else to explore.

BEYOND CAMP FREE

This is not a comprehensive guidebook. B.C. has hundreds of free campgrounds not described in *Camp Free*. Some are too far off main highways. We recognize there's a limit to most people's tolerance for dusty, rocky, bouncy backroads. And some final-access roads are forbiddingly rough. If you need 4WD and a kidney belt to get there, it's not in the book.

Few campgrounds listed in *Camp Free Volume I* are more than 30 km (18 mi) from pavement. Central B.C. has a more extensive backroad network and longer chains of remote campgrounds, so *Camp Free Volume II* describes full-day excursions off pavement.

If you have a burly vehicle and a questing mind, call or visit the FS office for the district you'll be exploring. They're listed in the back of this book. Ask if a recreation map is available. If so, it will help you find campgrounds beyond *Camp Free*.

With Camp Free *you'll avoid crowds like this at commercial and provincial-park campgrounds.*

When you see someone sacked out on the roadside, kindly suggest they buy this book.

GUERILLA CAMPING

It's late. You're tired. You're nowhere near an official, free camp-ground. You're also unaware of any commercial campgrounds in the area, but you don't want to pay to camp anyway. And you prefer to avoid hotels.

It's still possible to camp free.

Sniffing out places to free-camp is a skill you can develop. As you become proficient, you'll only pay to camp when you're desperate for a shower. Even then, you can just pay for the shower and camp free elsewhere. Unless the land is all fenced off or way too steep, or you absolutely must stop immediately, you probably don't have to pay to camp.

The free-camping spots you find on your own, however, might not be great places to hang around the next morning. They'll likely be adequate only for a night's sleep, nothing more. And it's much easier if you have a vehicle you can sleep in—at least the back of a truck or the bed of a mini-van. It's hard to find places you can safely, comfortably pitch a tent for free.

So what we're really talking about here is creative parking. We call it guerilla camping. It's the only way to cope with all the NO CAMPING signs that have appeared on public land during the last few years.

Is there a conspiracy to make us all pay to sleep? It's unwarranted. Campers who pull off the road for a night, whether they sleep in their vehicles or bravely pitch their tents, rarely harm the land or other people. They're just sleeping! If they're allowed to park there all day, why not at night? What's the harm?

Beat the system. Be a guerilla camper. The following questions will help you assess where and when. Just don't violate people's property rights. If you know it's private, don't camp without asking permission. And always respect the land. Never trash it. As a thank-you for a night's sleep, leave it cleaner than you found it.

What are the options? Be open-minded. Use your imagination. How far you must stretch your thinking depends on where you've free-camped before, what you consider safe, and how bold you are. Some people are audacious. They'll camp anywhere it's wide enough to pull a vehicle off the road. But you can also be a stealth camper, cautiously choosing tranquil, secretive locations.

What's your sense of the place? Does it feel inviting, or creepy? Trust your instinct. If it looks clean, you know people don't park there to drink and party. If it makes you feel vulnerable, that feeling will only grow with every noise you hear. You'll lie awake in the dark, straining to detect anything suspicious. A passing car will slow down and you'll be on edge until it's gone. That's not a good night's sleep. That's miserable. Find another spot where you can relax.

Is it secluded enough? Before you decide to stay, consider what might awaken you later. Are bright lights shining nearby? What's the noise level? How many cars or pedestrians are passing by? Even if you've pulled off what seems like a little-used road, sit there for ten minutes to gauge the traffic before you settle in for the night; you might be surprised.

Will you harm the land? Guerilla camping isn't crashing your way into places you shouldn't be. It's gliding in at night, then slipping out in the morning, without leaving a trace. Vegetation, even grass, should be left intact. Harm nothing, take nothing, leave nothing. If that's not possible, move on.

Have you tried residential areas? If you can sleep in your vehicle, you might feel safer parked in a town near homes, rather than on a road that's lonely but still close to civilization. Just outside a town, you're within range of malicious teenagers or other suspicious characters, and somewhat defenseless against them. In town, on a quiet, dark, residential street, it's unlikely you'll be hassled, because help is just a horn-honk away.

In a neighbourhood, never intrude on anyone's privacy. Try not to park directly in front of a house. You'll be less obvious beside a field or vacant lot. Ideally you won't be noticed. A resident who peeks out a window should assume you're guests of a neighbour.

Compared to urbanites, people in small towns are generally less jumpy about unfamiliar parked cars. Live and let live seems to be the rural attitude. Plus, small towns have fewer parking restrictions and often no police to enforce them.

Are you arriving late enough so you won't be noticed? At residential streets, university grounds, and hospital or church parking lots, the later you arrive the better your chances of an uninterrupted night. You want to be situated so you're inconspicuous—where it's normal to see a few cars parked overnight, but not many. If you're noticed, it shouldn't occur to anyone that you're sleeping in your vehicle. That means you have to finish cooking and arranging your bed elsewhere, before you park. You'll also have to depart early. By 7:30 a.m. you'll probably attract someone's attention, but at that point it might not matter.

If you're noticed, will anyone care? This is highly subjective. Parked close to anything of obvious importance or value, near any potential object of theft or vandalism, someone will probably care if they notice you. That means they might wake you up and tell you to move, which is always a pain and can be scary. It's better to invest a little more time finding a spot where nobody will care if they suspect you're sacked out.

You don't know B.C. until you've visited its far-flung communities. Camp Free *will get you there.*

RESPECT OTHER CAMPERS

Most people live cheek-by-jowl with their neighbors back home. They want a little privacy when they go camping. So don't barge in on someone who already occupies the limited space at a small campground. Make sure there's plenty of room for one more.   If you can't leave a buffer between your camp and others, and there's still daylight left to look elsewhere, please go. If it's late and you decide to stay, be as quiet as a deer mouse. Speak softly and ready yourself for sleep without commotion.

If you're the captain of a fully-equipped motorhome, please consider the rest of us before firing up your generator. Several times that wicked racket has forced us to pack and move late at night. Recognize that your generator, though a convenience to you, is a nuisance to others. It shatters what many of us cherish most about camping: peace. Make sure your system is fully charged before you arrive at a campground. If you must run your generator, do it midday when fellow-campers are most active. Everyone will appreciate that.

Some Neanderthals don't just go camping, they go wild—bellowing at each other, roaring with laughter, blasting stereos, letting their kids rampage. It's rude and obnoxious—night or day. Then there's the couple, inexperienced at backing their trailer into a campsite, who arrives late. The wife shouts directions for fifteen minutes while the husband rocks and rolls the rig. If any of these descriptions sound like you, please be quieter and more considerate.

Because of rowdy, disrespectful campers, a few campgrounds now charge a "keep the peace" fee to employ live-in attendants during summer. They make sure everyone's quiet after 10 p.m. It solves the late-night noise problem but degrades the camping experience and burdens you with an expense. Help prevent it from happening elsewhere.

CAMPGROUND DIPLOMACY

What should you do when Roseanne and family pull into the campsite next to yours and start screaming? Or worse, when Beavis, Butthead and friends crank up the stereo, intent on partying? (1) Don't assume the noise will stop or the offenders will leave. And don't rely on subtle hints to express your feelings. Be very upfront. Talk to them, or the situation and your anger will escalate. (2) Don't shout at them from your site. Walk over and calmly explain the problem. Maybe they were unaware you were bothered. A simple statement might solve it. (3) Kindly but firmly suggest a specific action. Don't be obnoxious, insulting, or demanding; it will only make them defensive. (4) If it's obvious that diplomacy won't work, move—to another campsite farther away, or to another campground if necessary. Yes, it's unfair. But the misery of enduring a joyless day or sleepless night is worse than the hassle of leaving.

BE REVERENT

Reverence is achingly absent from the world today. And if there's anyplace we can and should feel reverent, it's out in nature. Reverence is simply being aware of and respecting life in all its manifestations, including our forests, meadows, rivers and lakes. What you revere, you care for.

Most FS campgrounds are *User Maintained.* No trash cans. No garbage trucks. No cleaning crews. It's your responsibility to pick up after yourself. That's largely why all these campgrounds are free, and why the annual Camping Pass is modestly priced.

If campgrounds are trashed and abused, the price of the Camping Pass will increase. If maintenance costs mount, you'll eventually be slapped with an entry fee at every campground. Most of us can't imagine leaving garbage at a campsite or damaging the already minimal facilities. Please help spread that ethic.

Always carry a few extra garbage bags. If previous campers left anything behind, you can pick it up. You'll be doing your share of user maintenance. And anyone observing you will see reverence in action.

Always haul out your garbage.

Whenever trash is left, even in a fire pit, it encourages others to assume they can add to the mess. So take a few minutes to fill up your garbage bag. On your way home, drop it in a dumpster, preferably in a city. Small towns have limited garbage capacity and infrequent pickups.

Anything campers leave behind is trash. Orange and banana peels take years to biodegrade, and animals won't eat them. Cigarette butts are even worse. Smokers have been allowed to assume butts don't qualify as litter. It's time to change that. They give campgrounds a dirty, ravaged look that saddens and disgusts most campers. Never leave your cigarette butts at a campground. It's easy to haul them away with the rest of your trash.

In general, leave as little impact as possible. For example, you'll find more fire rings than are necessary at most campgrounds. If you light a campfire, use an existing ring so you don't further scar the land. Burn only small pieces of deadfall. The foliage is part of the scenery; don't destroy it for firewood. Be sure your fire is stone-cold dead before you leave or go to sleep. Also, never wash dishes near a lake or stream. Use a plastic basin, then dump the waste water in thick brush, well away from campsites. Always use biodegradable soap.

Wouldn't it be refreshing to arrive at a campground and find no evidence anyone had camped there before you? Do it for the next campers. Maybe someone will do it for you.

PRACTICAL STUFF

This is a how-to-get-there guidebook, not a how-to-do-it manual. You've probably camped many times and know what you need to take on a camping trip. It's not like backpacking, where you can haul only so much and you're a long way from a road. This is *car* camping. You can take whatever you want, or as much as your vehicle can hold. So, if you're not sure, just bring it. The more you camp, the better you'll get at keeping your load light and compact, without forgetting necessities. Until then, this list of practical stuff might be helpful.

• **Water.** Bring plenty. You'll almost never find a potable water source at a free campground.

• **Toilet paper, trowel, plastic bag.** FS campgrounds are basic, often referred to as primitive or rustic. Most have outhouses, which are usually stocked with toilet paper but not always. Bring a spare roll. Unofficial free campgrounds and overnight pullouts have no facilities whatsoever. There you'll need a trowel to bury your poop, and a plastic bag to hold used toilet paper.

• **Garbage bags.** Bring one for all your trash, and another to pick up after other campers less considerate than you.

• **Stove, fuel, matches.** Firewood might not be available. Besides, cooking over an open fire is difficult, time consuming and wasteful. Keep extra matches or a lighter in your vehicle.

• **Can Opener.** Ever try to open a can with a rock?

• **Flashlight and extra batteries.** You'll never see Tiki torches lining a cement walkway to a "comfort station" at a free campground. If you let your eyes adjust to the dark, it's surprising how well you can see without a flashlight. But there are times you'll need one.

B.C. STANDS FOR BEAR COUNTRY

The moment you leave any of B.C.'s major cities, you're in bear country. You can encounter a bruin anytime, anywhere—not just on remote hiking trails. Black bears are a common sight on backroads, even on some highways. Grizzly sightings are less frequent but always a possibility.

That doesn't mean bears are lurking behind every bush, stalking you, ready to pounce. They usually avoid human contact. They're generally calm, passive, shy. So don't be bearanoid. Just be practical.

Avoid inviting bears into your camp. Their strongest sense is smell, so never leave food untended. After you eat, keep leftovers sealed in plastic bags and containers, locked in your vehicle. At night, don't even leave your cooler out.

When walking, stay alert and make noise so you won't surprise a bear. Given sufficient warning, they'll usually depart before you see them. If startled, their instinctive response could be aggressive.

If you see a bear, don't look it in the eyes; it might think you're challenging it. Never run. Be still. If you must move, do it in

Keep your campsite clean. Food odours attract bears. This one's a grizzly.

slow motion. Bears are more likely to attack if you flee, and they're fast, much faster than humans. A grizzly can outsprint a racehorse. And it's a myth that bears can't run downhill. They're also capable swimmers. Remember: it's highly unlikely you'll provoke an attack as long as you stay calm, retreat slowly, and make soothing sounds to convey a nonthreatening presence.

What if a bear charges you?

Climbing a tree is an escape option. Some people have saved their lives this way, others have been caught in the process. Despite their ungainly appearance, bears are excellent climbers. To be out of reach of an adult bear, you'd have to climb at least 10 meters (33 feet), something few people are capable of. And you'd probably need to be at least two football fields from the bear to beat it up a tree.

Playing dead is debatable. It used to be the recommended response to a charge, but now some scientists, rangers and surviving victims say it might be better to fight back. It's your call. Every encounter involves different bears, people and circumstances, so the results vary. Even bear behaviour experts cannot suggest one all-purpose response technique. Black bears can be intimidated if you fight back. Grizzlies tend to break off

B.C. stands for Bear Country, so be alert.

their attack if you remain totally passive. But quickly identify-
ing a bear while under threat requires expertise. To learn more,
read Dave Smith's *Backcountry Bear Basics.*

Rating System for Campgrounds and Backroads

Scenery and Recreation

You'll enjoy staying longer at campgrounds with better scenery and more recreation. So that's the basis for these ratings. Just keep higher-rated campgrounds in mind for short stays too, because they're not necessarily farther from pavement.

DESTINATION
You could spend your vacation here. If it's a long drive, it's worth it. The scenery and the campground are wonderful. The recreation is excellent and varied.

WEEKEND
A couple days here might be pleasant, but any longer and you'd want a prettier campground or more impressive scenery. Recreation is available but limited.

OVERNIGHT
Stop here for a convenient place to sleep, but that's it. Don't expect anything special. Something's lacking: either the scenery or the site itself is poor to mediocre.

Note: Nearly all FS campgrounds have tables, pit toilets, and fire rings. Our descriptions warn you where these are absent. Unofficial, free campgrounds and overnight pullouts have no facilities whatsoever.

Access

At a glance, these ratings tell you the distance to the campground, the quality of the road surfaces, and the patience needed to follow the directions.

EASY
Right under your nose. Mr. Magoo could find it. The road is smooth and the distance short—usually less than 15 km (9.3 mi) from pavement.

MODERATE

Just around the corner. Probably 15 to 25 km (9.3 to 15.5 mi) from pavement. There could be a few rough stretches.

DIFFICULT

Back of beyond. You must be patient and adventurous. The navigating is difficult, the roads challenging, or the distances longer—up to 50 km (31 mi) from pavement.

Maps

In addition to the overview map of camping regions, each chapter begins with a regional map indicating campground locations. Even the regional maps, however, are for general reference only. They were simplified to help you quickly assess campground locations in relation to each other, and to determine which ones are within range. But *Camp Free's* directions are very precise and should provide you with all necessary details.

Tripometer

When you read *Set your tripometer to 0* in the directions, push the button to reset your trip odometer to 0 at that point. Odometer readings on different vehicles vary. Mechanics say this might be the result of road jostling, tires that are not the manufacturer's specified size, or an imprecise odometer. So your distances might differ slightly from those in *Camp Free*. Just be looking for the turns or landmarks near the stated distances. If you encounter a discrepancy of 0.5 km (0.3 mi) or more, we apologize. That might be an error, in which case we welcome your suggested changes.

Recreation Site Numbers

FS campgrounds are officially referred to as Recreation Sites. Each FS district numbers their sites. The numbers are printed on FS recreation maps. *Camp Free* uses these same numbers, enabling you to read FS recreation maps in conjunction with this book. If FS districts issue new recreation maps with revised numbers, then the *Camp Free* numbers will differ. But within the book, that won't matter. The numbers will still be consistent on *Camp Free* maps and route descriptions.

"Got Everything? Okay, let's go."

Directions to the Campgrounds

Occasionally, a well-signed junction will encourage you to plunge into the backcountry.

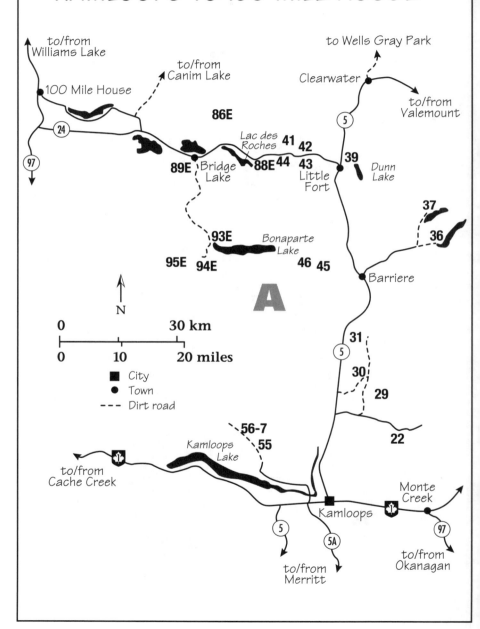

KAMLOOPS TO 100 MILE HOUSE

to/from
Williams Lake

to/from
Canim Lake

to Wells Gray Park

100 Mile House

Clearwater

86E

to/from
Valemount

5

24

Lac des
Roches 41 42

89E Bridge
Lake

88E 44 43

39

Dunn
Lake

Little
Fort

97

93E

95E 94E

Bonaparte
Lake

46 45

37

36

Barriere

A

31

5

30

29

22

N

0   30 km

0   10   20 miles

■ City
● Town
- - - Dirt road

56-7

55

Kamloops
Lake

to/from
Cache Creek

Monte
Creek

Kamloops

97

5

5A

to/from
Okanagan

to/from
Merritt

A: Kamloops to 100 Mile House

Most of these campgrounds are in **Kamloops FS District**.
E stands for **East Cariboo FS Region**.

22	Heffley Lake
29	Community Lake
30	Sullivan Lake
31	Badger Lake
36	East Barriere Lake
37	Vermelin Creek
39	Dunn Lake
41	Deer Lake
42	Goose Lake
43	Latremouille Lake
44	Long Island Lake
45	Gorman Lake
46	Allan Lake
55	Watching Creek
56	Tranquille Crossing
57	Tranquille Meadow
86E	Needa Lake
88E	Phinetta Lake
89E	Crystal Lake
93E	Bonaparte Lake
94E	Hammer Lake
95E	Scot Lake

Kamloops to 100 Mile House

NORTHWEST OF KAMLOOPS, page 36
NORTH OF KAMLOOPS, page 40
WEST ON HWY 24, page 51
SOUTH OF HWY 24, page 56
EAST ON HWY 24, page 62

Some backroads lead to lodges and private cottages, as well as campgrounds.

NORTHWEST OF KAMLOOPS

Kamloops is one city where you don't have to be cunning to camp free. Several free campgrounds are within easy range via good dirt roads. They're above the surrounding sagebrush country, in dry, open, conifer forests of big Douglas fir and Ponderosa pines. Even at night, you should have no problem reaching any of them following the directions below. But there is a drawback. The three campgrounds northwest of Kamloops—Watching Creek, Tranquille Crossing, and Tranquille Meadow—have been heavily used and abused. They're denuded, pitted, and rutted. Ranchers run cattle there, so cow pies are the dominant feature. Worn-out land caked with shit creates an atmosphere few people will be comfortable in for long. So think of these campgrounds simply as convenient places to sleep. Arrive late, leave early, and during daylight concentrate on the blue skies that are so reliable here, not on the ground underfoot.

From downtown Kamloops, you can be at Watching Creek campground in 45 minutes. The two Tranquille campgrounds are a bit farther. So, if you want to camp near the city, consider Heffley Lake (page 41). It too is just a 45-minute drive—north on Hwy 5, then east, entirely on pavement. And unlike the campgrounds northwest of Kamloops, Heffley won't creep you out. It's pleasant. It's also quite small, and the setting is surprisingly civilized, so come only for a brief overnight stay.

If you're heading south on Hwy 5 to Kamloops

Just north of Kamloops, watch for the signed and lighted turnoff to Paul Lakes Provincial Park. Across from it, turn right (west) where a green sign directs you to the North Shore and the airport. There's a Husky gas station and traffic lights at this turn.

Departing Hwy 5, follow signs for the airport. The road soon crosses railroad tracks and the North Thompson River. Several kilometers farther, bear left for the North Shore. Follow Tranquille Road west to the community of Tranquille, still heading toward the airport.

If you're entering Kamloops from either direction on Trans-Canada Hwy 1

Drive into downtown Kamloops. Near the west side of the city, turn north to cross the Thompson River bridge. Then head west on Tranquille Road. Proceed to the community of Tranquille, following signs for the North Shore and the airport.

For either approach, now follow the directions below

Continue about 15 minutes past the North Shore businesses, then through the residential district. Where the road curves right and the airport is visible left, set your tripometer to 0. In 1 km (0.6 mi), turn left before the railroad tracks; don't cross them. Pass the Kamloops Compost Facilities. At 6.6 km (4.1 mi) fork right to ascend Criss Creek Road. Reset your tripometer to 0.

0 km (0 mi)
Starting on Criss Creek Road. Soon cross railroad tracks.

1.8 km (1.1 mi)
Cross a bridge over the Tranquille River. Begin ascending the broad, smooth, gravel road.

4.4 km (2.7 mi)
Bear right on Tranquille-Criss Creek FS road.

7.4 km (4.6 mi)
Pass an **overnight pullout** on the right. The road levels. Proceed straight.

13.7 km (8.4 mi)
Turn right for Watching Creek campground.

Descend from the main road. In 200 meters fork right. Proceed another 200 meters on rough, rutted road to the campground: a large clearing ringed by ponderosa pines. Rain creates serious mud here. When dry, the ruts are like cement speed bumps and will severely jostle your vehicle. The Tranquille River is audible.

WATCHING CREEK RECREATION SITE #55
Overnight / Easy
8 campsites without tables
Accessible by motorhomes and 5th-wheels

Watching Creek campground

~

Continuing northwest on Tranquille-Criss Creek FS road, passing the turnoff to Watching Creek campground.

17.2 km (10.7 mi)
Cross a bridge and reach Tranquille Crossing campground on the left. You can camp by the river, but it's just 50 meters from the road, so you'll see and hear every passing vehicle.

TRANQUILLE CROSSING RECREATION SITE #56
Overnight / Easy
2 campsites without tables
Accessible by motorhomes and 5th-wheels

~

Continuing northwest on Tranquille-Criss Creek FS road, passing Tranquille Crossing campground.

18.8 km (11.7 mi)
Turn left for Tranquille Meadow campground. Big RVs and 2WD cars can descend the first rough 100 meters to a large clearing. The river is beyond, but 4WD might be necessary for the deeply rutted road, especially if muddy. The land looks punished.

TRANQUILLE MEADOW RECREATION SITE #56
Overnight / Easy
Many campsites without tables
Accessible by motorhomes and 5th-wheels

NORTH OF KAMLOOPS

Camp at some of the lakes north of Kamloops and you'll enjoy a bonus: a lovely drive on smooth, gently meandering roads. Heffley, Community, Sullivan and Badger lakes are particularly worth steering your wheels toward. The mixed forest en route includes studly ponderosa pines and burly Douglas firs and is occasionally broken by verdant grassland. In spring, the birch and aspen leaves are crisp, lime green. In fall, they're electric gold.

Heffley Lake (page 41) is just 20 minutes from Hwy 5. Access is entirely paved. But the campground is small, the road busy, the area rife with cabins and country homes. Don't expect solitude or wilderness. It's simply a handy, comfortable place for a night's sleep.

As for **Community, Sullivan and Badger lakes** (page 42), none is a garden of earthly delights. But you won't recoil in dismay when you see them either. They're just small lakes, with ordinary campgrounds, in scenically mediocre settings. Community is the least attractive. Sullivan Lake is across the road from the campground. Badger is on a treeless slope, so bring your own shade. Sullivan and Badger accommodate monster RVs. Big rigs should avoid Community. Oblivious cows—lovable despite their mental and physical lethargy—often loiter on the roads, so drive warily. The two Barriere lakes (page 46) are farther north, closer to Little Fort than to Kamloops. **East Barriere Lake** campground, though well designed, is virtually treeless. You'll have no privacy from fellow campers or from the homes a short distance away. **Vermelin Creek** campground is just a modest gravel beach on beautiful North Barriere Lake. Claim part of it for yourself, and you'll be a happy camper. Both lakes are accessible by motorhomes and 5th-wheels, but Vermelin Creek campground is too small for them.

Gorman and Allan lakes (page 49) are west of Barriere. Avoid them. The creature from the black lagoon probably crawled out of Gorman. The shore is a muddy quagmire. The tiny lake is little more than a swamp. The campground is just a big pullout that every cow in the area has dumped on repeatedly. Allan is even nastier. A watery graveyard for scraggly tree carcasses, it could be the setting of a Stephen King novel. The surrounding hills are low and dull. But fishermen love it. They say it's a whitefish hotspot. Access to both lakes is tedious, through grim forest. The road demands attention where it narrows, clinging to a steep slope. If this stretch is muddy, timid drivers will regret coming, even before they reach the horrific lakes. Small motorhomes and trailers can probably make it.

Dunn Lake (page 50) is northeast of Little Fort. Though the campground can accommodate huge RVs, the small ferry across the Thompson River can't. And it's the ferry that allows you to reach Dunn Lake quickly and easily. Otherwise it's a 38-km (24-mi) drive on dirt road from Barriere. Dunn isn't worth that much effort. The lake is beautiful, but the camp-ground is essentially just a dirt parking lot. There are only two lakeshore campsites. So consider Dunn Lake only for a brief overnight stay, and only if you're driving a modest vehicle.

HEFFLEY LAKE

If you're heading north on Hwy 5, from Hwy 1 at Kamloops

In 24.2 km (15 mi) turn right (east) onto paved Old Hwy 25, signed for Sun Peaks Resort. Set your tripometer to 0.

If you're heading south on Hwy 5, from Hwy 24 at Little Fort

In 69.5 km (43.1 mi) turn left (east) onto paved Old Hwy 25, signed for Sun Peaks Resort. Set your tripometer to 0.

For either approach, now follow the directions below

0 km (0 mi)
Starting east on paved Old Hwy 25, signed for Sun Peaks Resort.

0.2 km (0.1 mi)
Bear left at Heffley Creek store.

8.1 km (5 mi)
Proceed straight for Heffley Lake. Turn left (north) onto Sullivan Lake Road for Community, Sullivan or Badger lakes campgrounds; read further directions at the bottom of this page.

18 km (11.2 mi)
Pass Golden Horn Road, signed for Hitch and Reel Resort. Slow down after the long, cement, roadside barrier.

19 km (11.8 mi)
Pass the second access to Embleton Mtn. trail on the left. Just 50 meters beyond, turn right and descend for Heffley Lake campground.

In 40 meters reach a fork. The middle road leads to one campsite. Right leads in 100 meters to the main campground. The lake is not visible there. The small road between the first and third tables leads to a secluded, treed campsite without a table but overlooking the lake. Bear right, past the campsites, to reach a day-use area in 150 meters. It has tables on the shore.

HEFFLEY LAKE RECREATION SITE #22
Overnight / Easy
Elev: 948 m (3110 ft) / Lake: 4.5 km (2.8 mi) long, 172 ha
3 tables in a grassy clearing ringed by tall trees
Accessible by motorhomes and 5th-wheels

COMMUNITY, SULLIVAN AND BADGER LAKES

0 km (0 mi)
Starting north on Sullivan Lake Road, from the 8.1-km (5-mi) junction on Old Hwy 25, en route to Heffley Lake. Ascend through a small, upper valley.

Heffley Lake

9 km (5.6 mi)
Reach a junction. Turn right (east) for Community Lake. Proceed straight (north) for Sullivan or Badger lakes.

>**0 km (0 mi)**
>Starting east on Community Lake FS road. Rain can make this steep ascent dangerously muddy.

>**3.3 km (2 mi)**
>Reach a 3-way junction. Take the middle fork signed for Community Lake. Tall trees are on the left, a clearcut is on the right.

>**4.2 km (2.6 mi)**
>Bear right.

>**5.9 km (3.7 mi)**
>Go left at the 3-way junction.

>**6.1 km (3.8 mi)**
>Arrive at Community Lake campground.

COMMUNITY LAKE RECREATION SITE #29
Weekend / Moderate
Elev: 1372 m (4500 ft) / Lake: 1.5 km (0.9 mi) long, 36 ha
2 tables, boat launch, dock
Accessible by small motorhomes and trailers

Continuing north on Sullivan Lake Road, from the 9-km (5.6-mi) junction, passing the turnoff to Community Lake campground.

11.5 km (7.1 mi)
Proceed straight where a road forks right.

11.7 km (7.3 mi)
Reach a signed junction. Bear right for Sullivan Lake. Left descends to Hwy 5.

12.5 km (7.8 mi)
Proceed straight.

13.9 km (8.6 mi)
Turn right at the fork.

14.1 km (8.7 mi)
Turn left for Sullivan Lake campground. The lake is on the right. The access road rejoins the main road in 0.4 km (0.25 mi).

SULLIVAN LAKE RECREATION SITE #30
Weekend / Moderate
Elev: 1148 m (3765 ft) / Lake: 2 km (1.2 mi) long, 87 ha
4 tables (3 grouped, 1 separate)
Accessible by motorhomes and 5th-wheels

Continuing north on Sullivan Lake Road, passing Sullivan Lake campground.

14.9 km (9.2 mi)
Pass Knouff Lake Resort.

17 km (10.5 mi)
Pass a small lake.

20 km (12.4 mi)
Proceed straight through the 4-way junction.

21 km (13 mi)
Badger Lake is visible.

21.5 km (13.3 mi)
Fork left on Badger Creek FS road.

22.3 km (13.8 mi)
Reach a sign: PUBLIC ACCESS. Fork left on either of two roads.

22.7 km (14.1 mi)
Arrive at Badger Lake campground. A loop road accesses the campsites.

BADGER LAKE RECREATION SITE #31
Weekend / Moderate
Elev: 1082 m (3542 ft) / Lake: 2.3 km (1.4 mi) long, 53 ha
17 tables, good boat launch, no shade
Accessible by motorhomes and 5th-wheels

Departing Badger Lake, instead of returning the way you came, consider this shortcut to Hwy 5. With a mountain bike, and someone willing to drive your vehicle, you can bike down this road and enjoy a thrilling descent.

0 km (0 mi)
Starting west from the 11.7-km (7.3-mi) junction just south of Sullivan Lake.

7 km (4.3 mi)
Curve right on the main road after a major descent.

8 km (5 mi)
Stay left and continue descending.

12 km (7.4 mi)
Intersect Hwy 5. Turn left (south) for Kamloops. Turn right (north) for Barriere, Little Fort or Clearwater.

EAST AND NORTH BARRIERE LAKES

If you're heading north on Hwy 5, from Hwy 1 at Kamloops

In 63.7 km (39.5 mi) angle right off Hwy 5. Go through the *Welcome to Barriere* portal. About 2 km (1.2 mi) farther, cross a bridge over Barriere River. Just 300 meters beyond, across from the secondary school, turn right (northeast) onto the paved road signed for N. Barriere Lake Resort (33 km). Set your tripometer to 0.

If you're heading south on Hwy 5, from Hwy 24 at Little Fort

In 29 km (18 mi) turn left (east) onto Barriere Town Road, signed for Barriere and Dunn lakes. Reach a junction near the secondary school in 1.2 km (0.7 mi). Set your tripometer to 0 and proceed straight (northeast).

For either approach above, now follow the directions below

0 km (0 mi)
Starting northeast from the junction near the secondary school in Barriere.

1.9 km (1.2 mi)
Bear right.

16.6 km (10.3 mi)
Cross a bridge over Barriere River.

17.4 km (10.8 mi)
Reach a junction. There's a public phone here. Pavement ends. Set your tripometer to 0 before going either way. Proceed straight (northeast) for East Barriere Lake campground. Turn left (north) for Vermelin Creek campground on North Barriere Lake and read the directions on page 47.

0 km (0 mi)
Proceeding straight (northeast) from the 17.4-km (10.8-mi) junction, heading for East Barriere Lake.

0.5 km (0.3 mi)
Stay on the main road.

3.1 km (1.9 mi)
Bear left at the fork.

5.5 km (3.4 mi)
The road ends at the entrance to East Barriere Lake campground.

It's well designed, with level campsites on a 400-meter loop. But because many diseased trees were felled, it lacks forest cover and seems naked and exposed. Also, directly across the narrow west end of the lake are luxurious homes with huge windows. You might feel you're being watched.

EAST BARRIERE LAKE RECREATION SITE #36
Weekend / Easy
Elev: 640 m (2100 ft) / Lake: 12 km (7.4 mi) long, 1000 ha
12 tables, 16 campsites
Accessible by motorhomes and 5th-wheels

0 km (0 mi)
Starting north from the 17.4-km (10.8-mi) junction, heading for Vermelin Creek campground on North Barriere Lake.

4.5 km (2.8 mi)
Cross a bridge over Barriere River.

7.9 km (4.9 mi) and **8.9 km (5.5 mi)**
Proceed straight on the main road.

10.4 km (6.4 mi)
Cross a bridge over Harper Creek. Just after, bear right at the junction.

13.1 km (8.1 mi)
Pass a boat launch on the right.

Pitch your tent on the beach at Vermelin Creek campground on North Barriere Lake.

15.1 km (9.4 mi)

Turn right to enter Vermelin Creek campground. It's just after a yellow 15 KM sign, near a small peninsula in the lake.

> This is simply a gravel beach that you can drive onto. There's one individual campsite next to the road as you enter. Otherwise camp in the open on the beach. It would be crowded with three vehicles, but tolerable if everyone was quiet and considerate. The lakeshore is undeveloped. The forested, hilly setting is beautiful.

VERMELIN CREEK RECREATION SITE #37
Weekend / Easy
Elev: 610 m (2000 ft) / Lake: 7 km (4.3 mi) long, 497 ha
3 campsites without tables
Inaccessible by motorhomes and 5th-wheels

GORMAN AND ALLAN LAKES

If you're heading north on Hwy 5, from Hwy 1 at Kamloops

In 63.7 km (39.5 mi) bear left on Hwy 5 past the *Welcome to Barriere* portal. Continue 1.1 km (0.7 mi) beyond Barriere Town Road, then turn left (west) onto Westsyde Road. Set your tripometer to 0.

If you're heading south on Hwy 5,
from Hwy 24 at Little Fort

In 27.7 km (17.2 mi) turn right (west) onto Westsyde Road. Set your tripometer to 0.

For either approach above, now follow the directions below

0 km (0 mi)
Starting west on Westsyde Road, departing Hwy 5 just north of Barriere.

0.4 km (0.25 mi)
Bear right on dirt Westsyde Road. Begin a switchbacking ascent.

1.5 km (0.9 mi)
Go right and ascend the switchback.

4.3 km (2.7 mi)
Reach a Y-junction. Go right, onto Gorman Lake FS road.

6.9 km (4.3 mi)
Bear right. Having completed much of the ascent, proceed through an upper valley.

13.2 km (8.2 mi)
Go right.

14.5 km (9 mi)
Gorman Lake is visible.

15.7 km (9.7 mi)
Reach Gorman Lake campground and a lone table on the right. It's not recommended.

GORMAN LAKE RECREATION SITE #45
Overnight / Moderate
Elev: 1173 m (3847 ft) / Lake: 1 km (0.6 mi) long, 17 ha
Accessible by small motorhomes and trailers

Continuing generally west on Gorman Lake FS road, passing Gorman Lake campground.

17.7 km (11 mi)
Reach a junction. Turn right for Allan Lake.

20 km (12.4 mi) and **20.9 km (13 mi)**
Proceed on the main road.

21.2 km (13.1 mi)
Turn right to reach Allan Lake campground in 0.4 km (0.25 mi). It's not recommended.

ALLAN LAKE RECREATION SITES #46
Weekend / Moderate
Elev: 1235 m (4050 ft) / Lake: 4 km (2.5 mi) long, 130 ha
4 tables, dock, rough boat launch
Accessible by small motorhomes and trailers

DUNN LAKE

Drive to Little Fort, at the junction of Hwys 5 and 24. It's about 94 km (58.3 mi) north of Kamloops, and about 29 km (18 mi) north of Barriere. In the village, 300 meters east of Hwy 5, is the Thompson River ferry. It operates daily, on demand, 7 a.m. to 11:45 a.m., 1 p.m. to 4:45 p.m., and 6 p.m. to 6:45 p.m. It's too small to accommodate 5th-wheels or large motorhomes. Cross the river, then set your tripometer to 0 as you disembark the ferry on the east bank.

0 km (0 mi)
Disembarking the ferry on the east bank of the Thompson River,

across from Little Fort. Immediately go left. Cross railroad tracks. The road can be very muddy near the dilapidated house, but good gravel soon resumes as you ascend.

1 km (0.6 mi)
Proceed straight.

5.6 km (3.5 mi)
Curve right. Soon ascend steeply.

6.9 km (4.3 mi)
Slow down for a potentially very muddy stretch with an abrupt drop on the left.

8 km (5 mi)
Reach a junction. Left leads to Clearwater. Turn right to reach Dunn Lake in 100 meters. It's a large, impressive lake, walled-in by steep forested mountains. The campground is primarily just a dirt parking lot with room for several vehicles, but there are two lakeshore campsites.

DUNN LAKE RECREATION SITE #39
Overnight / Easy
Elev: 450 m (1476 ft) / Lake: 5 km (3.1 mi) long, 356 ha
2 tables, 2 lakeshore campsites, boat launch
Accessible by small motorhomes and trailers,
if the ferry allows

WEST ON HWY 24

Publicizing Hwy 24 would be easy. An advertising agency could forego the standard ploy of exaggeration and simply tell the truth. They could call it the *Aspenland Skyway*. Nobody would question the name's veracity.

This sleek ribbon of pavement links Hwy 5, at Little Fort, with Hwy 97, just south of 100 Mile House. It climbs modest mountains known for temperate weather and consistently blue skies. Then it careens through the range at about 1200 m (3935 ft) elevation, where aspen trees thrive. Their trunks are wedding-dress white. Their leaves are lime in spring, gold in fall. They lighten and brighten the forest. Add the occasional roadside

Camping Builds Confident, Caring Kids

Introducing children to the great outdoors can have a significant, long-lasting impact on their lives. Helping kids see, understand and appreciate nature encourages them to learn skills that will bolster their personal confidence and make them more competent at navigating the human and physical environments. Also, most adolescent love affairs with the outdoors continue into adulthood. In one study, 73% of Canadians said their passion for outdoor recreation is the direct result of fun times they had outdoors while growing up. 50% of those said their conservation ethic, their active concern for the earth, was sparked before the age of eight.

lake, and virtually traffic-free driving, and the result is a delightful, stress-relieving experience behind the wheel.

South of the Bridge Lake community are campgrounds on Bonaparte, Scot, and Hammer lakes. Bonaparte and Scot are hardly worth the necessary 45-minute drive from Hwy 24. Bonaparte is a big lake, but the campground is mediocre. It allows you no privacy and no view because it's just a clearing entirely framed by trees. Scot is a dinky lake, has a reedy shore and is surrounded by low hills. Hammer is a fine lake, bigger than Scot, but still small. It has a pleasant, medium-size campground set in tall trees near the shore. Check it out if you're likely to stay a couple nights.

Your stop-and-plop options include very convenient campgrounds at Latremouille, Phinetta and Crystal lakes. Phinetta is idyllic. Crystal is also appealing. Latremouille is closest to pavement, but even it should be quiet, because Hwy 24 is lightly travelled, especially at night.

If you're heading west on Hwy 24, from Hwy 5 in Little Fort

0 km (0 mi)
Starting west on Hwy 24 from Little Fort.

16.6 km (10.3 mi)
Turn left for Latremouille Lake campground.

Descend to reach the campground in 300 meters. The first loop on the right has 6 tables, 7 campsites. The left loop has 1 table and 3 sites near the lake. The highway is just above, but it's not busy, so noise might not be a problem for you.

LATREMOUILLE LAKE RECREATION SITE #69
Weekend / Easy
Elev: 1190 m (3903 ft) / Lake: 2.7 km (1.7 mi) long, 75 ha
7 tables, 10 campsites
Accessible by motorhomes and 5th-wheels

Continuing west on Hwy 24, passing the turnoff to Latremouille Lake campground.

17 km (10.5 mi)
Pass a big pullout with a bearproof garbage bin.

18.8 km (11.7 mi)
Turn right to reach Goose Lake campground in 200 meters.

GOOSE LAKE RECREATION SITE #72
Overnight / Easy
3 tables, many more campsites, rough boat launch
Accessible by motorhomes and 5th-wheels

Continuing west on Hwy 24, passing the turnoff to Goose Lake campground.

19.8 km (12.3 mi)
Turn right (north) onto Taweel FS road for Deer Lake campground.

Proceed north on the main road for about 5 km (3.1 mi). Watch for the access on the right. The campground is spacious, the lake is small.

DEER LAKE RECREATION SITE #41
Weekend / Easy
Elev: 1402 m (4600 ft) / 1 km (0.6 mi) long, 33 ha
8 tables, rough boat launch
Inaccessible by large motorhomes and 5th-wheels

Continuing west on Hwy 24, passing the turnoff to Deer Lake campground.

22 km (13.6 mi)
Reach 1311-m (4300-ft) McDonald Summit.

22.6 km (14 mi)
Turn left and descend to reach **Janice Lake campground** in 0.5 km (0.3 mi). Managed by BC Parks, it was fee-free in 1999. It's accessible by small motorhomes and trailers. The road narrows and gets brushy within 100 meters, but soon widens again. The campground is a small clearing with 2 tables, 3 campsites. The forest-ringed lake is tiny—5 hectares. Launching even a cartop boat is difficult.

30.2 km (18.7 mi)
Phinetta Lake is visible.

30.7 km (19 mi)
Turn left (south) onto Opax Road for Phinetta Lake campground.

0 km (0 mi)
Starting south on Opax Road.

0.2 km (0.1 mi)
Turn left at the Opax Mountain Cafe.

0.4 km (0.25 mi)
Proceed straight.

0.6 km (0.4 mi)
Turn right to enter the campground. At the fork, right leads 100 meters to a secluded campsite with a table. Left leads to 2 well-spaced tables by the lake. Big rigs can turn around 300 meters beyond the campground.

Though it's beside Hwy 24, Phinetta Lake campground is idyllic.

PHINETTA LAKE RECREATION SITE #88
Weekend / Easy
Elev: 1128 m (3700 ft) / Lake: 0.8 km (0.5 mi) long, 23 ha
3 tables
Accessible by motorhomes and 5th-wheels

Continuing west on Hwy 24, passing the turnoff to Phinetta Lake campground.

34.4 km (21.3 mi)
Pass the turnoff to Eagle Island Resort.

40.4 km (25 mi)
Pass a **rest area** on the left, overlooking Lac des Roches. Overnight parking was still allowed as of 1998. RVs can probably stop here for dinner and a night's sleep.

49.4 km (30.6 mi)
Pass Cottonwood Bay Road on the right. It leads north to Bridge Lake Provincial Park. Soon after, a blue sign announces the left turn for Green Lake and the community of Bridge Lake.

50.2 km (31.1 mi)
Turn left (south) onto Bridge Lake Business Route (the community's east access) for Crystal, Bonaparte, Hammer, or Scot lakes. In 1.1 km (0.7 mi) reach the junction at Bridge Lake store and set your tripometer to 0.

Or, proceeding west on Hwy 24, pass the west end of Bridge Lake Business Route at 51.8 km (32.1 mi). Set your tripometer 0, then continue following directions on page 60.

SOUTH OF HWY 24

0 km (0 mi)
Starting south on N. Bonaparte Road, from the signed junction at Bridge Lake store.

0.2 km (0.1 mi)
Pavement ends. Proceed straight on the main road.

1.5 km (0.9 mi)
Pass Burn Lake on the left.

2.3 km (1.4 mi)
Reach a junction. Set your tripometer to 0 before going either way. Left leads south to Eagan, Sharpe, Bonaparte, Hammer, and Scot lakes. Proceed straight for Crystal Lake campground.

> **0 km (0 mi)**
> Proceeding straight at the 2.3-km (1.4-mi) junction.
>
> **1 km (0.6 mi)**
> Crystal Lake is visible.
>
> **1.6 km (1 mi)**
> Turn left to reach Crystal Lake campground in 100 meters. The lake is surrounded by mixed forest and low hills.

CRYSTAL LAKE RECREATION SITE #89
Weekend / Easy
Elev: 1122 m (3680 ft) / Lake: 2.5 km (1.6 mi) long, 150 ha
4 tables, 6 campsites, boat launch
Accessible by small motorhomes and trailers

Crystal Lake

~

0 km (0 mi)
Starting south on Eagan Lake Road, from the 2.3-km (1.4-mi) junction. Alert drivers can safely motor at 80 kph (50 mph) on this wide, well-maintained thoroughfare.

8.6 km (5.3 mi)
Bear right.

12.6 km (7.8 mi)
Proceed straight on the main road where Eagan Crescent rejoins it. Pass a ranch.

14.7 km (9.1 mi)
Pass a barn and the turnoff to Eagan Lake Resort.

15.4 km (9.5 mi)
Reach a junction. Turn left for Bonaparte Lake. Right leads to **Sharpe Lake Recreation Site #92**—a tiny campground on a small, shallow lake.

21.5 km (13.3 mi)
Bear right.

22.6 km (14 mi)
Cross a little bridge and bear right.

23.4 km (14.5 mi), 25 km (15.5 mi) and **26.3 km (16.3 mi)**
Bear right.

26.7 km (16.6 mi)
Reach a fork. Set your tripometer to 0 before going either way. Bear left for Bonaparte Lake. Turn right (south) for Hammer or Scot lakes.

> **0 km (0 mi)**
> Bearing left at the 26.7-km (16.6-mi) fork.

> **0.4 km (0.25 mi)**
> Proceed straight and descend to reach Bonaparte Lake campground in 100 meters. It's just a big forest-enclosed clearing with no view.

BONAPARTE LAKE RECREATION SITE #93
Weekend / Moderate
Elev: 1170 m (3838 ft) / Lake: 18.5 km (11.5 mi) long,
3325 hectares
6 tables, good boat launch
Accessible by motorhomes and 5th-wheels

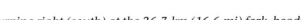

Turning right (south) at the 26.7-km (16.6-mi) fork, heading for Hammer or Scot lakes.

0 km (0 mi)
Starting south for Hammer and Scot lakes, from the 26.7-km (16.6-mi) junction.

1.9 km (1.2 mi)
Proceed straight past Bonaparte Lodge.

3 km (1.9 mi)
Bear right.

5.2 km (3.2 mi)
Reach a triangular junction. Go right. In 150 meters, go right again.

6 km (3.7 mi)
Reach a junction. Turn left and in 100 meters curve left again to arrive at Hammer Lake campground. Or, set your tripometer to 0 and continue right for Scot Lake.

HAMMER LAKE RECREATION SITE #94
Weekend / Difficult (due only to distance)
Elev: 1260 m (4133 ft) / Lake: 2.5 km (1.6 mi) long, 66 ha
9 tables on a loop, 6 lakeshore campsites, boat launch
Accessible by motorhomes and 5th-wheels

Continuing right at the 6-km (3.7-mi) junction, heading for Scot Lake.

0 km (0 mi)
Proceeding to Scot Lake from the Hammer Lake turnoff. The road ahead is rougher, with more potholes, but tolerable.

0.4 km (0.25 mi)
Stay right. Pass through regrowing clearcuts.

5.2 km (3.2 mi)
Turn left at the fork.

6.9 km (4.3 mi)
Arrive at Scot Lake campground. Go left or right for campsites.

SCOT LAKE RECREATION SITE #95
Weekend / Difficult (due only to distance)
Elev: 1204 m (3950 ft) / Lake: 1.5 km (0.9 mi) long, 34 ha
4 tables, 7 well-spaced campsites, boat launch
Inaccessible by motorhomes and 5th-wheels

Campers direct their straggling buddy to Bonaparte Lake.

Upon returning to Bridge Lake store, bear left at the junction to reach Hwy 24 in 0.9 km (0.5 mi). Turn left to continue west. Set your tripometer 0.

0 km (0 mi)
Resuming west on Hwy 24, from the west end of Bridge Lake Business Route.

9.5 km (5.9 mi)
Turn right (north) onto Shertenlib Road for Needa Lake camp-

ground. It's oddly located on a narrow, shallow arm of the lake, where views are nil. The shore is inhospitable. A boat is necessary to appreciate the lake.

0 km (0 mi)
Starting north on Shertenlib Road.

0.4 km (0.25 mi)
Bear left. The road is wide and fairly smooth.

1.9 km (1.2 mi) and **2.7 km (1.7 mi)**
Turn left.

5.5 km (3.4 mi)
Go right and ascend Windy Mountain FS road.

7.1 km (4.4 mi)
Cross the bridge.

9.2 km (5.7 mi) and **11.3 km (7 mi)**
Stay on the main road.

17.8 km (11 mi)
Turn right and reset your tripometer to 0. At 0.3 km (0.2 mi) descend right. At 0.4 km (0.25 mi) go right again. At 1.1 km (0.7 mi) go right yet again to enter small Needa Lake campground.

NEEDA LAKE RECREATION SITE #86
Weekend / Moderate
Elev: 1111 m (3645 ft) / Lake: 5 km (3.1 mi) long, 205 ha
5 tables, rough boat launch
Accessible by small motorhomes and trailers

Continuing west on Hwy 24, passing the turnoff to Needa Lake campground.

12.7 km (7.9 mi)
Pass Sheridan Lake store.

15.8 km (9.8 mi)
Reach a junction just past Interlakes store. Proceed straight

(west) on Hwy 24 to reach Hwy 97. Turn right (north) onto Horse Lake FS road to access superior campgrounds in the East Cariboo region via excellent backroads. The turn is signed for several lakes: Hathaway (14 km), Drewry (25 km), Canim (43 km), and Mahood (57 km). It's also the southwest approach to Wells Gray Provincial Park. Read page 160 for directions.

47.6 km (29.5 mi)
Intersect Hwy 97. Turn right (north) to quickly reach 100 Mile House. Turn left (south) for Clinton.

EAST ON HWY 24

0 km (0 mi)
Starting east on Hwy 24, departing Hwy 97 just south of 100 Mile House.

11.2 km (6.9 mi)
Pass the signed turnoff for Horse Lake on the left.

31.8 km (19.7 mi)
Reach a junction just before Interlakes store. Proceed straight (east) to access campgrounds along Hwy 24 en route to Hwy 5 at Little Fort. Turn left (north) onto Horse Lake FS road to access superior campgrounds in the East Cariboo region via excellent backroads. The turn is signed for several lakes: Hathaway (14 km), Drewry (25 km), Canim (43 km), and Mahood (57 km). It's also the southwest approach to Wells Gray Provincial Park. Read directions on page 160.

35 km (21.7 mi)
Pass Sheridan Lake store.

38.1 km (23.6 mi)
Turn left (north) onto Shertenlib Road for **Needa Lake campground**. Read further directions on page 61.

47.6 km (29.5 mi)
Proceed straight (east) on Hwy 24. Or turn right (south) onto Bridge Lake Business Route (the community's west access) for

campgrounds at Crystal, Bonaparte, Hammer, or Scot lakes. In 0.9 km (0.6 mi) reach the junction at Bridge Lake store, set your tripometer to 0, and read further directions on page 56.

49.2 km (30.5 mi)
Pass the east end of Bridge Lake Business Route.

59 km (36.6 mi)
Pass a **rest area** on the right, overlooking Lac des Roches. Overnight parking was still allowed as of 1998. RVs can stop here to cook a meal and maybe spend the night.

68.7 km (42.6 mi)
Turn right (south) onto Opax Road to quickly reach **Phinetta Lake campground**. Read further directions on page 54.

76.8 km (47.6 mi)
Turn right and descend to reach **Janice Lake campground** in 0.5 km (0.3 mi). Managed by BC Parks, it was fee-free in 1999. It's accessible by small motorhomes and trailers. Read page 54 for details.

77.4 km (48 mi)
Reach 1311-m (4300-ft) McDonald Summit.

79.6 km (49.4 mi)
Turn left (north) onto Taweel FS road for **Deer Lake campground**. Read further directions on page 53.

80.6 km (50 mi)
Turn left to reach **Goose Lake campground** in 200 meters. Read page 53 for details.

82.8 km (51.3 mi)
Turn right to reach **Latremouille Lake campground** in 300 meters. Read page 53 for details. Continuing west on Hwy 24, soon begin a long descent into the Thompson River valley.

99.4 km (61.6 mi)
Intersect Hwy 5 in Little Fort. Turn left (north) for Clearwater. Turn right (south) for Kamloops.

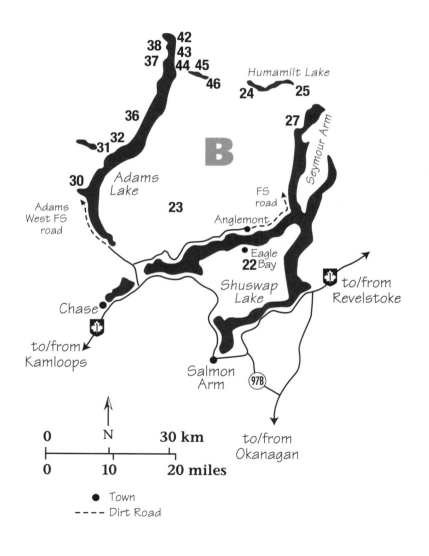

ADAMS AND SHUSWAP LAKES

38 42
37 43
44 45
46

Humamilt Lake

24 25

36 27

32
31

30 Adams
Lake

Adams
West FS
road

23

B

Seymour Arm

FS
road

Anglemont

Eagle
22 Bay

Shuswap
Lake

Chase

to/from
Revelstoke

to/from
Kamloops

Salmon
Arm

97B

to/from
Okanagan

0   N   30 km

0   10   20 miles

● Town
- - - - Dirt Road

B: Adams and Shuswap Lakes

These campgrounds are in different FS Districts: Clearwater, Kamloops or Salmon Arm. But all these campgrounds appear on the **Salmon Arm FS District** recreation map, so the numbers correspond with that map.

22	Herman Lake
23	Kwikoit Creek
24	Humamilt Lake West
25	Humamilt Lake East
27	Nellie Lake
30	Skwaam Bay
31	Johnson Lake
32	Sandy Point
36	Honeymoon Bay
37	Rocky Point
38	Gordon Bay
42	Tsikwustum Creek North
43	Tsikwustum Creek South
44	Momich River
45	Momich Lake West
46	Momich Lake East

Adams and Shuswap Lakes

ADAMS LAKE WEST, page 67
ADAMS LAKE EAST, page 75
ADAMS LAKE SOUTHEAST TO SEYMOUR ARM, page 78
SEYMOUR ARM NORTHWEST TO ADAMS LAKE, page 84
NEAR SHUSWAP LAKE, page 90

Premier camping on Adams Lake

Adams and Shuswap lakes are equally beautiful. Both are impressively long and wide, surrounded by high, forested mountains. Yet they are very different lakes.

The shoreline of Adams is almost undeveloped. Driving around it you'll enjoy frequent lake views and encounter plenty of free campgrounds—many of them provincial-park quality. Adams Lake is 62.5 km (39 mi) long and covers 13,108 hectares. The elevation is 412 m (1,350 ft).

Shuswap Lake is a popular summer vacation destination and retirement area. It's 71 km (44 mi) long and covers 30,512 hectares. The elevation is 346 m (1,135 ft). Houseboats toodle up and down its many arms, cottages and homes ring the shore, but you won't find a single Forest Service campground here. The undemocratic reality is that you must drive a long way off the Trans-Canada (81 km / 50 mi, nearly half of that on dirt), to reach the nearest free campground: a tiny one near the northwest end of Seymour Arm.

Nevertheless, the drive along Shuswap is worthwhile. So make a loop around both lakes. Head north along the west shore of Adams Lake. Cross the low mountains via Humamilt Lake. Then go south, down the west shore of Seymour Arm and the north shore of Shuswap Lake, back to the Trans-Canada.

ADAMS LAKE WEST

If you're heading west on Trans-Canada Hwy 1 from Sorrento

From the pedestrian walkway with flashing lights, drive 9.2 km (5.7 mi), then turn left off Hwy 1 and onto an overpass. The turn is signed for North Shuswap Resort Area, Roderick Haig-Brown, and Adams Lake. Set your tripometer to 0.

If you're heading east on Trans-Canada Hwy 1 from Kamloops

From the junction with Hwy 97, near Monte Creek, drive 27 km (16.7 mi), then turn right off Hwy 1 and onto an overpass. The turn is signed for North Shuswap Resort Area, Roderick Haig-Brown, and Adams Lake. Set your tripometer to 0.

For either approach above, now follow the directions below

0 km (0 mi)
Turning south off Hwy 1. Curve right to loop onto the overpass.

0.3 km (0.2 mi)
Bear right on the main road. (Turtle Valley Road forks left. It accesses Skimikin Lakes campground, described in *Camp Free in B.C. Volume I.*)

0.7 km (0.4 mi)
Midway across the South Thompson River bridge.

3.9 km (2.4 mi)
Turn left on Holding Road to proceed up the west side of Adams Lake. (Right, toward Scotch Creek and Anglemont, accesses the north side of Shuswap Lake, and Seymour Arm (page 84).

12.3 km (7.6 mi)
Pass Adams Lake store.

14.7 km (9.1 mi)
Arrive at a mill and a logging company sign: END OF PUBLIC ROAD. Don't be alarmed; you can continue by turning left. Set your tripometer to 0.

0 km (0 mi)
Turning left before the mill. Ascend the paved road past the house. Pavement soon ends. Continue on the wide gravel road. Bear left through the weigh-scale area. Immediately after is a 4-way junction. Stay straight on the main road.

3.4 km (2.1 mi)
Adams Lake Provincial Park is on the right.

12.8 km (7.9 mi)
Bear right and descend on the main road.

18.7 km (11.6 mi)
Left (northwest) is a pastoral valley. Cross a bridge. This is Squam Bay (spelled Skwaam on maps).

19 km (11.8 mi)
Reach a stop sign and 4-way junction. Continue straight on Adams West FS road.

20.5 km (12.7 mi)
Turn right for Skwaam Bay campground.

Descend from the main road. In 100 meters fork left for the easiest lake access. In 200 meters arrive at the first table, in forest above the lake. In 350 meters reach another fork. Left leads to private cottages. Turn right. Arrive at 2 tables on

Skwaam Bay campground on Adams Lake

the lakeshore, 450 meters from the main road. The view is across the lake to beautiful Douglas fir forest on high hillsides. Several cottages are visible to the right.

SKWAAM BAY RECREATION SITE #30
Destination / Moderate
3 tables, 4 campsites, pebble beach
Accessible by motorhomes and 5th-wheels

Continuing northeast on Adams West FS road, passing the turnoff to Skwaam Bay campground.

27.8 km (17.2 mi)
Samatosum FS road forks left here and climbs to Johnson Lake campground—not recommended. The lake is small, the forest scrawny, the campground desperate-looking. Your time is better invested reaching superior campgrounds on Adams Lake. Still want to see Johnson Lake? Here's how to get there:

0 km (0 mi)
Turning left onto Samatosum FS road from Adams West FS road.

2.7 km (1.7 mi)
Bear left.

4.5 km (2.8 mi)
Fork right and continue ascending.

6.5 km (4 mi)
Stay right on the larger road and ascend.

9.2 km (5.7 mi)
Fork left.

9.6 km (6 mi)
Fork right and descend on Camp Road.

9.8 km (6.1 mi)
Bear right. The lake is now visible through the trees. In 0.5 km (0.3 mi) reach an **overnight pullout** on the left, above the shore.

10.7 km (6.6 mi)
Turn sharply left and descend to **Johnson Lake Recreation Site #31**. It has 6 tables. The green lake has a sandy bottom and is shallow around the edge, but the shore is narrow and brushy.

Continuing northeast on Adams West FS road, passing the 27.8-km (17.2-mi) fork. Stay on the main road paralleling the lake. Ignore, narrower logging roads and private roads.

36.8 km (22.8 mi)
Reach a junction. To continue northeast up the lake, stay left on Adams West FS road. To reach the aptly named Sandy Point campground on Adams Lake, turn right at the sign: BRENNAN CREEK 2 KM.

The beach at Sandy Point campground on Adams Lake

In 1.4 km (0.9 mi) fork right and descend. In another 100 meters the road forks again. Left leads to the day-use area and beach. Right is the narrow road into the campground. A tiny school is nearby.

SANDY POINT RECREATION SITE #32
Destination / Moderate
12 tables in a cedar grove, big sandy beach, excellent swimming
Accessible by small trailers, but not motorhomes or 5th-wheels

Continuing northeast on Adams West FS road, passing the 36.8-km (22.8-mi) junction.

49.3 km (30.6 mi)
Stay right on the main road.

50.6 km (31.4 mi)
Watch carefully for the small, obscure, right fork descending to

Honeymoon Bay campground on Adams Lake

Honeymoon Bay campground on Adams Lake. Set your tripometer to 0 here, whether turning or continuing.

In 0.6 km (0.4 mi) reach the FS sign and another fork. Left descends to a small rocky beach. Right descends to the campground in 100 meters. The initial group of 5 tables is on the lake but fully exposed to sun, wind or rain. Proceed 0.5 km (0.3 mi) to other lake sites sheltered by trees. The first of these has a spring nearby. The fifth site is best. Despite large cutblocks visible across the lake, the setting is beautiful. RVs might be able to turn around at road's end.

HONEYMOON BAY RECREATION SITE #36
Destination / Moderate
11 tables, rocky lakeshore with small strips of sand
Accessible by small trailers or motorhomes, but not 5th-wheels

Continuing northeast on Adams West FS road, from the turnoff to Honeymoon Bay campground. Set your tripometer to 0.

0 km (0 mi)
On Adams West FS road, at the turnoff to Honeymoon Bay campground.

5 km (3.1 mi)
Stay right on the main road. A small road ascends left.

15.4 km (9.5 mi)
Turn right for Rocky Point campground. (The main road pulls away from the lake. Once the lake is again visible, watch for this unsigned road on the right.)

Arrive at the first table in 200 meters. Bear right and proceed 0.4 km (0.25 mi) to reach two more tables on the point. The surrounding topography is less dramatic here than farther south on the lake. RVs have room to maneuver.

ROCKY POINT RECREATION SITE #37
Weekend / Difficult (due only to distance)
3 unsheltered tables, boat launch
Accessible by motorhomes and 5th-wheels

Turn left at the first table to follow a narrow spur road north along the lakeshore. At 1 km (0.6 mi) turn right. At 1.2 km (0.7 mi) reach the **unofficial Gordon Bay camping area.** It's a grassy, birch-ringed clearing open to the lake. You'll find no outhouse or tables, but there's room for 3 separate campsites. Read page 26 under *Practical Stuff* to ensure you leave no trace of your stay.

Continuing north on Adams West FS road, passing the turnoff to Rocky Point campground.

16.7 km (10.4 mi)
A sharp right fork leads 200 meters to the **unofficial Gordon Bay camping area** described above.

17.7 km (11 mi)
Stay straight on the main road to round the north end of Adams Lake. Turn right for the official Gordon Bay campground.

View from Gordon Bay campground on Adams Lake

0 km (0 mi)
Turning right and descending.

0.4 km (0.25 mi)
Bear right.

0.6 km (0.4 mi)
The road divides into three. Left goes to two tables on the lake. The middle fork leads 400 meters to a large, open campsite ideal for 5th-wheels. It's across a narrow channel from an island. Right ascends 300 meters to a sandy loop with 5 tables in the trees. Honeymoon Bay and Brennan Creek campgrounds are prettier and their shorelines more spacious.

GORDON BAY RECREATION SITE #38
Weekend / Difficult (due only to distance)
7 tables, boat launch
Accessible by motorhomes and 5th-wheels

Continuing north on Adams West FS road, passing the turnoff to Gordon Bay campground.

21.3 km (13.2 mi)
Reach a major junction near the north end of Adams Lake. Set your tripometer to 0 and turn right on Adams East FS road.

ADAMS LAKE EAST

0 km (0 mi)
Heading northeast on Adams East FS road.

5.3 km (3.3 mi)
Cross a bridge over Adams River.

5.6 km (3.5 mi)
Stay straight.

7.6 km (4.7 mi)
Bear right where a left fork is signed for Gannett Lake. You're now heading south.

8.3 km (5.1 mi)
Ignore a minor right fork. Stay on the main road. Soon start descending.

10 km (6.2 mi)
Cross a small bridge over Gannett Creek, just before (north of) the KM 6 sign.

10.5 km (6.5 mi)
Cross a bridge over Michael Creek. The road is now following the east shore of Adams Lake.

11.7 km (7.3 mi)
The road veers right, toward the point.

12 km (7.4 mi)
Turn right for Silviculture campground, across from Michael Creek FS road.

A sign welcomes the public but warns that forestry work crews have precedence. Reach the campground 150 meters from the main road. The rocky lakeshore has a few patches of sand.

SILVICULTURE RECREATION SITE #42
Weekend / Difficult (due only to distance)
7 tables, many more campsites, good boat launch
Accessible by motorhomes and 5th-wheels

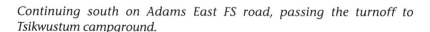

Continuing south on Adams East FS road, passing the turnoff to Silviculture campground.

12.1 km (7.4 mi)
Cross a bridge.

12.4 km (7.7 mi)
The main road widens. Turn right for Tsikwustum campground.

Descend to reach the campground in 0.5 km (0.3 mi). Right leads 100 meters to 2 separate campsites with tables. Left leads 100 meters to 1 table, 2 campsites, and enough room for RVs to turn around.

TSIKWUSTUM CREEK SOUTH RECREATION SITE #43
Weekend / Difficult (due only to distance)
3 tables, boat launch, rocky lakeshore
Narrow, brushy access road will scratch big RVs

Continuing south on Adams East FS road, passing the turnoff to Tsikwustum campground.

12.6 km (7.8 mi)
Stay on the main road curving right.

18.7 km (11.6 mi)
Reach a major junction. Bear right and descend for Momich River campground, beyond which there are no more camp-

grounds on the east shore of Adams Lake. Left is Momich-Stukemapten FS road, described on page 78. That's the way to Shuswap Lake's Seymour Arm. Set your tripometer to 0 here if turning left.

19 km (11.8 mi)
Turn right for BC Parks' Momich River campground (free in 1999).

Descend to enter the campground in 0.5 km (0.3 mi). Just before the sign, a right fork loops into the north section, passing 6 campsites (2 with tables, all in the trees, none with lake views) and reaching a cement boat launch. Stay straight at the sign to enter the main section where most campsites have lake views. Bear left for sites near the river, right for more privacy on the lake. An obnoxious generator across the river might be audible.

MOMICH RIVER CAMPGROUND #44
Destination / Difficult (due only to distance)
22 tables, pebble beach, boat launch, mega-wharf
Accessible by motorhomes and 5th-wheels,
but not on north-section loop

Momich River campground on Adams Lake

ADAMS LAKE SOUTHEAST TO SEYMOUR ARM

Turning left (east) onto Momich-Stukemapten FS road, before the turnoff to Momich River campground. Set your tripometer to 0.

0 km (0 mi)
Starting on Momich-Stukemapten FS road, from the 18.7-km (11.6-mi) junction on Adams East FS road.

0.5 km (0.3 mi)
Go right.

2.5 km (1.6 mi)
Small Momich Lake is on the right.

2.9 km (1.8 mi)
An obscure right fork leads to Momich Lake West campground—not recommended.

> The FS sign is hidden in foliage. The access road is narrow, overgrown, deeply potholed and rutted, and probably muddy—challenging for a 2WD vehicle. Reach **Momich Lake West campground #45** in 0.8 km (0.5 mi). It has 2 tables but room for only 1 vehicle. It's cramped, dark, viewless. The shore is mucky and brushy. Turning a big RV around here might be impossible. Leave this one to entropy, which already has a firm grasp on it.

6.9 km (4.3 mi)
The road is now high on a cliffside. Visible below is Momich Lake's east end.

7.9 km (4.9 mi)
Go right at the fork and descend.

8.4 km (5.2 mi)
Follow a hairpin turn right.

10.1 km (6.3 mi)
Cross the bridged inlet stream. Immediately after, turn right for Momich Lake East campground.

The 3 campsites are merely pullouts on the right side of the access road, which ends at 0.5 km (0.3 mi) in a turnaround. The forest is cool, shady, mossy. The green lake invites swimming.

MOMICH LAKE EAST CAMPGROUND #46
Weekend / Difficult (due only to distance)
2 tables, 3 campsites, boat launch, sandy beach, little privacy
Accessible by small trailers, but not motorhomes or 5th-wheels

Continuing east on Momich-Stukemapten FS road, passing the turnoff to Momich Lake East campground.

10.9 km (6.8 mi)
Turn left at a fork signed for Cayenne Camp.

12.2 km (7.6 mi)
Bear left on Cayenne Creek FS road.

12.5 km (7.8 mi)
Cross a bridged creek then immediately turn left at a T-junction.

13.5 km (8.4 mi)
Pass a lake on the left.

15.4 km (9.5 mi)
Bear left at the fork.

18 km (11.2 mi)
Bear left.

20.6 km (12.8 mi)
Reach a junction just before a bridged creek. Turn left, again following a sign for Cayenne Camp.

21 km (13 mi)
Turn right at the T-junction.

22.2 km (13.8 mi)
Turn right for **Stukemapten Lake campground.**

Descend from the main road. Fork right to reach 1 table in 150 meters. The left-fork campsite has no table. Both are inaccessible by trailers and motorhomes because there's no room to turn around.

26.2 km (16.2 mi)
Stay straight and soon descend.

27.5 km (17.1 mi)
Cross a bridged stream. Humamilt Lake is visible left.

28.9 km (17.9 mi)
Pass a KM 27 sign on the right. Slow down for Humamilt Lake campground.

29.5 km (18.3 mi)
Turn left for Humamilt Lake campground (photo on page 87). Stay straight on Celista Creek FS road for Seymour Arm. Set your tripometer to 0 here, whether turning or continuing.

Descend from the main road. Arrive at the first table in 100 meters. Proceed another 50 meters to the other 6 campsites scattered in a forest of cedar, fir and birch, near the southwest end of the lake.

HUMAMILT LAKE RECREATION SITE #24
Destination / Difficult (due only to distance)
Elev: 580 m (1902 ft) / Lake: 12 km (7.5 mi) long, 438 ha
7 tables, boat launch, exceptionally beautiful forest and lake
Inaccessible by motorhomes and trailers

Continuing east on Celista Creek FS road, from the turnoff to Humamilt Lake campground. Set your tripometer to 0.

0 km (0 mi)
On Celista Creek FS road, at the turnoff to Humamilt Lake campground.

0.9 km (0.5 mi)
Stay straight, along the south side of Humamilt Lake.

5.5 km (3.4 mi)
Stay left.

Free the Caveperson Within You

Technology has not delivered on its promise to reduce toil. Everywhere, people are working harder than ever. In a recent poll, 88% of workers said their jobs require them to work longer. 68% said they have to work faster. And 80% said their lives are more stressful now than five years ago, largely due to pressure at work. The result is a society of stressed-out wage slaves failing to keep pace in a techno-world where efficiency is everything. The solution to this crisis is complex. But the major symptom—stress—is easy to understand. According to brain research, humans have a Stone Age psychology that's struggling to adapt to modern life. So, whenever possible, turn your back on modern life. Go wild. Go camping. Embrace the simple life of your aboriginal ancestors. Become a hunter-gatherer. Gather a few essentials, then go hunt for a comfortable campsite. Cull your concerns down to food, water, warmth and shelter. You'll find the simple, outdoor life can relieve stress better than anything on pharmacy or video-store shelves.

10.5 km (6.5 mi)
Small islands are visible in the lake.

11.5 km (7.1 mi)
Reach **Humamilt Lake East Recreation Site #25**. It has 2 tables and an outhouse, but the sites are just overnight pullouts between the road and the marshy east end of the lake. During the day, the dust and noise of passing vehicles is annoying here.

12.2 km (7.6 mi)
Bear left on the main road. Pass a debris pile on the right.

14 km (8.7 mi)
Face a road looping toward you. Go left on the broader, main road.

14.9 km (9.2 mi)
Cross a bridge over Celista Creek and reach a T-junction. Turn right (south). The road is badly washboarded. Along the creek to your right is an ancient forest of cedar and hemlock—a rare delight in this heavily logged land.

18.8 km (11.7 mi)
Stay straight on the main road.

20.4 km (12.6 mi)
Cross under power lines.

21.7 km (13.4 mi)
Arrive at a well-signed major junction beside a mill, near the
north end of Shuswap Lake's Seymour Arm. Set your tripometer
to 0 here, whether turning or continuing. Turn left (east) on
Celista-Seymour FS road (also signed for Seymour Arm) to
quickly reach Nellie Lake campground. Continue straight
(south) on Celista Creek FS road and later Ross-Ruckell FS road
to reach Trans-Canada Hwy 1.

> **0 km (0 mi)**
> Turning left (east) onto Celista-Seymour FS road, from the
> 21.7-km (13.4-mi) junction on Celista Creek FS road.

> **0.3 km (0.2 mi)**
> Turn right to enter **Nellie Lake Recreation Site #27**. The
> 2 tables are in trees above a tiny lake. Though near a busy
> intersection, this campground is more appealing than
> Humamilt Lake East.

*Continuing south on Celista Creek FS road, from the junction at 21.7 km
(13.4 mi) with Celista-Seymour FS road. Set your tripometer to 0.*

0 km (0 mi)
On Celista Creek FS road, heading south to follow the west side
of Seymour Arm.

1 km (0.6 mi)
The signed access road for Albas Provincial Park is on the left. The
lakeside campground is several kilometers below the main road.

1.1 km (0.7 mi)
Bear left.

2.6 km (1.6 mi)
Stay straight.

3.1 km (1.9 mi)
Go right at this major junction and ascend on Ross-Ruckell FS road. Shuswap Lake's enormous Seymour Arm is visible left, far below.

7.1 km (4.4 mi)
Stay straight on the main road, then cross a bridged creek.

11.2 km (6.9 mi) to **28.1 km (17.4 mi)**
Stay straight on the main road.

30.8 km (19.1 mi)
The road is rough now and very close to the lakeshore.

32.3 km (20 mi)
Pavement begins. Pass a luxurious log home on the left.

41.3 km (25.6 mi)
Stay straight, along the lake.

63 km (39.1 mi)
Curve right.

65.3 km (40.5 mi)
Cross a bridge over Scotch Creek.

66 km (41 mi)
Bear left. Scotch Creek FS road forks right (north), reaching **Kwikoit Creek Recreation Site #23** in about 12.5 km (7.75 mi). It's a small campground, just north of the bridge over Sparkle Creek, near the confluence of Scotch and Kwikoit creeks.

76 km (47.1 mi)
Midway across the Adams River bridge.

76.6 km (47.5 mi)
Holding Road forks right, accessing the west side of Adams Lake. Proceed straight (south).

79.8 km (49.5 mi)
Midway across the South Thompson River bridge. Continue
onto the highway overpass and loop left.

80.6 km (50 mi)
Intersect Trans-Canada Hwy 1. Salmon Arm is right (east),
Kamloops is left (west).

SEYMOUR ARM NORTHWEST TO ADAMS LAKE

The best way to see Adams and Shuswap lakes is to follow the
clockwise loop previously described under *Adams Lake West*. It's a
faster route to the area's superior campgrounds. And it leads
directly into the less developed, more dramatic scenery surrounding Adams Lake. For whatever reason, however, you
might want to drive the loop counter-clockwise, beginning
along the north shore of Shuswap Lake. So here are the directions—but only as far as Adams Lake.

The approach to this counter-clockwise loop is the same as
described under *Adams Lake West*. On page 67 read the initial
directions to the turnoff from Trans-Canada Hwy 1.

0 km (0 mi)
Turning south off Hwy 1. Curve right to loop onto the overpass.

0.3 km (0.2 mi)
Bear right on the main road. (Turtle Valley Road forks left. It
accesses Skimikin Lakes campground, described in *Camp Free in
B.C. Volume I.*)

0.7 km (0.4 mi)
Midway across the South Thompson River bridge.

3.9 km (2.4 mi)
Bear right for Scotch Creek and Shuswap Lake's north shore.
Holding Road forks left here, accessing the west side of Adams Lake.

4.5 km (2.8 mi)
Midway across the Adams River bridge.

14.5 km (9 mi)
Bear right on the main paved road to pass through the communities of Scotch Creek, Celista, and Magna Bay. Scotch Creek FS road forks left (north) here, reaching **Kwikoit Creek Recreation Site #23** in about 12.5 km (7.75 mi). It's a small campground, just north of the bridge over Sparkle Creek, near the confluence of Scotch and Kwikoit creeks.

17.6 km (10.9 mi)
Curve left.

39.3 km (24.4 mi)
Bear right, along Shuswap Lake.

48.3 km (29.9 mi)
Pavement ends. Proceed on Ross-Ruckell FS road.

52.5 km (32.6 mi) to **69.4 km (43 mi)**
Stay straight on the main road.

73.5 km (45.6 mi)
Bear left.

77.5 km (48.1 mi)
Stay straight at this major junction.

78 km (48.4 mi) and **79.5 km (49.3 mi)**
Bear right.

79.6 km (49.4 mi)
The signed access road for Albas Provincial Park is on the right. The lakeside campground is several kilometers below the main road.

80.6 km (50 mi)
Arrive at a well-signed major junction beside a mill, near the north end of Shuswap Lake's Seymour Arm. Set your tripometer to 0 here, whether turning or continuing. Turn right (east) on Celista-Seymour FS road (also signed for Seymour Arm) to quickly reach Nellie Lake campground. Continue straight (north) on Celista Creek FS road for more campgrounds en route to Adams Lake.

0 km (0 mi)
Turning right (east) onto Celista-Seymour FS road, from the
80.6-km (50-mi) junction on Celista Creek FS road.

0.3 km (0.2 mi)
Turn right to enter **Nellie Lake Recreation Site #27**. The 2
tables are in trees above a tiny lake. Though near a busy
intersection, this campground is more appealing than
Humamilt Lake East.

*Continuing north on Celista Creek FS road, from the junction at 80.6 km
(50 mi) with Celista-Seymour FS road. Set your tripometer to 0.*

0 km (0 mi)
On Celista Creek FS road, heading north toward Humamilt
Lake.

2.9 km (1.8 mi)
Stay straight.

6.8 km (4.2 mi)
Go left.

7.7 km (4.8 mi)
Stay right on the main road.

9.5 km (5.9 mi)
Bear left.

10.2 km (6.3 mi)
Reach **Humamilt Lake East Recreation Site #25**. It has 2
tables and an outhouse, but the sites are just overnight pullouts
between the road and the marshy east end of the lake. During
the day, the dust and noise of passing vehicles is annoying here.

16.2 km (10 mi)
Stay right.

20.8 km (12.9 mi)
Bear right, along the south side of Humamilt Lake.

Humamilt Lake campsite

21.7 km (13.5 mi)
Turn right for Humamilt Lake campground. Set your tripometer to 0 here, whether turning or continuing.

> Descend from the main road. Arrive at the first table in 100 meters. Proceed another 50 meters to the other 6 campsites scattered in a forest of cedar, fir and birch, near the southwest end of the lake

HUMAMILT LAKE RECREATION SITE #24
Destination / Difficult (due only to distance)
Elev: 580 m (1902 ft) / Lake: 12 km (7.5 mi) long, 438 ha
7 tables, boat launch, exceptionally beautiful forest and lake
Inaccessible by motorhomes and trailers

Continuing northwest on Celista Creek FS road, from the turnoff to Humamilt Lake campground. Set your tripometer to 0.

0 km (0 mi)
On Celista Creek FS road, at the turnoff to Humamilt Lake campground.

3.3 km (2 mi)
Stay straight.

7.3 km (4.5 mi)
Turn left for **Stukemapten Lake campground.**

Descend from the main road. Fork right to reach 1 table in 150 meters. The left-fork campsite has no table. Both are inaccessible by trailers and motorhomes because there's no room to turn around.

8.6 km (5.3 mi)
Go left at the junction.

9 km (5.6 mi), 11.6 km (7.2 mi) and **14.1 km (8.7 mi)**
Go right.

17 km (10.5 mi)
Go right and immediately cross a bridged creek.

17.3 km (10.7 mi) and **18.6 km (11.5 mi)**
Bear right.

19.4 km (12 mi)
Turn left for Momich Lake East campground.

The 3 campsites are merely pullouts on the right side of the access road, which ends at 0.5 km (0.3 mi) in a turn-around. The forest is cool, shady, mossy. The green lake invites swimming

MOMICH LAKE EAST CAMPGROUND #46
Weekend / Difficult (due only to distance)
Elev: 472 m (1550 ft) / Lake: 3.8 km (2.4 mi) long, 206 ha
2 tables, 3 campsites, boat launch, sandy beach, little privacy
Accessible by small trailers, but not motorhomes or 5th-wheels

~

Continuing north on Momich-Stukemapten FS road, passing the turnoff to Momich Lake East campground

21.6 km (13.4 mi)
Go left and ascend.

22.6 km (14 mi)
The road is now high on a cliffside.

29 km (18 mi)
Stay left.

29.5 km (18.3 mi)
Reach a T-junction with Adams East FS road, above the northeast shore of Adams Lake. Set your tripometer to 0 here before turning either way. Turn left and descend for Momich River campground, beyond which there are no more campgrounds along Adams Lake. Turn right—following the page 76 directions in reverse from the 18.7-km (11.6-mi) point—to continue around the north end of Adams Lake.

0 km (0 mi)
Turning left onto Adams East FS road, from the 29.5-km (18.3-mi) junction on Momich-Stukemapten FS road.

0.3 km (0.2 mi)
Turn right for BC Parks' Momich River campground (free in 1999).

Descend to enter the campground in 0.5 km (0.3 mi). Just before the sign, a right fork loops into the north section, passing 6 campsites (2 with tables, all in the trees, none with lake views) and reaching a cement boat launch. Stay straight at the sign to enter the main section where most campsites have lake views. Bear left for sites near the river, right for more privacy on the lake. An obnoxious generator across the river might be audible.

MOMICH RIVER CAMPGROUND #44
Destination / Difficult (due only to distance)
22 tables, pebble beach, boat launch, mega-wharf
Accessible by motorhomes and 5th-wheels,
but not on north-section loop

NEAR SHUSWAP LAKE

As explained in this chapter's introduction, there are no free FS campgrounds on Shuswap Lake. But the area is immensely popular, so we've included a recreation site south of Shuswap Lake, at tiny Herman Lake. It's merely a day-use area on a marshy pond invisible from the road. Ringed by reeds and cattails, it's home to frogs and ducks protected by the BC Wildlife Federation. It's possible, however, to use the parking area for a quiet, dark, overnight pullout, or pitch a tent near the lone picnic table. Before driving here, realize that it accommodates only a couple vehicles. A much better option is Skwaam Bay campground on Adams Lake, described under *Adams Lake West*.

If you're heading west on Trans-Canada Hwy 1

0 km (0 mi)
In Salmon Arm, at the Safeway store.

9.4 km (5.8 mi)
Proceed straight. (Left, across from the mill, is Tappen Valley Road. It accesses Skimikin Lakes campground, described in *Camp Free in B.C. Volume I.*)

9.5 km (5.9 mi)
Cross a bridge over White Creek.

23.4 km (14.5 mi)
Turn right (north) on Balmoral Road. It's identified by a gas station, liquor store, and large blue-and-white sign: CAMPING, LODGING. South of the highway is a green sign: 5 BLIND BAY, 19 EAGLE BAY. Set your tripometer to 0.

If you're heading east on Trans-Canada Hwy 1

0 km (0 mi)
In Sorrento, at the pedestrian walkway with flashing lights.

9.7 km (6 mi)
Turn left (north) on Balmoral Road. It's identified by a gas station, liquor store, and large blue-and-white sign: CAMPING, LODGING. South of the highway is a green sign: 5 BLIND BAY, 19 EAGLE BAY. Set your tripometer to 0.

For either approach above, now follow the directions below

0 km (0 mi)
Turning north onto paved Balmoral Road. Bear left in 100 meters where White Lake Road forks right.

18.8 km (11.7 mi)
Pass Eagle Bay store.

19.8 km (12.3 mi)
Turn right onto Ivy Road, before a little church in the community of Eagle Bay.

21.3 km (13.2 mi)
Proceed through Eagle Ridge development and ascend.

21.9 km (13.6 mi)
Pavement ends and the road narrows.

22.4 km (13.9 mi)
Turn right at the historic cabin on which a sign states the lake is 2 km distant. This is Bastion-Ivy FS road.

22.6 km (14 mi)
Stay right and ascend.

23.4 km (14.5 mi)
Fork left.

24.3 km (15.1 mi)
Pass the private Herman Lake Wilderness Campground with its tall, wooden, ranch-style portico.

24.6 km (15.3 mi)
Arrive at the signed pullout for Herman Lake, on the left.

HERMAN LAKE RECREATION SITE #22
Overnight / Moderate
1 table, boardwalk, marshy pond, intended for day use
Accessible by all vehicles,
but too small for motorhomes or trailers

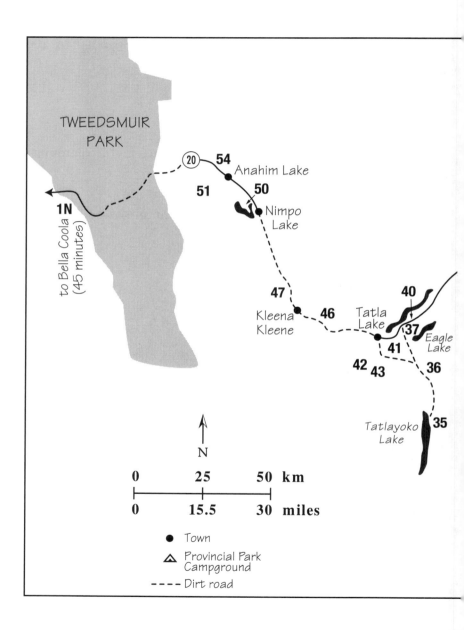

TWEEDSMUIR
PARK

20 **54**
● Anahim Lake

51   **50**

● Nimpo
Lake

1N

*to Bella Coola
(45 minutes)*

47

Kleena   **46**   Tatla
Kleene   Lake ●

40

37
Eagle
Lake

41

42 **43**   **36**

Tatlayoko   **35**
Lake

↑
N

| 0 | 25 | 50 | km |

| 0 | 15.5 | 30 | miles |

●   Town

△   Provincial Park
     Campground

- - - -   Dirt road

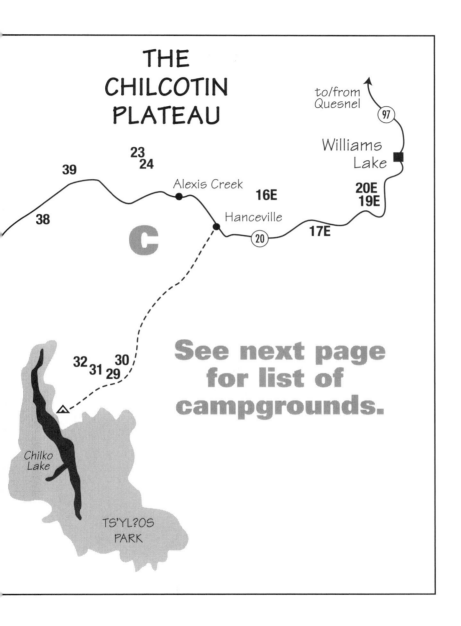

THE
CHILCOTIN
PLATEAU

to/from
Quesnel
97

Williams
Lake

39

23
24

Alexis Creek

16E

20E
19E

38

Hanceville

20

17E

C

32 31 30
29

See next page
for list of
campgrounds.

Chilko
Lake

TS'YL?OS
PARK

C: The Chilcotin Plateau

Most of these campgrounds are in **West Cariboo FS Region**.
E stands for **East Cariboo FS Region**. **N** stands for **North Coast FS District**.

1 N	McCall Flats
16 E	Raven Lake
17 E	Becher Pond
19 E	McIntyre Lake
20 E	Till Lake
23	Two Lakes
24	Alexis Lakes
29	Big Lake
30	Davidson Bridge
31	Vedan Lake
32	Chaunigan Lake
35	Tatlayoko Lake
36	Cochin Lake
37	Eagle Lake
38	Pyper Lake
39	Puntzi Lake
40	Tatla Lake
41	Pinto Lake
42	Sapeye Lake
43	Horn Lake
46	One Eye Lake
47	Clearwater Lake
50	Dean River (Fish Trap)
51	Kappan Lake
54	Little Anahim Lake

The Chilcotin Plateau

The Coast Mountains rise beyond Chilko Lake's west shore. In the foreground is a Russell fence, common throughout the Chilcotin.

Hunkered in the middle of central B.C. is the city of Williams Lake. Wedged into a narrow fiord that splits the Coast Range is the town of Bella Coola. Linking them is Hwy 20. It's 456 km (283 mi) long. A third of the distance is dirt—an often dusty, occasionally muddy reminder that this province is vast. So vast that paving all the main arteries isn't feasible, and that maybe what the initials really stand for is Big Country.

Hwy 20 traverses lonely terrain: the Chilcotin Plateau, virtually a big country unto itself. Driving west, you'll swoop into the Fraser River canyon, then climb onto the plateau. Until the rapid descent through mountainous Tweedsmuir Provincial Park to the Pacific Ocean, the highway bobs and weaves over hilly expanses of grass broken by forests of aspen and lodgepole pine. This is premier ranch land, where the vistas test the limits of your eyesight.

Across the plateau, as in other B.C. ranch lands such as Telkwa Valley outside Smithers, you'll see drift fences. They keep cattle from drifting—off the ranch, onto the road, into trouble. There are many styles of drift fence. The most artistic is the Russell fence. Like old covered bridges, Russell fences are certifiably quaint. They beg to be photographed.

Contrary to this grand setting, Chilcotin campgrounds tend to be small. But west of Williams Lake, no cities clog Hwy 20. The dots on the map are just hamlets. So there's no population pressure on these small campgrounds. Crowds don't seem to be a problem. At the campgrounds near Hwy 20, expect company. Those a day's journey from the highway just might be vacant when you arrive. Rub your lucky charm.

Concerned about too much solitude? Picturing yourself waiting hours for a saviour after your vehicle breaks down? The Chilcotin isn't *that* lonely. Actually, the Chilcotin is, but the roads aren't. That's because the traffic is not dispersed; it's confined to a relatively minimal network of roads. Traffic on Hwy 20 is light but steady. Huge ranches sprawl across the Chilcotin, keeping most backroads in regular use. There's always the occasional logging truck. And in big country like this, people tend to be open and trusting. They habitually offer help if it appears needed.

Heavy rain creates serious mud on Chilcotin backroads.

But you are hereby warned: watch your fuel gauge. Gas stations are rare as vegetarians out here. You can count on filling up in the communities of Alexis Creek, Tatla Lake, Nimpo Lake, and Anahim Lake (largest settlement in the West Chilcotin). Mega Fuels is the dominant gas station on Hwy 20. Most stations are open until 8 p.m. in summer. It's critical that you have plenty of gas and other necessities before driving southwest to Ts'yl?os Park and Chilko Lake.

Now, about that dust and mud. Dust is simply annoying. Mud can be dangerous. Surprised by a quagmire, your vehicle can swerve off the road no matter how quick or deft your are at the wheel. After a long, hard rain, slow down and stay alert. Shift into 4WD if you have it. With only 2WD be extra cautious, even on flat straight-aways. Any backroad or campground access road can get laundry-chute slick. Hwy 20 can have surprisingly long stretches of deep mud, particularly south of Nimpo Lake. The highway is unpaved (dirt and/or gravel) from Tatla Lake northwest to just south of Nimpo Lake, and from near Anahim Lake to the bottom of the Big Hill. Though the Big Hill is ski-run steep, its all-weather gravel surface offers better traction than the rest of unpaved Hwy 20, so you don't have to avoid it after encountering mud elsewhere.

Before travelling the Chilcotin Plateau, study the maps and brochures for Ts'yl?os and Tweedsmuir provincial parks. Write to BC Parks, 281 First Ave. North, Williams Lake, BC V2G 1Y7. Phone: (250) 398-4414. Fax: (250) 398-4686. They can also provide contact information for wilderness outfitters and charter transport services (planes and boats).

WEST ON HWY 20, FROM WILLIAMS LAKE

0 km (0 mi)
In Williams Lake, at the junction of Hwys 97 and 20. (It's a major intersection with traffic lights, near the rodeo grounds. You'll encounter no more traffic lights until Bella Coola.) Head southwest onto Hwy 20, soon ascending steeply.

2.6 km (1.6 mi)
Turn left (southeast) for **campgrounds on Chimney Lake Road**; read page 128 for further directions.

25 km (15.5 mi)
Midway across the Fraser River canyon bridge.

34 km (21.1 mi)
For campgrounds at McIntyre and Till lakes, turn right at the sign MELDRUM CREEK 31. (You're out of the canyon now, on the plateau.)

> **0 km (0 mi)**
> Starting north on Meldrum Creek FS road.
>
> **0.6 km (0.4 mi)**
> Reach McIntyre Lake campground, on the right, beside a shrinking, marshy lake ringed by meadow and trees.

MCINTYRE LAKE RECREATION SITE #19
Overnight / Easy
Elev: 930 m (3050 ft) / Lake: 16.4 ha
4 tables at well-spaced campsites
Accessible by motorhomes and 5th-wheels

Continuing north on Meldrum Creek FS road, passing McIntyre Lake campground.

3.8 km (2.4 mi)
Stay straight on the main road. Proceed through vast meadows and forested, rolling hills.

13.5 km (8.4 mi)
Turn left for Till Lake campground.

15.4 km (9.5 mi)
Go left at the 3-way junction.

16.3 km (10.1 mi)
Pass Till Lake's first campsite, on the right.

16.8 km (10.4 mi)
Reach Till Lake's last, best campsite. It has a large grassy area.

TILL LAKE RECREATION SITE #20
Weekend / Moderate
Elev: 869 m (2850 ft) / Lake: 2.5 km (1.6 mi) long, 102.5 ha
10 tables, more campsites
Accessible by motorhomes and 5th-wheels

Continuing west on Hwy 20, passing the turnoff to McIntyre and Till lakes campgrounds.

47.7 km (29.6 mi)
Pass the one-honk hamlet of Riske Creek. (Big Creek Ecological Reserve, Farwell Canyon, and Gang Ranch are south of here.)

50 km (31 mi)
Turn left (south) for Becher Dam campground.

> Take the right fork. In 200 meters, pass a house. Go right at the sign. The narrow road can be very muddy. The lake is tiny and shallow.

BECHER DAM RECREATION SITE #17
Overnight / Easy
Elev: approx. 930 m (3050 ft) / Lake: 9.5 ha
1 table across the lake from the highway
Inaccessible by motorhomes and 5th-wheels

~~

Continuing west on Hwy 20, passing the turnoff to Becher Dam campground.

69.3 km (43 mi)
Turn right onto Alex Graham FS road for Raven Lake campground. Set your tripometer to 0.

0 km (0 mi)
Starting north on well-graded Alex Graham FS road.

13 km (8.1 mi)
Stay straight on the main road.

15.8 km (9.8 mi)
Turn right (just before the KM 16 sign) to enter Raven Lake campground. It's less appealing than Till Lake.

RAVEN LAKE RECREATION SITE #16
Overnight / Moderate
Elev: 1252 m (4107 ft) / Lake: approx 45 ha
12 tables
Accessible by small motorhomes and trailers

~~

Continuing west on Hwy 20, passing the turnoff to Raven Lake campground.

83.6 km (51.8 mi)
Pass Hanceville Rest Area.

91.8 km (56.9 mi)
Reach Lee's Corner, in Hanceville. Set your tripometer to 0 whether turning or continuing. Turn left (south) for Chilko Lake and Ts'yl?os Provincial Park. The road is signed for Konni Lake (94 km), Taseko Lake (105 km), and Nemiah Valley (105 km).

Lee's Corner at Hanceville is where you turn south for Chilko Lake.

TS'YL?OS PROVINCIAL PARK

The following directions will guide you deep into the Chilcotin, through hilly grassland and forests of aspen and pine, to Ts'yl?os Park and 80-km (50-mi) long Chilko Lake. Nearing Nemiah Valley, your attention will be drawn toward the highest peak in the Chilcotin Range: 3066-m (10,056-ft) Mt. Tatlow, known as Ts'yl?os Mtn. to the people of the Tsilhquot'in Nation.

A sweeping view of a watery, icy wilderness is your reward for completing the drive to Chilko Lake. On sunny days it appears to be filled with turquoise paint, because of suspended glacial sediment. Guarding the lake and dialing up the scenic drama are the brawny, glacier-studded Coast Mountains. Chilko is the largest natural, high-elevation lake in North America, and an important spawning ground for Chinook and Sockeye salmon.

Because it's within a provincial park, the campground at Chilko Lake is not free. But it's cheap because it's remote. In 1999 the per-site, per-night fee was $8. Plan to stay there if you drive that far. Several campsites are on the shore. Most have tremendous views. Develop a deeper rapport with this awesome place by walking over the bluff north of the campground, to a small, rocky point. Don't have time to overnight at Chilko Lake? It's possible to see it in a day. Allow 7 hours for the roundtrip from Hwy 20. That includes 2 hours for a picnic and lakeshore stroll before returning.

Consider breaking up the journey at any of several free campgrounds. The first one is about two-thirds of the way to Ts'yl?os Park, at Davidson Bridge. The next is just beyond, at Big Lake. Another is at Vedan Lake—not far off the main road. It has a view of Mt. Tatlow and is often windy enough to excite boardsailors.

The road to Ts'yl?os Park is all-weather gravel, fairly wide and reasonably smooth—most of the way. It narrows and deteriorates (rutted dirt or mud) just west of Konni Lake, in Nemiah Valley. Unless it's muddy, even this last stretch is usually passable in a low-clearance 2WD car. Just drive the final 4.4 km (2.7 mi) to Chilko Lake slowly and cautiously, to avoid bottoming-out. Small motorhomes and trailers can probably make it to the 26.3-km (16.3-mi) junction beyond the Vedan Lake turnoff. The Coast Mtn. view is spectacular there, though Chilko Lake is not yet visible. Big-rig pilots should scout the final 4.4 km (2.7 mi) on foot. If you can't drive it, don't turn back; it's an enjoyable walk.

Want to hike in the cold, hard, unforgiving but beautiful mountains west of Chilko Lake? Be aware: this is prime bear habitat. Take all the necessary precautions for blacks and grizzlies. Listen to the audio cassette *Bears Beware: Warning Calls You Can Make to Avoid an Encounter.* It's described in the back of this book.

HANCEVILLE TO CHILKO LAKE

0 km (0 mi)
At Lee's Corner, in Hanceville, starting on the road south, heading for Konni Lake, Nemiah Valley, Chilko Lake and Ts'yl?os Provincial Park.

5.6 km (3.5 mi)
Turn left.

8.8 km (5.6 mi)
Turn right.

21.8 km (13.5 mi)
Go left at the T-junction.

71.2 km (44.1 mi)
Stay right where Road 4500 forks left.

72 km (44.6 mi)
Stay left.

75.8 km (47 mi)
Pass an **overnight pullout** on the right, beside Taseko River.
It's just after the road drops to the river.

78.4 km (48.6 mi)
Reach Davidson Bridge campground, on the right, just before
the bridge over Taseko River. (Left is a signed 4WD road leading
about 18 km / 11 mi to Fish Lake campground.)

DAVIDSON BRIDGE RECREATION SITE #30
Weekend / Difficult (due only to distance)
3 well-spaced campsites between the road and the river
Accessible by motorhomes and 5th-wheels

*Passing Davidson Bridge campground, crossing the bridge over Taseko
River, continuing southwest.*

83 km (51.5 mi)
Reach **Big Lake Recreation Site #29**, on the right. The campground has 2 sites with views southwest to Mt. Tatlow. The 97-
hectare lake is at 1326 m (4350 ft).

89.6 km (55.5 mi)
After descending part way into the valley, reach a signed junction. Set your tripometer to 0 whether turning or continuing. Turn
right for Vedan and Chaunigan lakes campgrounds. Continue on
the main road for Konni Lake, Nemiah Valley, Chilko Lake and
Ts'yl?os Provincial Park.

0 km (0 mi)
Starting northwest on Vedan-Elkins Lake FS road.

Looking south to Mt. Tatlow, from Vedan Lake

8.2 km (5.1 mi)
After crossing a stream between two lakes, reach a sign before a drift fence and house on the right. Proceed straight (south) for Vedan Lake. (Right ascends steeply to **Chaunigan Lake Recreation Site #32**, on the mesa above you, at 1494 m / 4900 ft. The road is steep and narrow, not recommended for big RVs. The campground has a pebble beach on the 440-hectare lake. Nearby is an airstrip.)

8.6 km (5.3 mi)
Stay straight.

9.1 km (5.6 mi)
Arrive at Vedan Lake campground, in a stand of pine and aspen. Mt. Tatlow is visible south.

VEDAN LAKE RECREATION SITE #31
Weekend / Difficult (due only to distance)
Elev: 1220 m (4002 ft) / Lake: 5 km (3 mi) long, 303 ha
3 tables, gravel boat launch
Inaccessible by large motorhomes and 5th-wheels

Continuing southwest on Nemiah Valley Road, passing the turnoff to Vedan Lake campground. Set your tripometer to 0.

0 km (0 mi)
Resuming the descent into Nemiah Valley.

7 km (4.2 mi)
Reach the east end of Konni Lake and Nemiah Valley.

14.5 km (9 mi)
Stay left at the fork.

26.3 km (16.3 mi)
Reach a signed junction. Go left for Ts'yl?os Park and Chilko Lake. When dry, the road beyond is usually passable in a 2WD car. The final 4.4 km (2.7 mi) to the lake is narrow and deeply rutted. It can be seriously muddy when wet.

29.6 km (18.4 mi)
Go right.

30.7 km (19 mi)
Fork left to arrive in 100 meters at Nu Chugh Beniz campground in Ts'yl?os Provincial Park, on the east shore of 18,447-hectare Chilko Lake, at 1172 m (3844 ft). It has about 12 campsites with tables. In 1999 the per-site, per-night fee was $8.

WEST ON HWY 20, FROM HANCEVILLE

0 km (0 mi)
At Lee's Corner, in Hanceville. Continuing west on Hwy 20, the scenery improves. Mountains are visible on the horizon.

22.2 km (13.8 mi)
Reach Alexis Creek store and gas station.

32.9 km (20.4 mi)
Turn right (northwest) for Alexis Lakes campground—not recommended for 2WD if the road's muddy.

At 2.4 km (1.5 mi) from the main road, fork right for a gentler ascent. The road proceeds northwest, staying above and just west of Alexis Creek. At 27 km (16.7 mi) arrive at narrow Alexis Lake. The campground is on the east side of the lake.

ALEXIS LAKES RECREATION SITE #24
Weekend / Moderate
Elev: 1038 m (3405 ft) / Lake: 5 km (3 mi) long, 91.5 ha
well-spaced campsites in a sandy pine forest
Inaccessible by motorhomes and 5th-wheels

~~~

Follow the main road north another 1.6 km (1 mi) up the west side of Alexis Lake to reach **Two Lake Recreation Site #23**. The campground and the lake are small.

~~~

Continuing west on Hwy 20, passing the turnoff to Alexis Lakes campground.

55.8 km (34.6 mi)
Cross a bridge over the Chilcotin River.

77.4 km (48 mi)
Pass a gas station in Redstone.

83.8 km (52 mi)
Reach Chilanko Forks (barely noticeable), where various signs urge you to visit Puntzi Lake. Set your tripometer to 0 whether turning or continuing. Turn right for Puntzi Lake campground—not recommended for big RVs.

 0 km (0 mi)
 Starting north on gravel Puntzi Lake road.

 4.4 km (2.7 mi)
 Go left at the fork. Proceed through an ugly, diseased, lodgepole-pine forest.

 6.5 km (4 mi)
 Turn right after passing a couple resorts. This final approach is steep and narrow. Arrive at the lakeside campground in 300 meters.

PUNTZI LAKE RECREATION SITE #39
Weekend / Moderate
Elev: 955 m (3132 ft) / Lake: 9 km (5.6 mi) long, 1688 ha
5 well-spaced campsites, rough boat launch
Inaccessible by motorhomes and trailers

Resuming southwest on Hwy 20, from the turnoff to Puntzi Lake campground. Set your tripometer to 0.

0 km (0 mi)
At Chilanko Forks.

9.4 km (5.8 mi)
Turn left for Pyper Lake campground.

> **0 km (0 mi)**
> Starting south on Chipman Road.

> **2.9 km (1.8 mi)**
> Go right at the fork.

> **3.4 km (2.1 mi)**
> Arrive at Pyper Lake.

PYPER LAKE RECREATION SITE #38
Overnight / Easy
Elev: 981 m (3218 ft) / Lake: 3.5 km (2.2 mi) long, 172 ha
2 tables at a small lakeside meadow
Accessible by motorhomes and 5th-wheels

Continuing southwest on Hwy 20, passing the turnoff to Pyper Lake campground.

37.2 km (23 mi)
Pass a **rest area** at a small lake on the southeast side of the highway.

39 km (24.2 mi)
Turn right (north) for Tatla Lake campground.

Low-clearance 2WD cars might struggle on this potholed access if it's muddy. Reach a fork 0.5 km (0.3 mi) off the main road. Right leads to campsites, left to the boat launch. RV pilots should scout the narrow, final 100 meters to the campsites; if impassable, park near the boat launch. The campground is on a meadowy, aspen-sprinkled hillside overlooking the long, narrow lake.

TATLA LAKE RECREATION SITE #40
Overnight / Easy
Elev: 910 m (2985 ft) / Lake: 30 km (18.6 mi) long, 1720 ha
2 tables, 3 campsites
Accessible by small motorhomes and trailers

Continuing southwest on Hwy 20, passing the turnoff to Tatla Lake campground.

39.7 km (24.6 mi)
Turn left (southeast), following directions on page 110, to quickly reach large Eagle Lake campground or to proceed farther south to the destination campground at Tatlayoko Lake. Set your tripometer to 0 whether continuing on Hwy 20 or turning.

Continuing southwest on Hwy 20, passing the turnoff to Eagle and Tatlayoko lakes campgrounds. Set your tripometer to 0.

0 km (0 mi)
On Hwy 20, where Eagle Lake Road forks southeast.

2.1 km (1.3 mi)
Turn left (south) for Pinto Lake campground.

Parallel the highway. Arrive at the campground in 1.4 km (0.9 mi). Big mountains are visible south. Proceed west to reach the highway in 0.3 km (0.2 mi).

PINTO LAKE RECREATION SITE #41
Overnight / Easy
Elev: 910 m (2985 ft) / Lake: 9.5 ha
3 tables beside the small lake
Accessible by motorhomes and 5th-wheels

3.8 km (2.4 mi)
Pass Pinto Lake's west access on the left.

8.5 km (5.3 mi)
The highway curves. Pass prominent signs for Chilko Lake (south).

9.9 km (6.1 mi)
Reach the general store in the town of Tatla Lake. Set your tripometer to 0. Hwy 20 proceeds northwest; for directions continue reading on page 115.

SOUTH OF HWY 20, TO TATLAYOKO LAKE

Though overshadowed by Chilko Lake, strikingly beautiful Tatlayoko Lake is another wonder of the Chilcotin. At its north end, 45 minutes south of Hwy 20, is a large, provincial-park-quality free campground. The sites are sheltered in a grand Douglas fir forest—a welcome change from the more common, unimpressive forests of lodgepole pine. Directly across the lake are the spectacular, snow-clutching Niut mountains.

The Niuts also create an exceptionally scenic backdrop for smaller Horn Lake, just 25 minutes south of Hwy 20. Like Tatlayoko, this spacious campground lives up to the setting. It's rated Destination.

The campgrounds at Tatlayoko and Horn lakes are inaccessible by motorhomes and 5th-wheels. But big rigs can easily glide into the sprawling campground at Eagle Lake, a mere 6 minutes south of Hwy 20. Rarely do campgrounds this convenient earn a Weekend rating. Eagle does, thanks to its pastoral, park-like atmosphere.

Tatlayoko Lake campground

0 km (0 mi)
Starting southeast on Eagle Lake Road (39.7 km / 24.6 mi southwest of Chilanko Forks), departing Hwy 20.

4.3 km (2.7 mi)
Continue straight.

5 km (3 mi)
Turn left (east) to enter Eagle Lake West campground, in a large clearing.

EAGLE LAKE RECREATION SITE #37
Weekend / Easy
Elev: 1060 m (3477 ft) / Lake: 10 km (6.2 mi) long, 1185 ha
2 tables, many more campsites
Accessible by motorhomes and 5th-wheels

Continuing south on Eagle Lake Road, passing Eagle Lake campground.

13.2 km (8.2 mi)
Proceed through a ranch.

16.2 km (10 mi)
Reach a T-junction with a bigger road. Turn left (south) for Cochin and Tatlayoko lakes. (Right leads northwest 12.4 km / 7.7 mi to a junction where you can turn left for Horn and Sapeye lakes, or right to reach the town of Tatla Lake on Hwy 20 in another 4.3 km / 2.7 mi. For directions continue reading on page 113.)

20 km (12.4 mi)
Turn left (east) for nearby Cochin Lake campground—not recommended for 2WD if the road's muddy. Bear right (south) for Tatlayoko Lake.

> **0 km (0 mi)**
> Starting east on Chilko Road.

> **0.6 km (0.4 mi)**
> Turn left (north) onto the rough, possibly muddy spur road to Cochin Lake. Chilko Road continues east to a junction where right (south) leads to the north end of Chilko Lake— a less scenic vantage than reached via Nemiah Valley (page 102).

> **0.9 km (0.6 mi)**
> Fork right.

> **1.1 km (0.7 mi)**
> Arrive at the campground. It's more confined than most in this area.

COCHIN LAKE RECREATION SITE #36
Weekend / Moderate
Elev: 1013 m (3323 ft) / Lake: 2.5 km (1.5 mi) long, 180 ha
4 tables, 5 campsites
Inaccessible by motorhomes and 5th-wheels

Continuing south, passing the turnoff to Cochin Lake campground.

22 km (13.6 mi) and **33 km (20.5 mi)**
Pass through ranches.

Getting Acquainted with Doug Fir

The outdoor activities you can enjoy with your child are limitless. This one develops empathy and perception. Blindfold your child, then lead him to a tree. Introduce them to one another. Urge your child to get acquainted with the tree. Suggest touching it, hugging it, talking to it, listening to it, smelling it. Nudge your child's curiosity by posing questions about the tree's life and history. Then lead your child back to camp, take off the blindfold and ask, "Where's your friend?" Let him find the tree. During your stay, occasionally ask "How's your friend doing?" After he visits it, question him about the experience. "Has the tree changed? Does it have a family nearby? Who are the tree's friends? Bugs? Birds? Chipmunks?" If you'll ever return to this campground, tell your child he can visit his friend again. Before you leave, let him say goodbye.

34.6 km (21.5 mi)
Bear right at the fork.

35.2 km (21.8 mi)
Reach Tatlayoko Lake.

36.1 km (22.4 mi)
Turn right to enter Tatlayoko Lake campground. It extends south along the lake, where one of the sites is on a scenic viewpoint. The Niut mountains are directly across the lake.

TATLAYOKO LAKE RECREATION SITE #35
Destination / Difficult (due only to distance)
Elev: 827 m (2713 ft) / Lake: 23 km (14 mi) long, 3928 ha
8 tables, 10 campsites
Inaccessible by motorhomes and 5th-wheels

Continuing south on the main road, passing Tatlayoko Lake campground.

37.3 km (23.1 mi)
Reach a community park at an old mill site, on the right.

Camping is allowed in the open field; donations are encouraged. The road proceeds south, staying above the lake. It drops to the shore and ends in about 15 km (9.3 mi).

Heading northwest from the 16.2-km (10-mi) T-junction on Eagle Lake Road (page 111). Set your tripometer to 0.

0 km (0 mi)
Starting on Tatla Lake Road, heading northwest. (This is the shortest route between Tatlayoko Lake and the town of Tatla Lake. It also accesses Horn and Sapeye lakes.)

12.4 km (7.7 mi)
Reach a 3-way junction. Set your tripometer to 0 again. Turn left for Horn and Sapeye Lakes. Right leads north 4.3 km (2.7 mi) to the town of Tatla Lake on Hwy 20.

Turning left at the 12.4-km (7.7-mi) junction on Tatla Lake Road.

0 km (0 mi)
Starting on Westbranch Road, heading southwest to Horn and Sapeye lakes.

10 km (6.2 mi)
Horn Lake and the Niut Range are visible south.

11.5 km (7.1 mi)
Turn right for homely Sapeye Lake campground. Bear left (south) for the superior campground at Horn Lake.

> **0 km (0 mi)**
> Starting on the spur road to Sapeye Lake campground. Mud could prohibit 2WD cars.
>
> **0.4 km (0.25 mi)**
> Turn right.
>
> **1.2 km (0.7 mi)**
> Turn left.

1.7 km (1 mi)
Arrive at the campground, above the lake.

SAPEYE LAKE RECREATION SITE #42
Overnight / Easy
Elev: 887 m (2910 ft) / Lake: 5 km (3 mi) long, 290 ha
5 campsites in a confined area
Inaccessible by motorhomes and 5th-wheels

Continuing south on Westbranch Road, passing the turnoff to Sapeye Lake campground.

13 km (8.1 mi)
Turn left to enter Horn Lake campground. The well-separated campsites even have gravel parking pads. The Niut mountains are visible south.

HORN LAKE RECREATION SITE #43
Destination / Easy
Elev: 915 m (3000 ft) / Lake: 4 km (2.5 mi) long, 190 ha
13 tables, good boat launch, provincial-park quality
Inaccessible by motorhomes and 5th-wheels

Horn Lake campground

NORTHWEST ON HWY 20, FROM TATLA LAKE

0 km (0 mi)
At the general store in the town of Tatla Lake. Set your tripometer to 0. Pavement soon ends as you head northwest on Hwy 20.

26.2 km (16.2 mi)
Turn right for One Eye Lake campground.

Drive 200 meters in on Holm Road. Then turn right. This spur road is narrow and rough but passable in 2WD when dry. At 1.2 km (0.7 mi) watch for a granddaddy pothole just before arriving at the campground.

ONE EYE LAKE RECREATION SITE #46
Weekend / Easy
Elev: 907 m (2975 ft) / 5 km (3 mi) long, 483 ha
3 tables, 4 campsites, boat launch
Inaccessible by motorhomes and 5th-wheels

Continuing northwest on Hwy 20, passing the turnoff to One Eye Lake campground.

32 km (19.8 mi)
Cross the bridge over Kleena Kleene River, in the otherwise barely noticeable hamlet of Kleena Kleene.

37.3 km (23.1 mi)
Turn left for Clearwater Lake campground. If muddy, the narrow access road will challenge 2WD cars.

Descend from the highway to reach the small campground in 0.4 km (0.25 mi). The treed lakeshore limits views of distant mountains.

CLEARWATER LAKE RECREATION SITE #47
Weekend / Easy
Elev: 960 m (3150 ft) / Lake: 3 km (1.8 mi), 210 ha
2 tables in a grassy clearing, rough boat launch
Inaccessible by large motorhomes and 5th-wheels

~

Continuing northwest on Hwy 20, passing the turnoff to Clearwater Lake campground.

67 km (41.5 mi)
Pavement resumes.

78 km (48.4 mi)
Reach Nimpo Lake store and gas station. Set your tripometer to 0.

~

Resuming northwest on Hwy 20, from the town of Nimpo Lake. Set your tripometer to 0

0 km (0 mi)
At Nimpo Lake store and gas station, heading northwest on Hwy 20.

4.8 km (3 mi)
Turn left for Fish Trap campground on Dean River. It's just 50 meters off the highway but behind a wall of trees.

FISH TRAP RECREATION SITE #50
Overnight / Easy
Elev: 1117 m (3664 ft)
3 tables, 5 campsites, rough boat launch
Accessible by motorhomes and 5th-wheels

~

Continuing northwest on Hwy 20, passing the turnoff to Fish Trap campground.

20 km (12.4 mi)
Reach the village of Anahim Lake. (Anahim Street leads to the store and gas station.)

21.1 km (13.1 mi)
Turn left for Kappan Lake campground.

0 km (0 mi)
Starting southwest on Kappan Mtn. FS road.

5 km (3 mi)
Proceed straight through the intersection.

9.6 km (6 mi)
Turn right for the final, steep descent to the lake.

11.3 km (7 mi)
Arrive at the campground on the lake's southeast end.

KAPPAN LAKE RECREATION SITE #51
Overnight / Easy
Elev: 1113 m (3650 ft) / Lake: 7 km (4.3 mi) long, 350 ha
6 tables, no privacy, sandy beach, good boat launch
Inaccessible by large motorhomes and 5th-wheels

Continuing northwest on Hwy 20, passing the turnoff to Kappan Lake campground.

23.7 km (14.7 mi)
Turn right for Little Anahim Lake campground. It's just 30 meters off the highway but minimal nighttime traffic should grant you uninterrupted sleep.

LITTLE ANAHIM LAKE RECREATION SITE #54
Overnight / Easy
Elev: 1083 m (3552 ft) / Lake: 3.5 km (2.2 mi) long, 165 ha
5 campsites, no tables, boat launch
Accessible by motorhomes and 5th-wheels

Continuing northwest on Hwy 20, passing the turnoff to Little Anahim Lake campground. Pavement soon ends.

53 km (32.9 mi)
Pass an **overnight pullout** on the left, near a creek.

56 km (34.8 mi)
Enter Tweedsmuir Provincial Park. Set your tripometer to 0. The highway soon tops 1524-m (5000-ft) Heckman Pass.

TWEEDSMUIR TO BELLA COOLA

The Chilcotin Plateau ends near Tweedsmuir Provincial Park's east boundary. You're entering the Coast Mountains here. But instead of climbing over them, the road descends through them. Pavement is finally halted by the sea at Bella Coola, on the tail of a fiord long ago gouged by a glacier.

This section of Hwy 20 is a marvel. Wrested from sheer cliffs, it allows vehicles to safely travel what would otherwise be the exclusive domain of mountain goats and eagles. Acrophobic passengers: blindfold yourself, or risk a catatonic reaction. Called the Big Hill, it rapidly drops 1244 m (4015 ft) between Heckman Pass and Atnarko Valley. The government refused to build the road, saying it was too costly and would serve too few people. So the locals built it themselves, finishing the task in 1953. It's Bella Coola's only land link to the rest of the planet.

Approaching Bella Coola, gazing up at the sheer valley walls, California's Yosemite National Park comes to mind. Hikers will be goggle-eyed. Sadly, not many trails pierce this lush, vertical world. The few in Tweedsmuir Park are well worth hoofing. A dayhike in the Rainbow Range reveals why the name is apt. Peaks averaging 2500 m (8200 ft) sport an array of Florentine colours: purple, rouge, mustard. Backpacking in the Rainbows is also possible, but an even better option is trekking into the alpine highlands above Hunlen Falls. Allow 3 to 4 days for the 58-km (36-mi) roundtrip. Hunlen tumbles 366 m (1200 ft) and comprises one of Canada's longest freefall cascades: 260 m (853 ft).

The area's greatest deficiency, however, isn't trailheads. It's free campgrounds. There's only one (McCall Flats) in the 197-km (122-mi) stretch between Little Anahim Lake and Bella Coola. At least it's conveniently located near Tweedsmuir's west boundary. Too bad it's in a graveyard of giant cedar stumps. Your other options are the two pay-campgrounds in the Park.

0 km (0 mi)
At Tweedsmuir Park's east boundary, heading west.

6.3 km (3.9 mi)
Pass the Rainbow Range trailhead on the right.

7 km (4.2 mi)
Begin descending the Big Hill. Atnarko Valley is 1244 m (4015 ft) below but only 19.2 km (11.9 mi) distant.

26.2 km (16.2 mi)
Pavement resumes here in Atnarko Valley. You've completed the Big Hill descent. A 4WD road on the left leads to Hunlen Falls trail-head. (The falls trail is steep, regaining most of the elevation you just lost on the Big Hill.) Young Creek picnic area is also on the left.

28 km (17.4 mi)
Pass Tweedsmuir Park Headquarters on the left. It's staffed only part-time, but maps are always available at the kiosk.

44 km (27.3 mi)
Pass the provincial park Fisheries Pool campground, where you can watch salmon spawning.

52 km (32.2 mi)
Proceed on Hwy 20 for Bella Coola. Turn left for McCall Flats campground.

> **0 km (0 mi)**
> Starting south on the spur road, departing Hwy 20.
>
> **0.7 km (0.4 mi)**
> Cross a bridge and turn right.
>
> **2 km (1.2 mi)**
> Pass an **overnight pullout** on the left, beside a rockslide.
>
> **2.2 km (1.4 mi)**
> Go right.
>
> **2.8 km (1.7 mi)**
> Arrive at McCall Flats campground on Bella Coola River.

MCCALL FLATS RECREATION SITE #1
Destination / Easy
5 tables, bearproof garbage cans
Accessible by small motorhomes and trailers

Backroad near Bella Coola River

Continuing west on Hwy 20, passing the turnoff to McCall Flats campground.

54 km (33.5 mi)
Pass Burnt Bridge picnic area on the left. Park here to hike the MacKenzie trail, a loop affording views south of 2677-m (8780-ft) Stupendous Mountain.

54.3 km (33.7 mi)
Cross the bridge over Burnt Creek—west boundary of Tweedsmuir Park.

64.8 km (40.2 mi)
Pass the Summer trail parking area on the right.

69.3 km (43 mi)
Cross the bridge over Bella Coola River.

86 km (53.3 mi)
Reach the community of Hagensborg. The original settlers were Norwegian descendants from Minnesota who felt at home in this fiord.

104 km (64.5 mi)
Arrive in Bella Coola.

EAST ON HWY 20, FROM BELLA COOLA

0 km (0 mi)
At the bridge over Burnt Creek—west boundary of Tweedsmuir Park. It's about 50 km (31 mi) east of Bella Coola.

0.3 km (0.2 mi)
Pass Burnt Bridge picnic area on the right. Park here to hike the MacKenzie trail.

2.3 km (1.4 mi)
Turn right for **McCall Flats campground**; read further directions on page 119.

26.3 km (16.3 mi)
Pass Tweedsmuir Park Headquarters on the right.

28.1 km (17.4 mi)
Pass Young Creek picnic area on the right. The 4WD road to
Hunlen Falls trailhead is also on the right. Pavement ends on
Hwy 20. Begin ascending the Big Hill.

47.3 km (29.3 mi)
You've completed the Big Hill ascent.

48 km (30 mi)
Pass the Rainbow Range trailhead on the left. Set your tripometer to 0 before continuing east on Hwy 20.

SOUTHEAST ON HWY 20, FROM TWEEDSMUIR

0 km (0 mi)
At the Rainbow Range trailhead, heading east on Hwy 20.

6.3 km (3.9 mi)
Cross Tweedsmuir Park's east boundary.

9.1 km (5.6 mi)
Pass an **overnight pullout** on the right, near a creek.

38.6 km (23.9 mi)
Soon after pavement resumes, turn left for **Little Anahim Lake
campground**. Just 30 meters off the highway, it's accessible by
motorhomes and 5th-wheels. It has 5 campsites but no tables.

41.2 km (25.5 mi)
Turn right (southwest) for **Kappan Lake campground**; read
further directions on page 117.

42.3 km (26.2 mi)
Reach the village of Anahim Lake. (Anahim Street leads to the
store and gas station.)

57.4 km (35.6 mi)
Turn right for **Fish Trap campground** on Dean River. Just 50
meters off the highway, it's accessible by motorhomes and 5th-
wheels. It has 5 campsites.

62.2 km (38.6 mi)
Reach Nimpo Lake store and gas station. Set your tripometer to 0 before continuing southeast on Hwy 20.

SOUTHEAST ON HWY 20, FROM NIMPO LAKE

0 km (0 mi)
At Nimpo Lake store and gas station, heading southeast on Hwy 20.

11.3 km (7 mi)
Pavement ends.

40.8 km (25.3 mi)
Turn right for **Clearwater Lake campground**; read further directions on page 115.

46 km (28.6 mi)
Cross the bridge over Kleena Kleene River.

51.7 km (32.1 mi)
Turn left for **One Eye Lake campground**; read further directions on page 115.

78 km (48.4 mi)
Soon after pavement resumes, reach the general store in the town of Tatla Lake. Set your tripometer to 0 before continuing northeast on Hwy 20.

NORTHEAST ON HWY 20, FROM TATLA LAKE

0 km (0 mi)
At the general store in the town of Tatla Lake, heading northeast on Hwy 20.

1.4 km (0.9 mi)
The highway curves. Prominent signs direct you to Chilko Lake, but before committing to this approach consider the more scenic vantage reached via Nemiah Valley from Hanceville (page 102). To reach provincial-park quality **Horn Lake campground**, turn right (south) here; in 4.3 km (2.7 mi) bear right on Westbranch Road; read further directions on page 113.

6.1 km (3.8 mi)
Turn right for **Pinto Lake campground**. Just 0.3 km (0.2 mi) from the highway, it's accessible by motorhomes and 5th-wheels. It has 3 campsites.

7.8 km (4.8 mi)
Pass Pinto Lake's east access on the right.

9.9 km (6.1 mi)
Turn right (southeast) to quickly reach large **Eagle Lake campground** or to proceed farther south to the provincial-park quality **Tatlayoko Lake campground**; read page 110 for further directions.

10.6 km (6.6 mi)
Turn left (north) for **Tatla Lake campground**; read page 108 for further directions.

40.2 km (24.9 mi)
Turn right (south) for **Pyper Lake campground**; read page 107 for further directions.

49.6 km (30.8 mi)
Reach Chilanko Forks. Turn left (north) for **Puntzi Lake campground**; read page 106 for further directions.

56 km (34.7 mi)
Pass a gas station in Redstone.

77.6 km (48.1 mi)
Cross a bridge over the Chilcotin River.

100.5 km (62.3 mi)
Turn left (northwest) for **Alexis Lake campground**—not recommended for 2WD if the road's muddy. Read page 105 for further directions.

111.2 km (68.9 mi)
Reach Alexis Creek store and gas station.

133.4 km (82.7 mi)
Reach Lee's Corner, in Hanceville. Set your tripometer to 0

whether turning or continuing. Turn right (south) for Chilko Lake and Ts'yl?os Provincial Park; read page 102 for further directions. Continue east on Hwy 20 to reach Williams Lake in 92.5 km (57.4 mi).

EAST ON HWY 20, FROM HANCEVILLE

0 km (0 mi)
At Lee's Corner, in Hanceville, heading east on Hwy 20.

7.8 km (4.8 mi)
Pass Hanceville Rest Area.

22.5 km (14 mi)
Turn left (north) for **Raven Lake campground**; read page 100 for further directions.

42.5 km (26.4 mi)
Turn right (south) for tiny **Becher Dam campground.** It's within view but inaccessible by motorhomes and 5th-wheels. Read the bottom of page 99 for details.

58.5 km (36.3 mi)
Turn left (north) for **McIntyre and Till Lakes campgrounds**; read page 98 for further directions. Continuing east, Hwy 20 soon descends off the Chilcotin Plateau, into the Fraser River canyon.

67.5 km (41.9 mi)
Midway across the Fraser River canyon bridge.

90 km (55.8 mi)
Turn right (southeast) for **campgrounds on Chimney Lake Road**; read page 128 for further directions.

92.6 km (57.4 mi)
Arrive in Williams Lake, at the junction of Hwys 20 and 97.

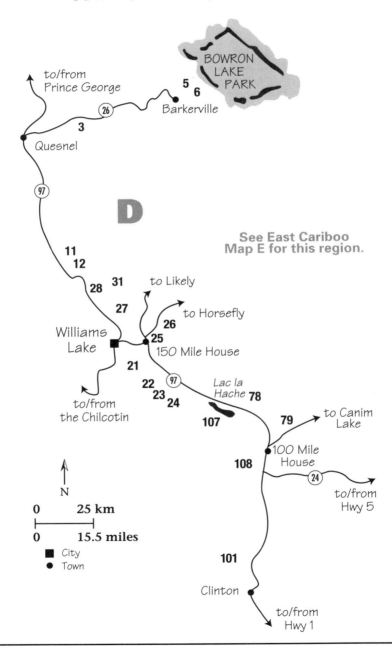

CLINTON TO QUESNEL

BOWRON
LAKE
PARK

to/from
Prince George

5 6

26

Barkerville

3

Quesnel

97

D

See East Cariboo
Map E for this region.

11
12

28   31

to Likely

27

to Horsefly

26

25

Williams
Lake

150 Mile House

21

22   97
23 24

Lac la
Hache   78

to/from
the Chilcotin

107

79

to Canim
Lake

100 Mile
House

108

24

to/from
Hwy 5

N

0   25 km

0   15.5 miles

■ City
● Town

101

Clinton

to/from
Hwy 1

D: Clinton to Quesnel

All these campgrounds are in the **East Cariboo FS Region**.

3	Lightning Creek
5	Atan Lake
6	Chisel Lake
11	Bushie Lake
12	Cuisson Lake
21	Brunson Lake
22	Felker Lake
23	Chimney Lake North
24	Chimney Lake Centre
25	Dugan Lake
26	Dewar Lake
27	Forest lake
28	Blue Lake West
31	Tyee Lake
78	Greeny Lake
79	Lower Lake
101	Beaverdam Lake
107	Helena Lake
108	Valentine Lake

Clinton to Quesnel

SOUTHEAST OF WILLIAMS LAKE, page 128
150 MILE HOUSE TO 100 MILE HOUSE, page 132
LOWER, CANIM, and HOWARD LAKES, page 139
NORTH TO 100 MILE HOUSE, page 143
WILLIAMS LAKE TO QUESNEL, page 146
NEAR BARKERVILLE, page 151

Picturesque access road leading to Brunson Lake campground, southeast of Williams Lake

SOUTHEAST OF WILLIAMS LAKE

The paved Chimney Lake Road links a rural bedroom community with the city of Williams Lake. It runs the length of a lovely, shallow valley. The pastoral scenery comprises meadows, marshes, lakes, forests, a meandering stream, and substantial country homes. You'll find several easy-to-reach free campgrounds here. They're even handy when travelling north or south on Hwy 97, because you can access Chimney Lake Road from Enterprise; read pages 136-37 for directions.

Enough people live along Chimney Lake Road that passing cars are frequently audible from the campgrounds. On weekdays, commuters start whizzing by at 6:30 a.m. They continue until 11:30 p.m. The quietest and prettiest campground is at small Brunson Lake. Felker and Chimney lakes are larger, and the campgrounds closer to the road. At Chimney Lake, the proximity of houses and the road create the feeling that you're camping in a city park. It's also popular with waterskiers.

CHIMNEY LAKE ROAD

0 km (0 mi)
In Williams Lake, at the junction of Hwys 97 and 20. (It's a major intersection with traffic lights, near the rodeo grounds.) Head southwest onto Hwy 20, soon ascending steeply.

2.6 km (1.6 mi)
Near the top of the hill, turn left (southeast) onto Chimney Lake Road. You'll continue climbing, then descend steeply.

10.5 km (6.5 mi)
Turn left.

15 km (9.3 mi)
Turn right for Brunson Lake campground.

Reach the first campsite 0.5 km (0.3 mi) off the pavement. The campground is on an open, grassy, lightly-treed promontory overlooking the small but picturesque lake. The shore is mostly forested. The resident loons seem to be unusually loud. Their robust calls echo among the surrounding low hills. Expect an onslaught of mosquitoes in June and July.

BRUNSON LAKE RECREATION SITE #21
Weekend / Easy
Elev: 808 m (2650 ft) / Lake: 53 ha
1 table, 4 well-spaced campsites
Accessible by small motorhomes and trailers

~

Continuing southeast on Chimney Lake Road, passing the turnoff to Brunson Lake campground.

25.4 km (15.7 mi)
The north end of Felker Lake and nearby houses are visible.

28 km (17.4 mi)
Turn right to enter Felker Lake campground. It's on the shore, beside a meadow.

FELKER LAKE RECREATION SITE #22
Weekend / Easy
Elev: 876 m (2873 ft) / 2.7 km (1.7 mi) long, 200 ha
10 tables, rough boat launch
Accessible by motorhomes and 5th-wheels

Continuing southeast on Chimney Lake Road, passing the turnoff to Felker Lake campground.

29.7 km (18.4 mi)
Turn right for Chimney Lake North campground. It's 100 meters off the pavement, near houses at the northwest end of the lake.

CHIMNEY LAKE NORTH RECREATION SITE #23
Weekend / Easy
Elev: 883 m (2896 ft) / Lake: 6 km (3.7 mi) long, 430 ha
4 tables, good gravel boat launch
Accessible by motorhomes and 5th-wheels

Continuing southeast on Chimney Lake Road, passing the turnoff to Chimney Lake North campground.

30.1 km (18.7 mi)
Turn right for Chimney Lake Centre campground, the largest on Chimney Lake. It's in a wide meadow peppered with trees. Shade is minimal. The shallow water is comfortably warm in summer.

Chimney Lake

CHIMNEY LAKE CENTRE RECREATION SITE #24
Weekend / Easy
Elev: 883 m (2896 ft) / Lake: 6 km (3.7 mi) long, 430 ha
20 campsites, many with tables, rough boat launch
Accessible by motorhomes and 5th-wheels

Continuing southeast on Chimney Lake Road, passing the turnoff to Chimney Lake Centre campground.

32.2 km (20 mi)
Turn right for Chimney Lake East campground.

CHIMNEY LAKE EAST RECREATION SITE
Weekend / Easy
Elev: 883 m (2896 ft) / Lake: 6 km (3.7 mi) long, 430 ha
4 tables
Accessible by motorhomes and 5th-wheels

Continuing southeast on Chimney Lake Road, passing the turnoff to Chimney Lake East campground, heading for Hwy 97.

35.4 km (21.9 mi)
Pavement ends.

40.7 km (25.2 mi)
Turn left at the 3-way junction.

47.8 km (29.6 mi)
Stay right, on the main road.

49.9 km (30.9 mi)
Cross railroad tracks.

50.7 km (31.4 mi)
Reach Hwy 97 at Enterprise. Turn left (northwest) for Williams Lake. Turn right (southeast) for Lac la Hache.

150 MILE HOUSE TO 100 MILE HOUSE

Several campgrounds are easily reached off Hwy 97 between 150 Mile House and 100 Mile House. All are at small or medium-sized lakes and are sufficiently pleasant for a weekend stay. But with little topography to speak of, the scenery is unexciting. So most of these campgrounds are best appreciated by travellers in need of a convenient one-night refuge.

The campgrounds on Chimney Lake, as well as those on Dugan, Helena and Greeny lakes, are accessible by motorhomes and 5th-wheels. Dugan Lake (pages 138-39) is very close to 150 Mile House, and not far from Williams Lake.

Lower Lake is an option if you must stay near 100 Mile House, but others are closer to Hwy 97. Try Greeny Lake, northeast of Lac la Hache. It's a bit more convenient and a lot more attractive. It's also bigger, so you're more likely to find a vacant site.

Howard Lake is about 50 minutes from Hwy 97, but the route is straight forward and the campground is rated Destination.

The one campground you shouldn't aim for late at night is Valentine Lake. Getting there can be frustrating even in broad

Helena Lake

daylight, because the area is laced with a confusing network of rough, heavily-used industrial roads.

If you're heading southeast on Hwy 97 from 150 Mile House

0 km (0 mi)
On Hwy 97 in 150 Mile House, at Mega Fuels gas station in 150 Centre.

19.3 km (12 mi)
For **campgrounds on Chimney Lake Road** (which continues northwest to Williams Lake) turn right onto initially paved Enterprise Road. Read further directions on page 137.

32 km (19.8 mi)
Pass a pullout with a litter barrel.

35 km (21.7 mi)
For Helena Lake campground, turn right (southwest) onto Wright Station Road, just before a sign welcoming you to Lac la Hache.

0 km (0 mi)
Starting on Wright Station Road (paved for 1 km, then good gravel).

100 meters
Cross a bridge and railroad tracks, then go left.

5.1 km (3.2 mi)
Turn left.

8.1 km (5.1 mi)
Turn right at the T-junction.

12 km (7.4 mi)
Arrive at Helena Lake campground. Don't follow the road left away from the lake; it departs the area. The lake is visible from most campsites.

HELENA LAKE RECREATION SITE #107
Weekend / Easy
Elev: 960 m (3150 ft) / Lake: 4.5 km (2.8 mi) long, 238 ha
4 tables, 10 campsites
Accessible by motorhomes and 5th-wheels

Continuing southeast on Hwy 97, passing the turnoff to Helena Lake campground.

37.5 km (23.3 mi)
Pass the turnoff to Lac la Hache Provincial Park.

51.4 km (31.9 mi)
For Greeny Lake campground, turn left (northeast) by the general store in the town of Lac la Hache, at the sign for Timothy Lake.

0 km (0 mi)
Starting northeast on paved Timothy Lake Road.

7.2 km (4.5 mi)
Turn right at the junction and continue on gravel.

Greeny Lake

11.5 km (7.1 mi)
Turn right at the lodgepole fence to enter Greeny Lake campground. Most campsites are in the open, along the shore. Those at the end are in the trees.

GREENY LAKE RECREATION SITE #78
Weekend / Easy
Elev: 937 m (3073 ft) / 2.6 km (1.6 mi) long, 72.5 ha
12 tables at a reedy-edged, narrow lake
Accessible by motorhomes and 5th-wheels

Continuing southeast on Hwy 97, passing the turnoff to Greeny Lake campground.

75 km (46.5 mi)
For **Lower Lake campground, Canim Lake, and Howard Lake campground** (rated Destination) turn left (east) across from Exeter Truck Route, at the north edge of 100 Mile House. Read further directions on page 139.

77 km (47.7 mi)
For **Valentine Lake campground**, turn right onto Exeter Station Road, by Marmot Ridge Golf Course. Read further directions on page 145.

77.6 km (48.1 mi)
Arrive in 100 Mile House, at the centre of town, between the Petro Canada gas station (left) and the Forest Service District Office (right).

~

If you're heading north on Hwy 97 from 100 Mile House

0 km (0 mi)
On Hwy 97 in the centre of 100 Mile House, between the Petro Canada gas station (right) and the Forest Service District Office (left).

0.6 km (0.4 mi)
For **Valentine Lake campground,** turn left onto Exeter Station Road, by Marmot Ridge Golf Course. Read further directions on page 145.

2.6 km (1.6 mi)
For **Lower Lake campground, Canim Lake, and Howard Lake campground** (rated Destination) turn right (east) across from Exeter Truck Route, at the north edge of 100 Mile House. Read further directions on page 139.

26.2 km (16.2 mi)
For **Greeny Lake campground**, turn right (northeast) by the general store in the town of Lac la Hache, at the sign for Timothy Lake. Read further directions on page 134.

42.6 km (26.4 mi)
For **Helena Lake campground**, turn left (southwest) onto Wright Station Road, just past the northwest end of Lac la Hache (the lake itself). Read further directions on page 134.

58.3 km (36.1 mi)
Proceed northwest on Hwy 97 to reach 150 Mile House (see page 138). For **campgrounds on Chimney Lake Road**, which continues northwest to Williams Lake, turn left onto Enterprise Road.

0 km (0 mi)
Starting southwest on Enterprise Road.

0.8 km (0.5 mi)
Cross railroad tracks. Pavement ends. Proceed on Chimney Lake FS road.

2.9 km (1.8 mi)
Stay left on the main road.

10 km (6.2 mi)
Turn right (west) at the 3-way junction.

14.5 km (9 mi)
The south end of Chimney Lake is visible.

15.3 km (9.5 mi)
Pavement begins.

18.5 km (11.5 mi)
Turn left for **Chimney Lake East campground**. Read page 131 for description.

20.6 km (12.8 mi)
Turn left for **Chimney Lake Centre campground**. Read page 131 for description.

21 km (13 mi)
Turn left for **Chimney Lake North campground**. Read page 130 for description.

22.7 km (14.1 mi)
Turn left for **Felker Lake campground**. Read page 130 for description.

35.7 km (22.1 mi)
Turn left for **Brunson Lake campground.** Read page 129 for description.

40 km (24.8 mi)
Turn right and ascend steeply for Williams Lake.

48 km (29.8 mi)
Turn right onto Hwy 20 to descend to Williams Lake.

50.6 km (31.4 mi)
Arrive in Williams Lake, at the junction of Hwys 20 and 97.

Continuing northwest on Hwy 97, passing the turnoff to the Chimney Lake Road campgrounds.

77.6 km (48.1 mi)
Arrive in 150 Mile House, at Mega Fuels gas station in 150 Centre. Proceed west on Hwy 97 for Williams Lake. Continue north for Likely, Horsefly, and campgrounds near Quesnel Lake; read page 188 for further directions. Just 10 minutes north of 150 Mile House is Dugan Lake campground; directions are below.

Continuing north from 150 Mile House, at Mega Fuels gas station in 150 Centre, heading for Dugan Lake campground. Set your tripometer to 0.

0 km (0 mi)
Starting north from 150 Mile House, following signs for Likely.

4.5 km (2.8 mi)
Turn right onto Horsefly Road, at the big white sign for Resort Lakes.

7.3 km (4.5 mi)
Turn right onto Dugan Lake Road.

7.7 km (4.8 mi)
Curve right, passing a home on the left, to enter Dugan Lake campground. The best sites are just beyond, between the trees and the lake. Tenters will find plenty of level grass. Road noise is audible.

DUGAN LAKE RECREATION SITE #25
Overnight / Easy
Elev: 930 m (3050 ft) / 94.5 ha
6 campsites, several tables around a pasture, boat launch
Accessible by motorhomes and 5th-wheels

Dugan Lake is a handy campground near 150 Mile House.

LOWER, CANIM, AND HOWARD LAKES

There are various ways to reach Canim Lake. The shortest route, and the only one that's paved, starts just north of 100 Mile House. It's described below. En route is a small campground at tiny Lower Lake.

Canim is a significant, beautiful lake, so it's unfortunate there are no free campgrounds on its shore. You will, however, find several nearby. Of special note is Howard Lake, rated Destination. It's located above and just south of Canim Lake.

0 km (0 mi)
Starting east on Canim Lake Road. It departs Hwy 97 across from Exeter Truck Route, 2.6 km (1.6 mi) north of the Forest Service District Office in 100 Mile House.

8 km (5 mi)
Proceed through the village of Edwards Lake.

15.3 km (9.5 mi)
Turn right for Drewry Lake West campground.

> In about 1 km (0.6 mi) bear right. FS directional signs should guide you the remaining 19 km to the lake's southwest end. The rough, winding road gets very muddy when wet.

DREWRY LAKE WEST RECREATION SITE #80
Weekend / Difficult
Elev: 1067 m (3500 ft) / Lake: 5 km (3 mi) long, 577 ha
6 campsites with tables, boat launch
Inaccessible by motorhomes and 5th-wheels

Continuing northeast on Canim Lake Road, passing the turnoff to Drewry Lake West campground.

18 km (11.2 mi)
Turn left (west) onto Archie Meadow Road for Lower Lake campground.

0 km (0 mi)
Starting west on Archie Meadow Road.

3 km (1.9 mi)
Turn right.

4.2 km (2.6 mi)
Arrive at Lower Lake campground—a small grassy clearing beside the road, just above the tiny lake.

LOWER LAKE RECREATION SITE #79
Overnight / Easy
Elev: 930 m (3050 ft) / 15 ha
no tables, level tentsites
Accessible by small motorhomes and trailers

Continuing northeast on Canim Lake Road, passing the turnoff to Lower Lake campground.

29 km (18 mi)
Reach a junction. Proceed left (northeast) on Canim Lake Road for campgrounds north of Canim Lake; read further directions on page 163. Bear right (east) onto Canim Lake South Road for Howard Lake campground. Set your tripometer to 0.

0 km (0 mi)
Starting east on Canim Lake South Road. This is at the junction of Canim Lake Road and Canim Lake South Road, near the west end of Canim Lake, about 29 km (18 mi) northeast of Hwy 97 and 100 Mile House.

9.4 km (5.8 mi)
Turn right and ascend for Howard Lake campground. See photo on page 162.

The road soon levels and widens but remains bumpy. In 3.8 km (2.4 mi) reach the first campsites—one on the left, another on the lakeshore. The main campground is 200 meters farther, in a large clearing. Secluded lakeshore sites are slightly beyond.

HOWARD LAKE RECREATION SITE #81
Destination / Easy
Elev: 937 m (3073 ft) / Lake: 3.8 km (2.4 mi) long, 175 ha
20 campsites with tables, good boat launch
Accessible by motorhomes and 5th-wheels

Continuing north on Canim Lake South Road, passing the turnoff to Howard Lake campground.

25 km (15.5 mi)
Reach a junction with Mahood Lake FS road. Turn left (northeast) for Mahood Lake. Bear right (south) to reach Hwy 24 in about

The National Bird of Canada

Canadian winters can be torture. Constant numbing cold. Oppressive, dismal dark. Repeatedly shoveling snow. By February it can seem unbearable, and you begin to pray for spring. But when your prayers are answered, you step outside and you're assaulted. In your craving for light and warmth, you'd forgotten about mosquitoes—the national bird of Canada.

They come down the chimney. They rush in before the door is fully open. They seem to squeeze through cracks in the walls. And that unmistakable high-pitched whine gnaws at your nerves. There's no sound more horrifying to some of us. Not the wail of a fire alarm in the middle of the night. Not the shriek of an incoming SCUD missile. For this is the sound of a demon intent on extracting your blood. The blood that should be coursing through your veins. Oxygenating your tissues. A researcher in the far north supposedly recorded 9,000 bites per minute on a human volunteer. That's enough to drain half your blood in under two hours. Theoretically, mosquitoes could kill you.

To go camping is to offer yourself to the feast. What's the best defense? Well, mosquitoes are primarily attracted to carbon dioxide and lactic acid, which are uncontrollably expelled from your body. But there are attractants you can control: scented products (cologne, perfume), strong-smelling soaps, lotions, hair-care products. Adults are bitten more than children. Men are bitten more than women. The middle-aged are bitten more than the elderly. The bigger you are, the more mosquitoes you'll attract, possibly due to greater carbon-dioxide output. So, other than repellent or proboscis-proof clothing, the best mosquito defense is to choose your campmates carefully. Large, heavy-breathing, 40-something men who use hair spray are ideal.

43 km (27 mi). En route to Hwy 24, stay right on the main road at all junctions; for details follow pages 159-62 directions in reverse.

NORTH TO 100 MILE HOUSE

North of Clinton, you'll notice a transition: from dry, rolling, sagebrush country, to flater, cooler forests and grasslands. The lone free campground between Clinton and 100 Mile House is at shallow **Beaverdam Lake**. The distant scenery includes the southern Chilcotin Mtns. Specifically, you can see 2270-m (7445-ft) Mt. Kerr in Marble Range Provincial Park. Beaverdam's gorgeous lakeside meadow and the showy blue skies that often prevail might lull you into a relaxing stay—if the mosquitoes have abated. Heading south? Stop here for a peaceful interlude prior to forging into combat on Hwy 1.

Not far from 100 Mile House, **Valentine Lake** is best approached in broad daylight, with patience, good humour, and low expectations. The area is laced with a confusing network of rough, heavily-used industrial roads. Cattle roam the extensively clearcut land. They sometimes congregate on the roads, staring you down until you can coax them out of the way. The lake provides visual relief from the grim surroundings, but otherwise is not noteworthy. The campground is minimal. Though the campsites are well spaced, and the lake is accessible by RVs, even small motorhomes and trailers will have difficulty turning around. Most campers should head elsewhere. That said, you might find solitude here.

BEAVERDAM LAKE

If you're heading south on Hwy 97 from 100 Mile House

Drive south to 70 Mile House and the southern access to Green Lake. From this junction, continue nearly another 15 km (9.3 mi), then turn right (northwest) onto Meadow Lake Road. Set your tripometer to 0.

Beaverdam Lake

If you're heading north on Hwy 97 from Clinton

Drive 17 km (10.5 mi) north, then turn left (northwest) onto Meadow Lake Road. (It's 1.5 km / 0.9 mi north of the turnoff to Chasm Provincial Park.) Set your tripometer to 0.

For either approach above, now follow the directions below

0 km (0 mi)
Starting northwest on Meadow Lake Road, signed for Gang Ranch and Alkali. Proceed through vast meadowlands.

10.4 km (6.4 mi)
Turn left to enter Beaverdam campground. Be prepared for mosquitoes at this shallow, reedy lake.

BEAVERDAM RECREATION SITE #101
Weekend / Easy
Elev: 1110 m (3640 ft) / Lake: 1.4 km wide and long, 143 ha
3 tables, many more campsites
Accessible by motorhomes and 5th-wheels

VALENTINE LAKE

0 km (0 mi)
Starting west on paved Exeter Station Road. It departs Hwy 97 at the north edge of 100 Mile House, by Marmot Ridge Golf Course, 0.6 km (0.4 mi) north of the Forest Service District Office.

3.2 km (2 mi)
Cross railroad tracks and reach a T-junction. Turn left. Immediately after, go left again. Continue parallel to the nearby railroad tracks.

4 km (2.5 mi)
Pavement ends. Drive past the lumber mill.

5.7 km (3.5 mi)
Reach a fork. Bear right and ascend. Continue right uphill at the next minor fork.

6.1 km (3.8 mi)
Turn left at the 4-way junction. Stay on the main road.

8.4 km (5.2 mi)
Bear left on the main road.

13 km (8.1 mi)
Go left.

13.2 km (8.2 mi) and **15.8 km (9.8 mi)**
Bear right.

16 km (10 mi)
Fork left.

17.5 km (10.9 mi)
Arrive at Valentine Lake campground. The first table is on the left. The next is 30 meters farther.

18.3 km (11.3 mi)
Reach the boat launch. Another campsite is 0.6 km (0.4 mi) farther.

VALENTINE LAKE RECREATION SITE #108
Weekend / Difficult
Elev: 1204 m (3950 ft) / Lake: 1.2 km (0.7 mi) long, 64 ha
2 tables, 4 campsites, boat launch
Inaccessible by motorhomes and trailers

WILLIAMS LAKE TO QUESNEL

Five handy campgrounds ensure you'll find a home for the night near Hwy 97 between Williams Lake and Quesnel.

Forest Lake (11.2 km / 6.9 mi off the highway) has beautiful trees and a meadow. Tyee Lake (16.7 km / 10.4 mi off the highway) has a large clearing but isn't special. Blue Lake West (2.7 km / 1.7 mi off the highway) feels like it's in a mountain setting. All are accessible by motorhomes and 5th-wheels.

Cuisson Lake (8.3 km / 5.1 mi off the highway) and Bushie Lake (16 km / 10 mi off the highway) are tiny and unremarkable. The access is mostly paved, but neither campground is accessible by big RVs.

If you're heading north on Hwy 97 from Williams Lake

0 km (0 mi)
In Williams Lake, at the junction of Hwys 97 and 20. (It's a major intersection with traffic lights, near the rodeo grounds.) Proceed north on Hwy 97. Set your tripometer to 0.

25 km (15.6 mi)
For **campgrounds at Forest and Tyee lakes**, turn right (northeast) onto Lynes Creek FS road. Reset your tripometer to 0. Read further directions on page 147.

33.2 km (20.6 mi)
For **Blue Lake West campground**, turn right (northeast) onto Blue Lake Road. Reset your tripometer to 0. Read further directions on page 149.

44 km (27.3 mi)
Pass McCleese Lake store and gas station.

44.7 km (27.7 mi)
For **campgrounds at Cuisson and Bushie lakes**, turn right (east) onto Beaver Lake Road. It's signed for Cuisson Lake and Horsefly. Reset your tripometer to 0. Read further directions on page 150.

If you're heading south on Hwy 97 from Quesnel

From the south end of Quesnel, by Maple Park Mall, drive south 69.5 km (43.1 mi) to a **rest area** at the north end of McCleese Lake. Reset your tripometer to 0.

0.2 km (0.1 mi)
For **campgrounds at Cuisson and Bushie lakes**, turn left (east) onto Beaver Lake Road. It's signed for Cuisson Lake and Horsefly. Reset your tripometer to 0. Read further directions on page 150.

11 km (6.8 mi)
For **Blue Lake West campground**, turn left (northeast) onto Blue Lake Road. Reset your tripometer to 0. Read further directions on page 149.

19.2 km (11.9 mi)
For **campgrounds at Forest and Tyee lakes**, turn left (northeast) onto Lynes Creek FS road. Reset your tripometer to 0. Directions continue below.

For FOREST AND TYEE LAKES,
now follow the directions below

0 km (0 mi)
Starting northeast on Lynes Creek FS road. Begin ascending.

0.4 km (0.25 mi)
Pavement ends.

8.1 km (5 mi)
Reach a junction. For Tyee Lake, bear left and proceed north, ignoring minor right forks into private land. For more attractive Forest Lake, turn right (southeast).

0 km (0 mi)
Turning right (southeast) at the 8.1-km (5-mi) junction, heading for Forest Lake.

Forest Lake

2 km (1.2 mi)
Turn right at the junction.

3.1 km (1.9 mi)
Arrive at Forest Lake campground. The lake is reedy-edged.
There's a meadow on the shore and beautiful trees nearby.

FOREST LAKE RECREATION SITE #27
Weekend / Easy
Elev: approx. 900 m (2950 ft) / Lake: 2 km (1.2 mi) long, 98 ha
1 table, 6 well-spaced campsites
Accessible by motorhomes and 5th-wheels

*Continuing north on Lynes Creek FS road, passing the turnoff to Forest
Lake campground.*

16.2 km (10 mi)
Fork left and descend gradually.

16.7 km (10.4 mi)
Bear left to enter Tyee Lake campground. Many campsites are bunched together in a large clearing. The last campsite is a bit higher, with a lakeshore table and secluded level tentsite.

TYEE LAKE RECREATION SITE #31
Weekend / Easy
Elev: 915 m (3000 ft) / Lake: 7 km (4.3 mi) long, 408 ha
8 tables, boat launch
Accessible by motorhomes and 5th-wheels

For BLUE LAKE WEST, now follow the directions below

0 km (0 mi)
Starting northeast on Blue Lake Road.

0.2 km (0.1 mi)
Bear left and ascend steeply.

2.7 km (1.7 mi)
Turn right to reach Blue Lake West campground in 400 meters.

The lake is small, narrow, steep-sided. Unlike most pastoral, plateau lakes, the setting here feels mountainous. Half the campsites are on the shore, the rest have lakeviews. One is on a bench 15 meters above the lake. There's no boat launch, but with a canoe or kayak you can camp on an island.

BLUE LAKE WEST RECREATION SITE #28
Weekend / Easy
Elev: 820 m (2690 ft) / Lake: 34 ha
6 tables, 9 campsites
Accessible by motorhomes and 5th-wheels

For CUISSON AND BUSHIE LAKES,
now follow the directions below

0 km (0 mi)
Starting east on Beaver Lake Road (initially paved). Climb a big hill.

4.2 km (2.6 mi)
Reach a junction. Turn left onto Gibraltar Mine Road. Beaver Lake Road continues right.

7.1 km (4.4 mi)
Reach a junction. For Bushie Lake, bear right. To quickly reach Cuisson Lake, turn left onto dirt Rimrock Road, signed for Cuisson Lake Resort.

> **0 km (0 mi)**
> Starting on Rimrock Road, heading for Cuisson Lake.
>
> **0.9 km (0.6 mi)**
> Turn right onto a narrow, overgrown road.
>
> **1.2 km (0.7 mi)**
> Reach the south end of narrow Cuisson Lake and two tables. If the tiny campground is full, the meadow you passed 150 meters back will suffice as an overnight pullout.

CUISSON LAKE RECREATION SITE #12
Overnight / Easy
Elev: 884 m (2900 ft) / Lake: 5 km (3 mi) long, 170 ha
Inaccessible by motorhomes and 5th-wheels

Bearing right at the 7.1-km (4.4-mi) junction, passing the turnoff to Cuisson Lake campground.

14.7 km (9.1 mi)
Turn left onto gravel.

15 km (9.3 mi)
Go right at the fork.

16 km (10 mi)
Bear left. The lake is visible. Just 100 meters farther, turn sharply right. Arrive at Bushie Lake campground in another 50 meters.

The lake is marshy with lily pads. The tiny campground is between several big trees. There's room for only one vehicle, so don't arrive late assuming you'll camp here. If you find it vacant and don't mind the small lake and limited view, a weekend stay could be enjoyable.

BUSHIE LAKE RECREATION SITE #11
Overnight / Easy
Elev: approx. 890 m (2920 ft) / Lake: approx. 9.5 ha
1 campsite with a table
Inaccessible by motorhomes and 5th-wheels

NEAR BARKERVILLE

The best free campground in this area is closer to Quesnel than to Barkerville. It's just off Hwy 26, beside Lightning Creek. The campgrounds at Atan and Chisel lakes are northeast. As the snow flies, they're closer to Barkerville. But they're on backroads, so reaching them takes just as long. And they're small. Each has only two campsites. Unless they're vacant when you arrive (not likely), you're equally apt to enjoy quiet and privacy at Lightning Creek.

Plan on spending a day at Barkerville. It's an impeccably restored gold-rush town where actors in period costume carry on as if it were 1860. Without stepping out of character, they even interact with visitors. The result is often hilarious, as well as educational. In its prime, Barkerville appeared destined to become a major city. But when the gold rush died, so did the town. It was empty and silent for 75 years. Restoration began in 1958. Today, you'll see more than 40 buildings that look exactly as they did in the 1800's. Many of the original businesses— including the bakery, restaurants, general store, blacksmith, printer, and photographer—are operating and open to the public. You can visit Barkerville any day of the year. Phone (250) 994-3332 for details.

Lightning Creek campground

Heading east from the junction of Hwys 97 and 26

0 km (0 mi)
Starting east on Hwy 26, departing Hwy 97 just north of Quesnel.
It's about 5.2 km (3.2 mi) north of where Carson Avenue and
Front Street intersect along the river. Hwy 26 is signed for Wells
(74 km / 46 mi) and Barkerville (81 km / 50 mi).

26 km (16.1 mi)
Pass the historic site at Cottonwood.

32.5 km (20.2 mi)
Turn right, onto Swift River FS road, for Lightning Creek campground.

> In 200 meters, just before a bridge, turn left to enter the
> campground. Pass campsites right and left to reach a large,
> secluded site at road's end in about 400 meters. Spurs fork right
> to gravel sites on the creek. Aspen brighten the pretty forest.

LIGHTNING CREEK RECREATION SITE #3
Overnight / Easy
7 tables, 10 campsites
Accessible by motorhomes and 5th-wheels

~

Continuing east on Hwy 26, passing the turnoff to Lightning Creek campground.

75.5 km (46.8 mi)
Pass the RCMP office on the northeast edge of Wells.

81 km (50.2 mi)
For Barkerville, proceed a few minutes farther south. For Atan and Chisel lakes campgrounds, turn left (northeast) onto Bowron Lake Road, signed for Bowron Lakes Provincial Park (28 km). The precise location of this turn might vary slightly due to an extensive mining operation, but it should still be obvious. Set your tripometer to 0.

0 km (0 mi)
Starting northeast on Bowron Lake Road. The mining operation near this turn might vary the following distances slightly.

0.6 km (0.4 mi)
Bear left at the sign for Bowron Park.

4 km (2.5 mi)
Pass the Yellowhawk Trail parking area on the right.

7 km (4.2 mi)
Pass the Jubilee Trail parking area on the right.

16.7 km (10.4 mi)
Reach a major fork. Turn right on 2900 FS road (smaller, worse), signed for Atan and Chisel lakes.

17.4 km (10.8 mi)
Fork left at an old cabin. Slow down as the road starts descending. (Within 0.8 km / 0.5 mi, a 30-meter stretch of road gets dangerously muddy when wet.)

20.7 km (12.8 mi)
Cross a bridged creek. Immediately after, pass an **overnight pullout** on the right, near a small, derelict building.

21.3 km (13.2 mi)
Follow the middle road. The right fork was decommissioned.

23.3 km (14.4 mi)
Turn left to reach Atan Lake campground in 100 meters.

ATAN LAKE RECREATION SITE #5
Overnight / Moderate
Elev: 1030 m (3378 ft) / Lake: 1 km (0.6 mi) long, 29 ha
1 table, 2 campsites, gravel boat launch
Inaccessible by motorhomes and trailers

Continuing on the main road, passing the turnoff to Atan Lake campground.

25.6 km (15.9 mi)
Turn left for Chisel Lake campground. Descend on a good, stony road to reach the lake in 300 meters. A private cabin is visible across the water. The blunt, forested mountains of Bowron Lakes Park are beyond.

CHISEL LAKE RECREATION SITE #6
Overnight / Moderate
Elev: 1030 m (3378 ft) / Lake: 1 km (0.6 mi) long, 32 ha
2 tables, 3 campsites, gravel boat launch
Accessible by small motorhomes and trailers

Barkerville is educational and fun.

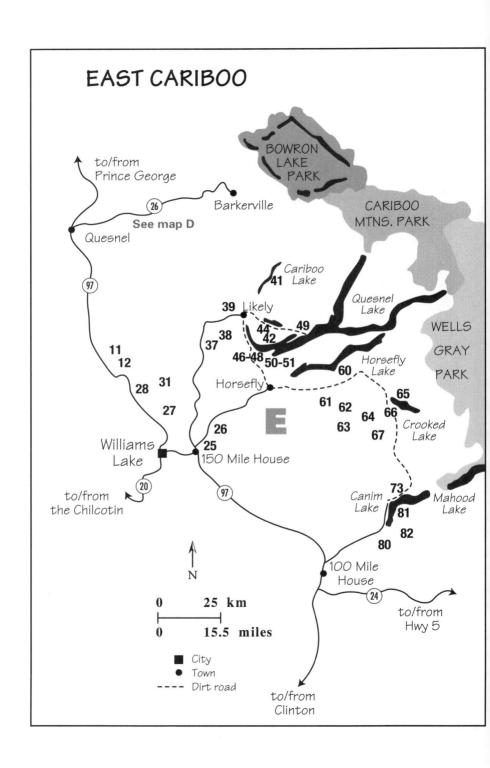

EAST CARIBOO

BOWRON
LAKE
PARK

CARIBOO
MTNS. PARK

to/from
Prince George

㉖ Barkerville

See map D

Quesnel

㊳

41 Cariboo
Lake

Quesnel
Lake

WELLS
GRAY
PARK

39 Likely

38

37

44   49

42

46-48 50-51

Horsefly
Lake

Horsefly

60

65

61   62

64   66

63   67

Crooked
Lake

26

25

150 Mile House

Williams
Lake

㉕

to/from
the Chilcotin

㉗

73

Canim
Lake

81

Mahood
Lake

82

80

100 Mile
House

㉔

to/from
Hwy 5

11
12

28

31

27

N

0   25 km

0   15.5 miles

■ City
● Town
- - - - Dirt road

to/from
Clinton

E

E: East Cariboo

All these campgrounds are in the **East Cariboo FS Region**.

11	Bushie Lake	49	Abbott Creek
12	Cuisson Lake	50	Squaw Flats
25	Dugan Lake	51	Horsefly Bay
26	Dewar Lake	60	Prairie Creek
27	Forest Lake	61	Horsefly River
28	Blue Lake West	62	McKinley Lake
31	Tyee Lake	63	Tisdall Lake
37	Jacobie Lake	64	Elbow Lake
38	Bootjack Lake	65	Crooked Lake North
39	Quesnel Forks	66	Crooked Lake South
41	Ladies Creek	67	Bosk Lake
42	Winkley Creek	73	Christmas Lake
44	Spanish Lake	80	Drewry Lake West
46	Polley Lake	81	Howard Lake
47	Raft Creek	82	Drewry Lake East
48	Mitchell Bay		

East Cariboo

Witness a fall-colour extravaganza on East Cariboo backroads, where aspen and birch thrive among the conifers.

BETWEEN HWY 24 AND CANIM LAKE

Well-maintained gravel roads at consistently low elevation allow easy travel to the sensuously long lakes between Hwy 24 and Canim Lake. And the area supports a healthy mix of deciduous and coniferous trees. Add those two facts to reach an obvious conclusion: leaf peepers should come here to enjoy an autumn drive. Vibrant reds, oranges, yellows and golds woven into the green forest fabric are dazzling. For the deluxe tour, depart Hwy 24 at the Interlakes Store just north of Sheridan Lake. Go north, past Hathaway and Drewry lakes, to Canim Lake. Pavement resumes near the southwest end of Canim Lake. Loop back to 100 Mile House and Hwy 97 via Forest Grove.

If you're heading west on Hwy 24 from Little Fort

At the junction of Hwys 5 and 24 in Little Fort, set your tripometer to 0 as you head west on Hwy 24. Proceed 67.6 km (42 mi) to the signed junction at Interlakes Store, just north of Sheridan Lake. Reset your tripometer to 0.

If you're heading north on Hwy 97 from Clinton

About 9.4 km (5.8 mi) before 100 Mile House, turn right (east) onto Hwy 24. Set your tripometer to 0 and proceed 29.4 km (18.2 mi) east to the signed junction at Interlakes Store, just north of Sheridan Lake. Reset your tripometer to 0.

If you're heading southeast on Hwy 97 from Williams Lake

About 9.4 km (5.8 mi) south of 100 Mile House, turn left (east) onto Hwy 24. Set your tripometer to 0 and proceed 29.4 km (18.2 mi) east to the signed junction at Interlakes Store, just north of Sheridan Lake. Reset your tripometer to 0.

For all approaches above, now follow the directions below

0 km (0 mi)
Starting north on Horse Lake FS road, departing Hwy 24 at Interlakes Store. The junction is signed for several lakes: Hathaway (14 km), Drewry (25 km), Canim (43 km), and Mahood (57 km). This is also the southwest approach to Wells Gray Provincial Park.

4.6 km (2.9 mi)
Reach a 3-way junction. Follow the paved middle fork: Mahood Lake Road, the southwest approach to Wells Gray Park.

9.3 km (5.8 mi)
Proceed straight for Hathaway Lake. Pavement soon ends.

14.4 km (8.9 mi)
Pass Hathaway Resort, where there's a public phone.

17.1 km (10.6 mi)
Reach a spacious, treed, one-vehicle **campsite** on the right. It's attractive, beside 5-km (3-mi) long Hathaway Lake, but the nearby road can be busy, especially on summer weekends. A sign labels this a Dispersed-Use Site and threatens closure or development if campers don't keep it clean.

17.9 km (11.1 mi)
Pass the north end of Hathaway Lake.

21.2 km (13.1 mi)
Pass Drewry Lake Ranch.

24.6 km (15.3 mi)
Bear left where Bowers-Decka FS road forks right.

25.4 km (15.7 mi)
Bear left where Bowers Lake FS road forks right.

26 km (16.1 mi)
Reach Drewry Lake East campground on the left. It's set in mixed forest between the road and the lake.

DREWRY LAKE EAST RECREATION SITE #82
Weekend / Difficult (due only to distance)
Elev: 1067 m (3500 ft) / Lake: 5 km (3 mi) long, 577 ha
4 tables, 6 campsites, boat launch
Accessible by small motorhomes, but not 5th-wheels

26.3 km (16.3 mi)
Pass Drewry Lake boat launch. Proceed north on the main road for Canim or Mahood lakes.

33 km (20.5 mi)
Stay straight.

39 km (24.2 mi)
Bear left and descend.

42.6 km (26.4 mi)
Reach a junction. Right leads northeast to Mahood Lake and Wells Gray Park. Turn left (northwest) onto Canim Lake South Road to reach 25-km (15.5-mi) long Canim Lake and return to pavement. It passes homes and cabins and grants only occasional views of the lake. Canim has no free campgrounds, but Howard Lake is nearby.

58.2 km (36.1 mi)
Fork sharply left, off Canim Lake South Road, for Howard Lake campground.

The road ascends, soon levels and widens, but remains bumpy. Reach the first campsites (one on the left, another on the lakeshore) in 3.8 km (2.4 mi). The main campground is 200 meters farther, in a large clearing. Secluded lakeshore sites are slightly beyond.

HOWARD LAKE RECREATION SITE #81
Destination / Difficult (due to distance from Hwy 24)
Elev: 937 m (3073 ft) / Lake: 4 km (2.5 mi) long, 175 ha
20 campsites with tables, good boat launch
Accessible by motorhomes and 5th-wheels

Camp in the open or snuggled into the trees at Howard Lake.

Continuing southwest on Canim Lake South Road, passing the turnoff to Howard Lake campground.

61.8 km (38.3 mi)
Pavement resumes.

67.6 km (42 mi)
Reach a junction. Left leads 30 km (18.6 mi) southwest to 100 Mile House; for details read page 141 directions in reverse starting at the 29-km (18-mi) point. Right (northeast) follows Canim Lake's west shore, then proceeds on excellent backroads through the East Cariboo to Crooked Lake and eventually Horsefly and Quesnel lakes. Set your tripometer to 0 and read the directions below.

CANIM LAKE TO HORSEFLY

The deeper you explore the East Cariboo, the more rewarding your journey. The mixed forest here can be quite scenic. In early summer, multiple shades of green are an inspirational sight. In fall, various hues of amber rustle overhead as you go. And the main Hendrix Creek road north of Canim Lake allows fast, easy travel, just like the road between Canim Lake and Hwy 24.

Here's a grand East Cariboo loop: from Sheridan Lake on Hwy 24, drive north to 25-km (15.5-mi) long Canim Lake, swing around its west shore, head north on Hendrix Creek Road to Crooked Lake, then west to Horsefly, and finally southwest to 150 Mile House, where you can follow Hwy 97 southeast back to Hwy 24. Allow two days of continuous driving, or 4 to 5 days if you linger at a few lakes. Lacking the obvious presence of aspen and birch, the road from Bosk Lake west to Horsefly is less enjoyable than roads farther south. Nevertheless, the ultimate East Cariboo week would include the drive from Horsefly north to Quesnel Lake, Likely, and Spanish Lake, following directions on page 171.

Horsefly FS District deserves appreciation. Their campgrounds are superbly organized and maintained. They've made the district a special resource for campers. Many of the lakes have inviting gravel beaches allowing you to easily dive in for a brisk swim. For the optimal view of the Cariboo Mountains, check out Crooked Lake South and Elbow Lake campgrounds.

0 km (0 mi)
Starting northeast on paved Canim Lake Road, from the 67.6-km (41.9-mi) junction on Canim Lake South Road, near the southwest end of Canim Lake.

8 km (5 mi)
Pass Canim Beach Provincial Park on the right.

12.6 km (7.8 mi)
Pavement ends.

17.6 km (10.9 mi)
Proceed straight on the main road, heading for Hendrix Lake.

19.1 km (11.8 mi)
Turn right and descend to reach Christmas Lake campground in 150 meters.

CHRISTMAS LAKE RECREATION SITE #73
Overnight / Difficult (due only to distance)
Elev: 915 m (3000 ft) / Lake: 32 ha
1 table, room for only 1 vehicle
Accessible by small motorhomes and trailers

Continuing northeast on the main road, passing the turnoff to Christmas Lake campground.

30.3 km (18.8 mi)
Bear left and ascend on the main road paralleling Hendrix Creek.

46.8 km (29 mi)
Bear right on the main road.

51.2 km (31.7 mi)
Bear left on the main road.

53 km (32.9 mi)
Proceed straight on the main road.

54.9 km (34 mi)
Bear right, still heading for Crooked Lake.

55.5 km (34.4 mi)
Bosk Lake is visible through trees on the left.

57.6 km (35.7 mi)
For Crooked Lake, stay right on the road signed for Eureka Peak Lodge. For Bosk Lake campground, turn left just before crossing a bridged creek. It's 200 meters off the main road in a large clearing.

BOSK LAKE RECREATION SITE #67
Weekend / Difficult (due only to distance)
Elev: 994 m (3260 ft) / Lake: 6 km (3.7 mi) long, 500 ha
4 tables, sandy beach, bearproof garbage bin
Accessible by motorhomes and 5th-wheels

Continuing northeast on the main road, passing the turnoff to Bosk Lake campground.

57.9 km (35.9 mi)
After crossing the bridged creek, proceed straight. Hendrix-Gotchen FS road forks right.

60.1 km (37.3 mi)
Bear right.

65.2 km (40.4 mi)
Reach a junction. Set your tripometer to 0 before going either way. Proceed straight (north) for **Crooked Lake**—worth a look even if you don't camp there. It's a beautiful lake beneath the Cariboo Mountains, near 2426-m (7957-ft) Eureka Peak. Turn left onto Black Creek-Bosk Lake FS road (following directions on page 167) to head northwest toward **Elbow, Tisdall and McKinley lakes**, as well as Horsefly.

> **0 km (0 mi)**
> Proceeding north for Crooked Lake, from the 65.2-km (40.4-mi) junction.
>
> **1.4 km (0.9 mi)**
> Pass small Cruiser Lake on the left.
>
> **5.1 km (3.2 mi)**
> Stay left.
>
> **6.7 km (4.2 mi)**
> Bear right and descend.
>
> **7.4 km (4.6 mi)**
> Reach Crooked Lake South campground on the right. Views of the mountains and the lake are much better here than at the north campground.

Crooked Lake

CROOKED LAKE SOUTH RECREATION SITE #66
Destination / Difficult (due only to distance)
Elev: 933 m (3060 ft) / Lake: 10.5 km (6.5 mi) long, 1092 ha
3 well-spaced tables, sandy beach, bearproof garbage bin
Accessible by motorhomes and 5th-wheels

Continuing north, passing the turnoff to Crooked Lake south campground.

9 km (5.5 mi)
Cross a bridged creek. Just beyond, go right at the junction.

9.7 km (6 mi)
Reach Crooked Lake North campground on the right. It's a large clearing tucked into a cove with no beach. The lake appears smaller here.

CROOKED LAKE NORTH RECREATION SITE #65
Destination / Difficult (due only to distance)
Elev: 933 m (3060 ft) / Lake: 10.5 km (6.5 mi) long, 1092 ha
4 tables, many more campsites, rough boat launch,
bearproof garbage bin
Accessible by motorhomes and 5th-wheels

0 km (0 mi)
Starting on Black Creek-Bosk Lake FS road, from the 65.2-km (40.4-mi) junction (page 165), heading northwest toward Elbow, Tisdall and McKinley lakes, as well as Horsefly. The road is narrow but generally smooth.

3.7 km (2.3 mi)
Bear left.

3.9 km (2.4 mi)
Proceed straight. Grass is growing in mid-road. Slow down to avoid a few potholes. Elbow Lake is soon visible.

7.2 km (4.5 mi)
Proceed straight along the lake. The road gets rougher.

9.3 km (5.8 mi)
Turn right for Elbow Lake campground. A 300-meter loop accesses the campsites, most of which have views of the lake and mountains.

ELBOW LAKE RECREATION SITE #64
Destination / Difficult (due only to distance)
Elev: 908 m (2978 ft) / Lake: 4 km (2.5 mi) long, 338 ha
5 tables, more campsites, gravel beach
Accessible by motorhomes and 5th-wheels

Continuing generally west on Black Creek-Bosk Lake FS road, passing the turnoff to Elbow Lake campground.

11.2 km (6.9 mi)
Stay right. In 100 meters cross a bridged creek.

12.1 km (7.5 mi)
Bear left.

17 km (10.5 mi)
Go right at the triangular junction.

Campfire Questions

Add spark to your evening powwow by asking your campfire mates unusual questions. Go around in a circle. Limit answers to a few minutes, to keep everyone involved. No judging allowed. The person who asks is the last person to answer. Here are suggestions. If you had time to learn, and money to hire the best instructors, what would you like to master? What character in what movie would you most like to be? What was your most embarrassing moment? If you could experience the outcome of a path you didn't take, what juncture in life would you return to? Of anyone in the world, past or present, who would you most like to be friends with? What personal trait would you like to improve? When did you feel most proud of yourself?

18.5 km (11.5 mi)
Reach another triangular junction and set your tripometer to 0. Left leads southwest to Tisdall Lake campground. Right (northwest) continues to McKinley Lake and Horsefly.

0 km (0 mi)
Turning left for Tisdall Lake campground, from the 18.5-km (11.5-mi) junction on Black Creek-Bosk Lake FS road.

2.2 km (1.4 mi)
Turn right.

3.4 km (2.1 mi)
Arrive at Tisdall Lake campground. The campsites are well spaced. Several have lakeviews. The mountains are less impressive here than at Crooked or Elbow lakes.

TISDALL LAKE RECREATION SITE #63
Destination / Difficult (due only to distance)
Elev: 960 m (3150 ft) / Lake: 5.5 km (3.4 mi) long, 490 ha
11 tables, good boat launch, bearproof garbage bin
Accessible by motorhomes and 5th-wheels

~

Continuing northwest on Black Creek-Bosk Lake FS road, from the 18.5-km (11.5-mi) junction and turnoff to Tisdall Lake campground. Set your tripometer to 0.

0 km (0 mi)
Continuing northwest on Black Creek-Bosk Lake FS road, heading for McKinley Lake and Horsefly.

1.6 km (1 mi) and **5.3 km (3.3 mi)**
Proceed straight on the main road.

6.7 km (4.2 mi)
Turn right for McKinley Lake campground.

> Drive through an aspen grove. At 1.8 km (1.1 mi) bear right where the left fork is signed for private cottages. Reach the campground at 2.2 km (1.4 mi). It's beautiful, at the lake's narrow west end, near the outlet stream. The campsites are well-spaced, near the shore, backed by trees. A water temperature control structure keeps the water favourably cool for salmon. In late August or September you'll see Sockeye salmon spawning here. You'll also see eagles converging to feed on the dead fish.

MCKINLEY LAKE RECREATION SITE #62
Weekend / Moderate (from Horsefly)
Elev: 863 m (2830 ft) / Lake: 7.5 km (4.7 mi) long, 514 ha
5 tables, good boat launch, bearproof garbage bin
Accessible by small motorhomes and trailers

Continuing west on Black Creek-Bosk Lake FS road, passing the turnoff to McKinley Lake campground.

10.7 km (6.6 mi)
Turn right to reach Horsefly River campground in 100 meters. It's accessible by RVs, but only tiny ones can squeeze in or turn around. By late September, the stench of rotting salmon carcasses is intense here.

HORSEFLY RIVER RECREATION SITE #61
Overnight / Moderate (from Horsefly)
2 tables in a tiny clearing
Too small for motorhomes and 5th-wheels

Continuing west on Black Creek-Bosk Lake FS road, passing the turnoff to Horsefly River campground.

12.2 km (7.6 mi)
Proceed straight on the main road.

12.3 km (7.6 mi)
Reach a major junction. Bear left (west) to reach the town of Horsefly in 28 km (17.4 mi). (For Horsefly Lake turn right / northeast. At the major junction, turn left / north. Near the south shore, fork left for **Prairie Creek Recreation Site #60**. It's a tiny campground about midway on the 45-km / 28-mi long lake.)

27.7 km (17.2 mi) and **29.7 km (18.4 mi)**
Stay straight on the main road.

39.3 km (24.4 mi)
Pavement resumes.

40.2 km (24.9 mi)
Reach a junction. The Horsefly Forest District office is on the right. Proceed street to reach the town of Horsefly.

40.6 km (25.2 mi)
Cross a single-lane bridge over the Horsefly River and arrive in the town of **Horsefly**, near Clarke's General store on paved Horsefly Road. A green sign states distances to various points. Left leads 53 km (32.9 mi) southwest to Hwy 97. Right leads 22 km (13.6 mi) north to Quesnel Lake, and 25 km (15.5 mi) to Mitchell Bay. Also turn right to drive northeast 11 km (6.8 mi) to the southwest end of Horsefly Lake. Black Creek is 29 km (18 mi) east, behind you. To continue, set your tripometer to 0 and follow the directions on the next page.

HORSEFLY TO LIKELY

The forest is noticeably lusher north of Horsefly compared to farther south in Cariboo country. You'll even see a few big cedar trees here. That, plus the sheer size of Quesnel Lake, lends the region a coastal atmosphere. It's refreshing.

This is also where you'll find B.C.'s highest concentration of provincial-park-quality free campgrounds. Mitchell Bay and Raft Creek are outstanding examples. They earn Destination ratings because they have striking mountain scenery and are on tremendous Quesnel Lake. It's among the biggest bodies of water in the province. From the northwest end, it measures 80 km (50 mi) to the tip of the north arm, and 104 km (64 mi) to the tip of the east arm. Boaters must be wary of the powerful winds that sometimes whip the lake into dangerously oceanic conditions. From the safety of the shore, however, these storms can be wildly entertaining.

You can quickly reach Horsefly via paved road. It's a mere 30-minute drive from 150 Mile House (page 188). But backroad nomads will want to journey from Hwy 24 near Sheridan Lake, all the way north to Horsefly, keeping their tires on dirt nearly the entire way. Prominent landmarks on this route are Canim Lake, and Hendrix and Black Creeks. Directions start on page 159.

0 km (0 mi)
At the junction in Horsefly, by Clarke's General Store, where a large blue sign marking the road east to Crooked Lake states: LODGING, CAMPING.

If you arrived here via Black Creek FS road, turn right (north) onto paved Horsefly Road. If you arrived here via paved Horsefly Road, stay on the main road. From either approach, follow the main road as it curves left (north) between the school and the Cornerhouse Place Stores.

0.8 km (0.5 mi)
The road bends right.

1.2 km (0.7 mi)
Pavement ends.

Squaw Flats campground on Horsefly River

2.4 km (1.5 mi)
Bear right at a sign for Mitchell Bay.

5.3 km (3.3 mi)
Proceed straight. This winding road gets rough, but the hard dirt-and-gravel surface provides traction even when wet. A comfortable speed is about 50 kph (30 mph). Watch for livestock.

10.7 km (6.6 mi)
Bear right. The Horsefly River is along here.

13.4 km (8.3 mi)
Cross a small bridge and reach a tiny campground above a noisy riffle.

SQUAW FLATS RECREATION SITE #50
Overnight / Moderate
2 tables, bearproof garbage bin
Accessible by motorhomes and small trailers

Continuing on the main road, passing Squaw Flats campground. Soon ascend high above the river and attain broad views.

16.7 km (10.4 mi)
Bear right at the fork and descend.

19.4 km (12 mi)
Reach a junction. For Horsefly Bay campground on Quesnel Lake, turn right (east) on Horsefly-Quesnel Lake FS road. For the larger Mitchell Bay or Raft Creek campgrounds farther west on Quesnel Lake, turn left (northwest).

Drive east 1.9 km (1.2 mi) on Horsefly-Quesnel Lake FS road to small Horsefly Bay campground. It's accessible by big RVs, but only tiny ones will be comfortable. The river enters the southwest end of Quesnel Lake here, creating a wide, delta-like mudflat where tall grass and cattails grow.

HORSEFLY BAY RECREATION SITE #51
Overnight / Moderate
Elev: 728 m (2388 ft) / Quesnel Lake: 27,013 ha
1 table, 2 campsites
Too small for motorhomes and 5th-wheels

Continuing left (northwest) from the 19.4-km (12-mi) junction, passing the turnoff to Horsefly Bay campground.

21.1 km (13.1 mi)
Stay left.

21.6 km (13.4 mi)
Bear left and proceed on Horsefly-Likely FS road. Pass a sign stating this is the end of maintained public road. Mitchell Bay Landing is right.

24.1 km (15 mi)
Turn right and descend to reach Mitchell Bay campground in 150 meters.

This provincial-park quality campground is in a grassy clearing, surrounded by birch trees, just 4 meters above the

Raft Creek campground on Quesnel Lake

lakeshore. The campsites are well-spaced but within view of each other.

MITCHELL BAY RECREATION SITE #48
Destination / Moderate
Elev: 728 m (2388 ft) / Quesnel Lake: 27,013 ha
5 tables, rock and gravel beach, boat launch
Accessible by small motorhomes and trailers

Continuing northwest on Horsefly-Likely FS road, passing the turnoff to Mitchell Bay campground.

28.1 km (17.4 mi)
Giant cottonwoods line the road ahead.

29.8 km (18.5 mi)
Turn right for Raft Creek campground.

In 50 meters reach two tables in a clearing on the right. At 100 meters is another secluded campsite. The last site, the one best-suited for big RVs, is 300 meters from the main road. It's on the beach and has 3 tables. Just beyond is a large turnaround.

RAFT CREEK RECREATION SITE #47
Destination / Moderate
Elev: 728 m (2388 ft) / Quesnel Lake: 27,013 ha
7 tables, a few secluded campsites, good boat launch
Accessible by motorhomes and 5th-wheels

Continuing northwest on Horsefly-Likely FS road, passing the turnoff to Raft Creek campground.

31.2 km (19.3 mi)
Go right for Likely. Left is Moorehead-Gavin Lake FS road.

33 km (20.5 mi)
Reach an **exceptional viewpoint** on the right. There's a table and outhouse on the left. You can survey a tremendous expanse of Quesnel Lake, about 200 m (656 ft) below you. Prominent above the north shore is (1570-m (5150-ft) Spanish Mtn. Farther northeast is 2057-m (6747-ft) Mt. Brew.

35.7 km (22.1 mi)
Bear right for Likely. Turn left (west) for Polley Lake campground. Just beyond is a yellow KM 14 sign.

0 km (0 mi)
Starting west on Polley Lake FS road.

1 km (0.6 mi)
Bear left and ascend. Stay on the main road through a regrowing forest.

3.7 km (2.3 mi)
Reach a bearproof garbage bin and two tables.

3.9 km (2.4 mi)
Arrive at the main Polley Lake campground—a clearing ringed by six tables. The view is dismal: cutblocks on the surrounding low hills.

POLLEY LAKE RECREATION SITE #46
Weekend / Moderate
Elev: 926 m (3037 ft) / Lake: 6.5 km (4 mi) long, 378 ha
8 tables, good boat launch
Accessible by motorhomes and 5th-wheels

Continuing north on Horsefly-Likely FS road, passing the turnoff to Polley Lake campground.

47.7 km (29.6 mi)
Intersect the paved Likely Road. Turn right to quickly reach the town of Likely, where Quesnel River departs the northwest end of Quesnel Lake. Left leads 81.6 km (50.6 mi) south to 150 Mile House and Hwy 97; read directions on page 186.

50.1 km (31.1 mi)
Cross the long bridge over Quesnel River where it departs the northwest end of Quesnel Lake. The town of **Likely** is just beyond. The bridge offers exciting entertainment—salmon watching—from August through early October. For campgrounds beyond Likely, set your tripometer to 0 midway across the bridge and continue reading directions on page 178.

Traffic sign for salmon in Quesnel River, near the bridge at Likely

LIKELY TO HORSEFLY

Two of Cariboo country's premier campgrounds—Raft Creek and Mitchell Bay—are on the west shore of hugely impressive Quesnel Lake. They're easily reached within a half-hour drive of Likely, en route to Horsefly.

0 km (0 mi)
In Likely, midway across the Quesnel River bridge, heading west on paved Likely Road.

2.4 km (1.5 mi)
Turn left onto Horsefly-Likely FS road.

14.4 km (8.9 mi)
Bear left and proceed south for Raft Creek and Mitchell Bay campgrounds. Turn right (west), following directions on page 175, for **Polley Lake campground**.

17.2 km (10.7 mi)
Reach an **exceptional viewpoint of Quesnel Lake**. You can survey a tremendous expanse of Quesnel Lake, about 200 m (656 ft) below you. Prominent above the north shore is 1570-m (5150-ft) Spanish Mtn. Farther northeast is 2057-m (6747-ft) Mt. Brew.

Quesnel Lake

18.9 km (11.7 mi)
Go left. Right is Moorehead-Gavin Lake FS road.

20.3 km (12.6 mi)
Turn left for **Raft Creek campground**. Read pages 174-75 for details and a photo.

26 km (16.1 mi)
Turn left and descend to reach **Mitchell Bay campground** in 150 meters. This provincial-park quality campground is in a grassy clearing, surrounded by birch trees, just 4 meters above the lakeshore. The campsites are well-spaced but within view of each other.

MITCHELL BAY RECREATION SITE #48
Destination / Moderate
Elev: 728 m (2388 ft) / Quesnel Lake: 27,013 ha
5 tables, rock and gravel beach, boat launch
Accessible by small motorhomes and trailers

Continuing generally south, it's another 24.1 km (15 mi) to Horsefly. Stay on the main road, bearing right at major junctions. For details follow the directions—in reverse—from the bottom of page 173.

BEYOND LIKELY

You're about to hit the motherlode. Four out of the five free campgrounds beyond Likely are rated Destination. Take your pick from this campers' bonanza.

(1) Winkley Creek is 20.7 km (12.8 mi) southeast, on 104-km (64.5-mi) long Quesnel Lake. It has a large gravel beach. The campsites are in the open. It's lovely when the sky is blue and the temperature mild. But keep in mind the potential exposure to rain, wind or blazing sun. Motorhomes and 5th-wheels should have no trouble getting here.

(2) Spanish Lake is 14.3 km (8.9 mi) east-southeast. The campsites are wonderfully secluded, more so than those at most provincial parks. The gorgeously forested setting rivals any campground in this book. Mountains rise 1000 m (3280 ft) above the 8-km (5-mi) long lake. As for access, the final 0.7 km (0.4 mi) is steep and narrow. Small motorhomes and trailers can make it, but only with good brakes and plenty of torque.

(3) Abbott Creek is 30.6 km (19 mi) east-southeast, on Quesnel Lake. The mountains appear less dramatic here than at Spanish Lake, but it's still an exceptional campground. The sandy beach is divine. This is just about the lake's widest point. The far shore is 3.5 km (2.2 mi) distant. The immensity of it is a compelling sight. If you can stand the paint-shaker effect on the last 3 km (2 mi), Abbott is accessible by motorhomes and 5th-wheels. This final approach is also steep, so big RVs need lots of torque to power out.

(4) Ladies Creek is 36 km (22.3 mi) northeast, on 9.5-km (6-mi) long Cariboo Lake. It looks remote on the map, but the wide, gravel road is generally smooth, allowing you to average 80 kph (50 mph). So it's easily accessible by motorhomes and 5th-wheels. Despite visible clearcuts, the lake has a wild atmosphere. So does the campground, framed by tall, thick-girthed hemlock and spruce. The large sandy beach seems luxurious in such a setting. Music, provided by the namesake creek, is audible. You might also hear a creek tumbling to the lake's far shore.

(5) Quesnel Forks, 12.3 km (7.6 mi) northwest, is rated merely Overnight. It doesn't warrant a longer stay. Though the setting is dramatic, it's difficult to appreciate from the campground. And while it does have historical significance, you'll be crushed if you expect to see a ghost town. Only a couple structures still stand. Others will supposedly be restored. Better to clear away the remaining timbers and encourage visitors to enjoy the time-less beauty of the confluence of two mighty rivers: the Quesnel and Cariboo. It's accessible by motorhomes and 5th-wheels.

(1) WINKLEY CREEK

0 km (0 mi)
In Likely, on the northeast side of the Quesnel River bridge. Just beyond, proceed straight (east) on Keithley Creek Road.

The provincial-park-quality campground at Spanish Lake has several secluded campsites.

0.5 km (0.3 mi)
Proceed straight. The road ascending left leads to Quesnel Forks campground.

1.5 km (0.9 mi)
Reach a fork. Both ways are paved. Turn right (southeast) for Winkley Creek campground on Quesnel Lake. Left leads to campgrounds at Spanish Lake, Abbott Creek (Quesnel Lake), and Ladies Creek (Cariboo Lake).

5.6 km (3.5 mi)
Pass Cedar Point Park on the right.

6.4 km (4 mi)
Stay left at the fork and ascend. Pavement ends.

9.4 km (5.8 mi)
Proceed straight. The road levels.

16 km (9.9 mi)
Go right at the fork. It's signed for Winkley Creek.

18.1 km (11.2 mi)
Go right at the fork and continue descending.

20.4 km (12.6 mi)
Turn right.

20.7 km (12.8 mi)
Arrive at Winkley Creek campground.

WINKLEY CREEK RECREATION SITE #42
Destination / Moderate
Elev: 728 m (2388 ft) / Lake: 1.2 km (0.7 mi) wide here
9 well-spaced tables, bearproof garbage bin, good boat launch
Accessible by motorhomes and 5th-wheels

(2) SPANISH LAKE

0 km (0 mi)
In Likely, on the northeast side of the Quesnel River bridge. Just beyond, proceed straight (east) on Keithley Creek Road.

0.5 km (0.3 mi)
Proceed straight. The road ascending left leads to Quesnel Forks campground.

1.5 km (0.9 mi)
Reach a fork. Both ways are paved. Turn left for campgrounds at Spanish Lake, Abbott Creek (Quesnel Lake), and Ladies Creek (Cariboo Lake). Right leads southeast to Winkley Creek campground on Quesnel Lake.

2.3 km (1.4 mi)
Pavement ends.

2.7 km (1.7 mi)
Reach a fork near a well-preserved rustic cabin. For Spanish Lake and Abbott Creek, turn right and ascend steeply on the road signed for Tasse Lake. Left leads northeast to Ladies Creek.

3.6 km (2.2 mi)
The steep ascent ends.

7.5 km (4.7 mi)
Proceed straight (southeast) on the main road.

13.6 km (8.4 mi)
Turn left to reach Spanish Lake campground in 0.7 km (0.4 mi). RVs must be capable of negotiating steep terrain. Secluded campsites are on the point. One is on a small cove.

SPANISH LAKE RECREATION SITE #44
Destination / Moderate
Elev: 937 m (3073 ft) / Lake: 8 km (5 mi) long, 448 ha
6 tables, bearproof garbage bin, good boat launch
Accessible by small motorhomes and trailers

(3) ABBOTT CREEK ON QUESNEL LAKE

Follow directions to the Spanish Lake turnoff at 13.6 km (8.4 mi) and continue straight (southeast) on the main road.

19.2 km (11.9 mi)
Bear left on the main road.

20.7 km (12.8 mi)
Go right at the fork and ascend.

24.5 km (15.2 mi)
Go right and descend. Attain a view east into the Cariboo Mountains of Wells Grey Park.

25.1 km (15.6 mi)
Proceed straight and descend.

27.6 km (17.1 mi)
Go left and descend steeply on a rougher road.

29.2 km (18.1 mi)
Go right. Left is signed for Shoals Bay Rd.

30.2 km (18.7 mi)
The final descent is very steep.

30.6 km (19 mi)
Arrive at Abbott Creek campground on Quesnel Lake's north shore.

ABBOTT CREEK RECREATION SITE #49
Destination / Difficult
Elev: 728 m (2388 ft) / Lake: 3.5 km (2.2 mi) wide here
6 spacious campsites with tables
Accessible by motorhomes and 5th wheels

(4) LADIES CREEK ON CARIBOO LAKE

0 km (0 mi)
In Likely, on the northeast side of the Quesnel River bridge. Just beyond, proceed straight (east) on Keithley Creek Road.

0.5 km (0.3 mi)
Proceed straight. The road ascending left leads to Quesnel Forks campground.

1.5 km (0.9 mi)
Reach a fork. Both ways are paved. Turn left for campgrounds at Ladies Creek (Cariboo Lake), Spanish Lake, and Abbott Creek (Quesnel Lake). Right leads southeast to Winkley Creek campground on Quesnel Lake.

2.7 km (1.7 mi)
Reach a fork near a well-preserved rustic cabin. Bear left (north) on the flat road for Ladies Creek. The road ascending steeply right (signed for Tasse Lake) leads to Spanish Lake and Abbott Creek.

8 km (5 mi) and **8.1 km (5.1 mi)**
Proceed straight on the main road.

9 km (5.6 mi)
Follow the main road through a big, sweeping curve left.

10.8 km (6.7 mi)
Cross a large, high bridge over the Cariboo River.

11.2 km (6.9 mi)
Bear right on the main road.

16.8 km (10.4 mi)
Proceed straight on the main road. Kangaroo Creek FS road forks left.

22.7 km (14.1 mi)
Go right. The road is rougher now, with potholes.

23.5 km (14.6 mi)
Cross a bridge over the broad, wild Cariboo River.

23.7 km (14.7 mi)
Turn left at the T-junction.

26.8 km (16.6 mi) and **29.2 km (18.1 mi)**
Proceed straight on the main road.

36 km (22.3 mi)
Turn left and descend to reach Ladies Creek campground on Cariboo Lake in 100 meters.

LADIES CREEK RECREATION SITE #41
Destination / Difficult (due only to distance)
Elev: 812 m (2663 ft) / Lake: 9.5 km (6 mi) long, 1010 ha
6 spacious campsites with tables, gravel boat launch
Accessible by motorhomes and 5th-wheels

(5) QUESNEL FORKS

0 km (0 mi)
In Likely, on the northeast side of the Quesnel River bridge. Just beyond, proceed straight (east) on Keithley Creek Road.

0.5 km (0.3 mi)
Turn left and ascend on the paved road.

Ladies Creek campground on Cariboo Lake

0.9 km (0.6 mi)
Go left on pavement and descend.

2.2 km (1.4 mi)
Pavement ends. A steeper ascent begins as the road switchbacks.

3 km (1.9 mi)
Bear left at the fork. The ascent eases.

6.2 km (3.8 mi)
Stay straight on the main road.

10.3 km (6.4 mi)
Begin a steep descent.

11.6 km (7.2 mi)
Reach a pullout and viewpoint on the left. From the log fence, you can peer down on Quesnel Forks.

12.3 km (7.6 mi)
Fork left to enter the campground and historic area in 200 meters. A loop road passes several campsites in a grassy area.

QUESNEL FORKS RECREATION SITE #39
Overnight / Moderate
3 tables
Inaccessible by large motorhomes and 5th-wheels

LIKELY TO 150 MILE HOUSE

0 km (0 mi)
In Likely, midway across the Quesnel River bridge, heading west on paved Likely Road.

2.4 km (1.5 mi)
Proceed straight (west) on paved Likely Road. Left is Horsefly-Likely FS road. It leads south to campgrounds at Polley Lake and on the west shore of Quesnel Lake; directions continue on page 177.

9.3 km (5.8 mi)
Bear left on Likely Road.

13.8 km (8.6 mi)
Turn left for Bootjack Lake campground.

> **0 km (0 mi)**
> Starting south on Bootjack Lake FS road.
>
> **0.2 km (0.1 mi)**
> Stay straight on the main road.
>
> **0.5 km (0.3 mi)** and **0.8 km (0.5 mi)**
> Bear right on the main road.
>
> **1.3 km (0.8 mi)**
> Morehead Lake is visible on the right.
>
> **6.8 km (4.2 mi)**
> Bear left on the main road.
>
> **8.8 km (5.5 mi)**
> Go right at the junction.
>
> **9.1 km (5.6 mi)**
> Arrive at Bootjack Lake campground. The area is treed.

The brushy shore has no beach. Low, forested hills provide mediocre scenery. The campgrounds at Spanish Lake, and Raft Creek on Quesnel Lake, are superior.

BOOTJACK LAKE RECREATION SITE #38
Weekend / Easy
Elev: 985 m (3231 ft) / Lake: 4.5 km (2.8 mi) long, 251 ha
6 tables, 3 more campsites, gravel boat launch, dock
Accessible by motorhomes and 5th-wheels

Continuing southwest on Likely Road, passing the turnoff to Bootjack Lake campground.

22.4 km (13.9 mi)
Turn left to quickly reach Jacobie Lake campground.

0 km (0 mi)
Starting southeast on Jacobie Lake FS road.

1.5 km (0.9 mi)
Stay straight on the main road.

3.2 km (2 mi)
Reach a fork. Bear right and descend.

3.4 km (2.1 mi)
Arrive at Jacobie Lake campground. The lake is small. The view is of low forested hills and a huge clearcut. Bootjack Lake campground is a bit better because the area's more forested.

JACOBIE LAKE RECREATION SITE #37
Overnight / Easy
Elev: 1122 m (3680 ft) / Lake: 1.8 km (1.1 mi) long, 85 ha
8 tables, gravel boat launch, dock
Accessible by motorhomes and 5th-wheels

Continuing southwest on Likely Road, passing the turnoff to Jacobie Lake campground.

30.3 km (18.8 mi)
Pass Morehead-Gavin FS road on the left. It heads east, reaching the small campground at **Gavin Lake Recreation Site #36**, next to the Forest Education Centre, in about 6.7 km (4.2 mi). The lake is 2.6 km (1.6 mi) long.

34.8 km (21.6 mi)
Pass Beaver Valley FS road on the left. It leads southeast about 40 km (24.8 mi) to Horsefly.

48.3 km (30 mi)
Pass Big Lake store.

79.5 km (49.3 mi)
Proceed straight (south) to intersect Hwy 97 at 150 Mile House. Turn left onto Horsefly Road and follow directions on page 189 (from 4.5 km / 2.8 mi) for campgrounds at Dugan or Dewar lakes, or to reach Horsefly in 48 km (29.8 mi). Dugan Lake is only 5 minutes away.

84 km (52 mi)
Intersect Hwy 97 at 150 Mile House. Williams Lake is right (west). Left leads south to Lac la Hache and 100 Mile House.

150 MILE HOUSE TO HORSEFLY

Access to Quesnel Lake from Hwy 97 is fast and easy via Horsefly Road. It starts just north of 150 Mile House. Within 10 minutes it passes campgrounds at Dugan and Dewar lakes. Neither is special, but both are convenient. Dugan is open, Dewar is treed. Passing cars and trains are sometimes audible at both. Horsefly Road ends at, you guessed it, the town of Horsefly. Pavement ends there too. But it's not far north to Quesnel Lake, and the unpaved road is decent. Follow directions on page 171. You'll find two provincial-park-quality campgrounds on the west shore: Mitchell Bay and Raft Creek. From there, it's a short drive up the lake's northwest arm to Likely, beyond which there are four more campgrounds rated Destination.

Marvel at the grandeur of Quesnel Lake from Mitchell Bay campground.

0 km (0 mi)
Starting north on Likely Road, departing Hwy 97 at 150 Mile House.

4.5 km (2.8 mi)
Turn right (northeast) onto Horsefly Road, at the big white sign for Resort Lakes.

7.3 km (4.5 mi)
For Dugan Lake campground, turn right onto Dugan Lake Road.

> In 0.4 km (0.2 mi) curve right, passing a home on the left, to enter the campground. The best sites are just beyond, between the trees and the lake. Tenters will find plenty of level grass. Road noise is audible.

DUGAN LAKE RECREATION SITE #25
Overnight / Easy
Elev: 930 m (3050 ft) / Lake: 1.2 km long and wide, 94 ha
6 campsites, several tables around a pasture, boat launch
Accessible by motorhomes and 5th-wheels

Continuing northeast on Horsefly Road, passing the turnoff to Dugan Lake campground.

12.8 km (7.9 mi)
For Dewar Lake campground, turn right onto Spokin Lake Road.

In 300 meters, turn right onto a spur road. A huge sign here warns about thin ice in winter. Reach the lake in another 50 meters.

DEWAR LAKE RECREATION SITE #26
Overnight / Easy
Elev: 990 m (3247 ft) / Lake: 1.2 km (0.7 mi) long, 43 ha
4 tables
Accessible by motorhomes and 5th-wheels

Continuing northeast on Horsefly Road, passing the turnoff to Dewar Lake campground.

52.5 km (32.6 mi)
Arrive in Horsefly. For Crooked Lake, continue reading the *East of Horsefly* directions below. For Mitchell Bay and Raft Creek campgrounds on Quesnel Lake, read the *Horsefly to Likely* directions on page 171.

EAST OF HORSEFLY

The section *Canim Lake to Horsefly* (page 162) covers in detail the area from Canim Lake, north to Crooked Lake, then generally west to Horsefly. But if you're going the opposite way—heading east from Horsefly—the following directions will guide you as far as the two Destination-rated campgrounds at Crooked Lake.

0 km (0 mi)
In Horsefly, near Clarke's General store, starting east on Black Creek FS road. It's signed for Crooked Lake. There's also a big blue sign here: LODGING, CAMPING. Set your tripometer to 0 and immediately cross a single-lane bridge over the Horsefly River.

0.4 km (0.25 mi)
Bear right and pass the Horsefly Forest District office. Pavement ends within a kilometer.

11 km (6.8 mi) and **13.1 km (8.1 mi)**
Stay straight on the main road.

28.4 km (17.6 mi)
Reach a major junction. Go right (east).

28.5 km (17.7 mi)
Proceed straight on the main road.

29 km (18 mi)
Cross a long bridge over the Horsefly River.

30 km (18.6 mi)
Turn left to reach small **Horsefly River campground** in 100 meters. Read the bottom of page 169 for details.

34 km (21.1 mi)
Turn left for **McKinley Lake campground**. Read further directions on page 169.

35.4 km (21.9 mi) and **39.1 km (24.2 mi)**
Proceed straight on the main road.

40.7 km (25.2 mi)
Reach a triangular junction. Right leads southwest to **Tisdall Lake campground**; read further directions on page 168. Continue left (southeast) for Elbow and Crooked lakes.

42.3 km (26.2 mi)
Bear left at the triangular junction.

47.2 km (29.3 mi)
Stay right.

48 km (29.8 mi)
Cross a bridged creek, then stay left.

50 km (31 mi)
Turn left for **Elbow Lake campground**. Read page 167 for details.

52.1 km (32.3 mi)
Proceed straight along the lake.

55.3 km (34.3 mi)
Proceed straight.

55.5 km (34.4 mi)
Bear right.

59.2 km (36.7 mi)
Reach a junction. Set your tripometer to 0 before going either way. Turn left (north) for the two **Crooked Lake campgrounds**. Right is Hendrix Creek FS road. It quickly passes Bosk Lake campground on the right, then continues south. Pavement resumes along the west shore of Canim Lake. Reach the junction of Canim Lake Road and Canim Lake South Road, near the lake's southwest end, in 65.2 km (40.4 mi). From there, it's 32 km (20 mi) southwest to 100 Mile House and Hwy 97.

0 km (0 mi)
Proceeding north for Crooked Lake, from the 59.2-km (36.7-mi) junction.

1.4 km (0.9 mi)
Pass small Cruiser Lake on the left.

5.1 km (3.2 mi)
Stay left.

6.7 km (4.2 mi)
Bear right and descend.

7.4 km (4.6 mi)
Reach **Crooked Lake South campground** on the right. Read page 166 for details.

9 km (5.5 mi)
Cross a bridged creek. Just beyond, go right at the junction.

9.7 km (6 mi)
Reach **Crooked Lake North campground** on the right. Read page 166 for details.

F: Around Francois Lake

The letter indicates which FS district the campground is in. **L** stands for **Lakes FS District**. **M** stands for **Morice FS District**. **V** stands for **Vanderhoof FS District**.

1 L	Augier Lake		11 V	Anzus Lake
1 M	Aspen		12 L	West Francois Lake
1 V	Peterson's Beach		13 L	Noralee West
2 L	Pinkut Lake		14 L	Noralee East
2 M	Owen Lake		15 L	Colleymount
3 L	Division Lake		15 M	Sunset Lake
3 M	Owen Flats A		16 L	Indian Bay
3 V	Ormond Lake		18 L	Eastern Lake
4 L	Taltapin Lake		19 L	Lund Lake
4 M	Owen Flats B		20 L	Takysie Lake
4 V	Oona Lake		21 L	Uncha Lake
5 L	Maxan Lake		22 L	Binta Lake North
5 M	Lamprey Creek		23 L	Binta Lake South
6 M	Morice Lake		24 L	Trout Lake
7 L	Co-op Lake		25 L	Ootsa Lake
8 M	Nadina Pool		32 V	Hogsback Lake
8 V	Sawmill Point		33 V	Cobb Lake
9 M	Nadina Lake		39 V	Burner Bay
9 V	Meuoon Lake			

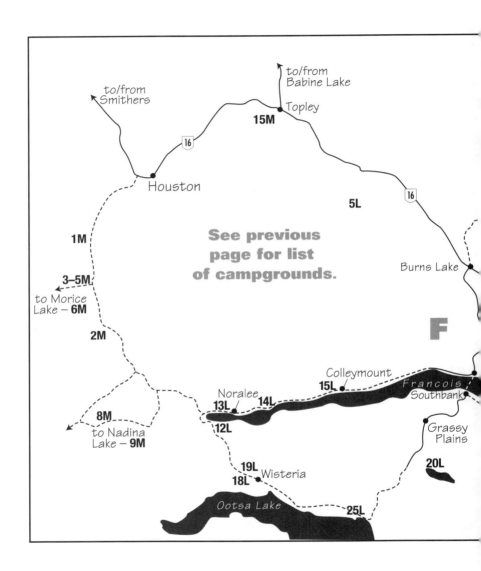

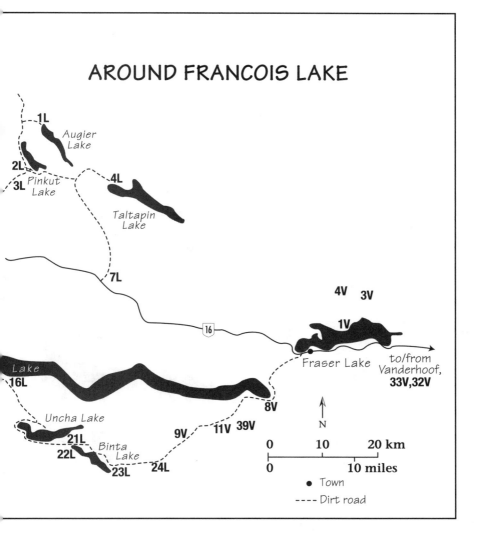

AROUND FRANCOIS LAKE

1L
Augier Lake
2L
3L Pinkut Lake
4L
Taltapin Lake
7L
16
4V 3V
1V
Lake
16L
Fraser Lake to/from Vanderhoof, 33V,32V
8V
Uncha Lake
9V 11V 39V
21L Binta Lake
22L
23L 24L

N

0   10   20 km
0   10 miles

● Town
---- Dirt road

Around Francois Lake

Binta Lake campgrounds can get crowded on weekends.

PRINCE GEORGE TO FRASER LAKE

Between Prince George and the town of Fraser Lake, Hwy 16 pierces the geographic heart of the province: Vanderhoof. But it's still an uneventful drive. So even if you're not ready to pitch the tent, veer off the pavement and check out Hogsback Lake campground. Mere minutes from the highway, it has a relaxing, park-like atmosphere. The lake is pretty, adorned with lily pads, ringed by Douglas fir. And the water is warm; dive in and refresh yourself. Your other campground option along here is Cobb Lake. It lacks charm, but it's convenient for a brief overnight stay. If you want to string up the tarp and establish a home in the outdoors for a few days, you'll probably want a bigger lake, grander surroundings, and a more spacious campground than Hogsback or Cobb. Follow the directions to Augier Lake (page 215), northeast of Burns Lake.

If you're heading west on Hwy 16 from Prince George

Set your tripometer to 0 at the junction of Hwys 97 and 16 in Prince George and head southwest on Hwy 16.

For Cobb Lake, drive 63 km (39.1 mi), then turn right (north) onto Finmoore Road. (It's 300 meters before the rest area.) Reset your tripometer to 0.

For Hogsback Lake, drive to 82.4 km (51.1 mi), then turn left (south) onto Mapes Road. Reset your tripometer to 0.

If you're heading east on Hwy 16 from Vanderhoof

Near the top of a rise, at Vanderhoof's east end, set your tripometer to 0 as you pass the tan Forest Service building.

For Hogsback Lake, drive 14.3 km (8.9 mi), then turn right (south) onto Mapes Road. Reset your tripometer to 0.

For Cobb Lake, drive 33.7 km (20.9 mi), then turn left (north) onto Finmoore Road. (It's 300 meters beyond the rest area.) Reset your tripometer to 0.

For COBB LAKE, now follow the directions below

0 km (0 mi)
Starting north on Finmoore Road.

6.1 km (3.8 mi)
Turn right onto a smaller, rougher road—passable in a 2WD car.

6.6 km (4.1 mi)
Turn right.

7.2 km (4.5 mi)
Arrive at Cobb Lake campground. It's on the lily-pad end of the forest-rimmed lake. The scenery is typical of the region: a vast expanse of virtually flat tree-prairie.

COBB LAKE RECREATION SITE #33
Overnight / Easy
Elev: 777 m (2550 ft) / Lake: 4 km (2.5 mi) long, 216 ha
5 tables, more campsites, rough boat launch
Inaccessible by large motorhomes and 5th wheels

Hogsback Lake campground

For HOGSBACK LAKE, now follow the directions below

0 km (0 mi)
Starting south on Mapes Road.

10.1 km (6.3 mi)
Reach a T-junction. Turn left onto Blackwater Road.

11.9 km (7.4 mi)
Turn right onto Hogback Lake Road, then immediately fork left.

13 km (8.1 mi)
Continue straight through the intersection.

13.6 km (8.4 mi)
Go left at the sign.

13.8 km (8.6 mi)
Arrive at Hogsback Lake. A clearing at the boat launch has 2 tables and is the only place big RVs should attempt to park. The road left rises then drops to 2 lakeshore campsites. Right leads to 2 sites above a lily-padded cove.

HOGSBACK LAKE RECREATION SITE #32
Weekend / Easy
Elev: 730 m (2395 ft) / Lake: 1 km (0.6 mi) long, 45 ha
6 tables, boat launch, historic hiking trail
Inaccessible by large motorhomes and trailers

NEAR FRASER LAKE

No other campground in this book draws crowds like Peterson's Beach, on the north shore of Fraser Lake. All summer, especially weekends and holidays, the scene here is precisely what free camping should enable you to avoid: raucous crowds, whining jet skis, roaring water-ski boats, blasting stereos, screaming brats. If you're very sociable, this provincial-park quality campground has advantages: easy access to a long, lovely beach; warm water, ideal for swimming; a shallow area for kids to play in. But even if you prefer bears to people, Peterson's is convenient to Hwy 16 and might be worth trying in spring or fall when a crowd is less likely. You can always push on north to Ormond Lake. The shore is brushy, unattractive for swimming and sunning, but Ormond can be vacant when Peterson's is throbbing with humanity. Ringed by higher hills, Ormond is prettier than Uncha and Binta lakes, off Hwy 16, south of Fraser Lake. As for Oona Lake, just west of Ormond, it's strictly for misanthropes. The rough access and grim campground will discourage others from bothering you there.

If you're heading west on Hwy 16 from Vanderhoof

From the junction of Hwys 16 and 27 (the Fort St. James turnoff) just west of Vanderhoof, drive Hwy 16 west 34.5 km (21.4 mi), then turn right (north) toward Nautley. This turnoff is 2.2 km (1.4 mi) west of the Nechako River bridge. Set your tripometer to 0.

If you're heading east on Hwy 16 from the town of Fraser Lake

From the Visitor Info Centre (located next to Fraser Lake Recreation Centre, on the east side of town), drive Hwy 16 east 16.8 km (10.4 mi), then turn left (north) toward Nautley. Set your tripometer to 0.

For either approach above, now follow the directions below

Pass Beaumont Provincial Park. In 3.6 km (2.2 mi), cross the bridge over Nautley River—the shortest river in B.C. Proceed through the village of Nautley. At 4.3 km (2.7 mi) reach a junction where pavement ends. Turn right onto Sutherland FS road to reach Ormond and Oona lakes; for directions continue reading at the bottom of page 201. Turn left onto Stella Road East to reach Peterson's Beach on Fraser Lake. Set your tripometer to 0 before turning either way.

Turning left (west) onto Stella Road East, from Nautley village.

0 km (0 mi)
Starting on Stella Road East, heading west to Peterson's Beach on Fraser Lake.

10.7 km (6.6 mi)
Turn left at the large signboard for Peterson's Beach.

> The gated entry is open 7 a.m. to 10 p.m. ATVs are prohibited. Quiet hours are 11 p.m. to 7 a.m. Many campsites are close together. A few along the lake are divided by trees and have their own pebble beach. Opposite the campground entrance is the signed Ormond Creek trail. It leads 13.2 km (8.2 mi) north to Ormond and Oona lakes. A short way up are lake views.

Peterson's Beach campground on Fraser Lake

PETERSON'S BEACH RECREATION SITE #1
Weekend / Easy
Elev: 670 m (2198 ft) / Lake: 18.5 km (11.5 mi) long, 5385 ha
25 tables, excellent swimming beach
good boat launch, hiking trail
very popular, often crowded, provincial-park quality
Accessible by motorhomes and 5th-wheels

Turning right (northeast) onto Sutherland FS road, from Nautley village.

0 km (0 mi)
Starting on Sutherland FS road, heading initially northeast to Ormond and Oona lakes.

2.1 km (1.3 mi)
Turn left (northwest) at the signed junction. Dog Creek Road forks right.

15 km (9.3 mi)
Turn left at the signed junction, onto Sutherland-Oona FS road.

15.1 km (9.4 mi)
A narrow, rough road on the left leads 1 km (0.6 mi) to the single table at tiny **Etcho Lake campground**.

15.9 km (9.6 mi)
Turn left for Ormond Lake campground.

Descend to reach the campground in 100 meters. It's set in forest with a few aspen. A treed bowl back from the lack shelters a spacious campsite with 2 tables—ideal for a large group.

ORMOND LAKE RECREATION SITE #3
Weekend / Moderate
Elev: 838 m (2750 ft) / Lake: 4 km (2.5 mi) long, 317 ha
11 tables, several secluded campsites, 2 good boat launches
Accessible by motorhomes and 5th-wheels

Continuing west on Sutherland-Oona FS road, passing the turnoff to Ormond Lake campground.

17.8 km (11 mi)
Bear right.

18.6 km (11.5 mi)
Pass the signed north end of Ormond Creek trail on the left. The road deteriorates.

20 km (12.4 mi)
Cross a bridge over Angly Creek and ascend steeply.

21.2 km (13.1 mi)
The road is badly rutted but still passable in 2WD if it's dry.

21.3 km (13.2 mi)
Turn left for Oona Lake campground.

Descend to reach the campground in 200 meters. Where the tables are visible, bear right to find a lone table. The trees are scrawny, mostly lodgepole pine. Though the sites overlook the lake, the water is an unappealing brown. Access to the meager, rocky shore is rough.

OONA LAKE RECREATION SITE #4
Overnight / Moderate / Not recommended
Elev: 838 m (2750 ft) / Lake: 4.8 km (3 mi) long, 321 ha
4 tables, boat launch in cove west of campground
Inaccessible by motorhomes and 5th-wheels

FRANCOIS LAKE SOUTHEAST

Francois Lake is a 104-km (64.3-mi) long horizontal streak across the map. It stretches east nearly to Hwy 16 and Fraser Lake, where the town of Fraser Lake is located. The land surrounding Francois Lake is not dramatic. A free ferry plies the middle of the 25,164-hectare lake, between the north-shore town of Francois Lake and the south-shore town of Southbank. Indian Bay campground is near Southbank. The remote west end of Francois Lake has four campgrounds. You'll find only a tiny one on the more convenient east end. But approaching Francois Lake from its east end, following the directions below, is the shortest route to a string of campgrounds on smaller lakes (Borel, Anzus, Binta, Uncha) amid forested hills. The topography there is a bit steeper and slightly more scenic than around Francois.

If you're heading west on Hwy 16
from the town of Fraser Lake

Drive 4 km (2.5 mi) past the Visitor Info Centre (located next to Fraser Lake Recreation Centre, on the east side of town), then turn left onto Francois Lake East Road. Set your tripometer to 0.

If you're heading east on Hwy 16
from the town of Burns Lake

Fraser Lake is the next town. Approaching its west end, set your tripometer to 0 on the bridge over the railroad tracks. In 1 km (0.6 mi) cross the Stellako River bridge. At 1.2 km (0.7 mi) turn right onto Francois Lake East Road. Reset your tripometer to 0.

For either approach above, now follow the directions below

0 km (0 mi)
Turning southwest onto Francois Lake East Road.

Sawmill Point on Francois Lake

7.4 km (4.6 mi)
Turn left onto dirt Nithi Road.

9.4 km (5.8 mi)
Turn right at the 3-way junction.

13.7 km (8.5 mi)
Watch carefully for the small, obscure, right fork dropping steeply to Sawmill Point campground on Francois Lake.

Directly below the main road is a table tucked into the trees; another is near the shore. The hills across the lake were denuded by the Endako molybdenum mine.

SAWMILL POINT RECREATION SITE #8
Weekend / Moderate
Elev: 715 m (2345 ft)
2 tables, boat launch
Accessible by motorhomes and 5th-wheels

~

Continuing west along Francois Lake, passing the turnoff to Sawmill Point campground.

17 km (10.5 mi)
The signed **Black Point trail** is on the right. It descends to a campsite on Francois Lake.

20.7 km (12.8 mi)
Bear right and proceed southwest on the main road.

23 km (14.3 mi)
Reach a junction and bear right on Holy Cross-Francois FS road. Left (east) leads to **Burner Bay Recreation Site #39** on Borel Lake in 5 minutes; read directions on page 236.

26 km (16.1 mi)
Turn left for **Anzus Lake Recreation Site #11**. It has 3 campsites and offers no privacy from the main road. This 304-hectare lake is at 868 m (2847 ft) elevation.

32.3 km (20 mi)
Turn right for Meuoon Lake campground.

The lone table is 40 meters off the main road. Faint tracks continue right to a possible second campsite.

MEUOON LAKE RECREATION SITE #9
Overnight / Difficult (due only to distance)
1 table, marshy 9-hectare pond
Inaccessible by motorhomes and trailers

Continuing southwest on Binta FS road, passing the turnoff to Meuoon Lake campground.

32.4 km (20.1 mi)
Bear left on the main road.

35 km (21.8 mi) and **41.2 km (25.5 mi)**
Stay straight on the main road.

47.3 km (29.3 mi)
Stay straight. Binta North Road forks right.

49.4 km (30.6 mi)
Turn right for Binta South campground.

> Arrive at the campground in 0.8 km (0.5 mi). The campsites ring a clearing on the southeast end of Binta Lake. The sunset view northwest up the lake is a treat.

BINTA SOUTH RECREATION SITE #23
Weekend / Difficult (due only to distance)
Elev: 820 m (2690 ft) / Lake: 8.7 km (5.4 mi) long, 833 ha
7 tables, beach, boat launch
Inaccessible by large motorhomes and trailers

Continuing northwest on Binta FS road, passing the turnoff to Binta South campground.

51 km (31.6 mi)
Stay right at the signed fork. Left is a narrow, rough, winding road to small campgrounds (suitable for tenting only) on Knapp and Moose lakes.

Binta Lake North

61.5 km (38.1 mi)
Stay straight.

63 km (39 mi)
Turn right for Binta North campground.

In 1.5 km (0.9 mi) reach a sign and go left. At 3.2 km (2 mi) fork left to 7 tables with lake views, or right to 2 more tables.

BINTA NORTH RECREATION SITE #22
Weekend / Difficult (due only to distance)
Elev: 820 m (2690 ft) / Lake: 8.7 km (5.4 mi) long, 833 ha
9 tables, boat launch
Inaccessible by large motorhomes and trailers

Continuing northwest on Binta FS road, passing the turnoff to Binta North campground.

64 km (39.7 mi)
Turn right for Uncha Lake campground. Set your tripometer to 0 whether turning or continuing.

Arrive at the campground in 1 km (0.6 mi). It's confined, and most sites are not on the lake.

UNCHA LAKE RECREATION SITE #21
Weekend / Difficult
Elev: 786 m (2578 ft) / 13.5 km (8.4 mi) long, 1340 ha
7 tables, boat launch
Inaccessible by large motorhomes and trailers

Continuing northwest on Binta FS road, from the turnoff to Uncha Lake campground. Set your tripometer to 0.

0 km (0 mi)
On Binta FS road, at the turnoff to Uncha Lake campground.

5 km (3.1 mi)
Stay right, passing a left fork. Continue around the northwest end of Uncha Lake.

9.7 km (6 mi)
Bear right.

12.4 km (7.7 mi)
Go left at the junction.

14.1 km (8.7 mi)
Go left (northwest) at the signed junction.

19.7 km (12.2 mi)
Pavement begins.

23.6 km (14.6 mi)
Turn right for Indian Bay campground. It's on Francois Lake, 1.2 km (0.7 mi) from the main road.

INDIAN BAY RECREATION SITE #16
5 tables, more campsites, convenient to Francois Lake ferry
Inaccessible by large motorhomes and trailers

Continuing northwest on Ancha Lake Road, passing the turnoff to Indian Bay campground.

26 km (16.1 mi)
Reach the ferry landing in the community of Southbank, on the south shore of Francois Lake. The ferry is free. It departs hourly, on the hour, 5 a.m. to 12 a.m., every day. The north-shore ferry landing is at the community of Francois Lake. From there, paved Hwy 35 leads 25 km (15.5 mi) north to the town of Burns Lake on Hwy 16.

FRANCOIS LAKE WEST

You'll find four campgrounds on the west end of 104-km (64.3-mi) long Francois Lake. All are small, none is special. But they're en route to other, more remote campgrounds, like those on Ootsa Lake (page 230), Nadina Lake (page 225), and Morice Lake (page 224).

Direct access to the west end of Francois Lake is from Hwy 16 at the town of Burns Lake. Drive paved Hwy 35 south about 25 km (15.5 mi) to the community of Francois Lake. Turn right (west) onto dirt Colleymount Road and proceed along the north shore of Francois Lake for about 30 km (18.5 mi) to Colleymount campground. It's beyond the community of Colleymount and just past the signed boundary between Lakes and Morice FS districts. Continue west, as described below, to reach the Noralee campgrounds. West Francois campground (page 228) is a bit farther, around the west end of the lake.

The north-shore landing for the ferry across Francois Lake is at the community of Francois Lake. The ferry is free. It departs hourly, on the half hour, 5:30 a.m. to 12:30 a.m., every day. The south-shore landing is at the community of Southbank. There you can turn left for Indian Bay campground (page 232) and others beyond, or stay straight for campgrounds on Takysie and Ootsa lakes (page 231).

COLLEYMOUNT RECREATION SITE #15
Weekend / Difficult (due only to distance)
5 tables, 2 lakeshore campsites, cooking shelter with a woodstove
large open area, good boat launch, gravel beach
Accessible by motorhomes and 5th-wheels

Continuing west on Colleymount Road, from the turnoff to Colleymount campground. Set your tripometer to 0.

0 km (0 mi)
On Colleymount Road, at the turnoff to Colleymount campground.

Francois Lake, from Noralee West campground

15.2 km (9.4 mi)
Turn left for Noralee East campground.

NORALEE EAST RECREATION SITE #14
Overnight / Difficult (due only to distance)
4 tables, large open area on short peninsula
boat launch, small pebble beach
Accessible by motorhomes and 5th-wheels

Continuing west on Colleymount Road, passing the turnoff to Noralee East campground.

18.6 km (11.5 mi)
Turn left for Noralee West campground.

NORALEE WEST RECREATION SITE #13
Overnight / Difficult (due only to distance)
4 tables, beside the road, good boat launch, small pebble beach
Accessible by motorhomes and 5th-wheels

Continuing west on Colleymount Road, passing the turnoff to Noralee West campground.

22 km (13.6 mi)
Arrive at a signed junction near the west end of Francois Lake. Turn right (northwest) to reach Owen Lake campground (page 225) in 21 km (13 mi), or Hwy 16 and Houston in 67 km (41.5 mi). Turn left to head southeast to Ootsa Lake (page 230) and loop back to the Francois Lake ferry landing at Southbank.

NORTHEAST OF BURNS LAKE

A network of good roads allows easy travel to a cluster of sizable lakes and their attendant campgrounds northeast of the town of Burns Lake.

Augier Lake is the area's most picturesque. Its campground is also the best. Though smaller than gigantic Babine or Francois lakes, at about 10 km (6.2 mi) long Augier is no bird bath. And its setting has enough topographical relief to be dramatic. Forested hills rise 274 m (900 ft) above the shore. You can admire them from a pebble beach. The direct route to Augier—north on Old Babine Road from the town of Burns Lake—is described on page 215.

For a weekend stay, also consider Taltapin or Division lakes. Boaters prefer Taltapin because it's bigger. Division is a mere pond but has a more attractive campground.

Simply need a place to crash for the night? Co-op Lake is convenient, east of town, just a few minutes north of Hwy 16.

If you're heading west on Hwy 16 from Vanderhoof

0 km (0 mi)
At the BC Hydro building (right) and community museum (left) in Vanderhoof, heading west on Hwy 16.

62.2 km (38.6 mi)
After passing through the town of Fraser Lake, turn left (southwest) onto Francois Lake Road, then follow directions on page 203 for campgrounds southeast of Francois Lake.

82.6 km (51.2 mi)
Pass a sign welcoming you to Lakes Resort District.

102 km (63.2 mi)
Pass a pullout with a garbage can, on the left. Slow down. A few kilometers farther is the first turnoff for campgrounds to the north.

106.5 km (66 mi)
Turn right (north) onto Augier FS road for Co-op or Taltapin Lakes. For Division, Pinkut and Augier lakes, continue northwest on Hwy 16 to the town of Burns Lake; read further directions on page 215. Set your tripometer to 0 whether turning or continuing.

Turning right (north) off Hwy 20, onto Augier FS road, 106.4 km (66 mi) west of Vanderhoof. Set your tripometer to 0.

0 km (0 mi)
Starting north on Augier FS road.

2.2 km (1.4 mi)
Turn right for Co-op Lake campground. It's 300 meters off the main road.

CO-OP LAKE RECREATION SITE #7
Overnight / Easy
Elev: 900 m (2952 ft) / Lake: 34 ha
5 tables around a big clearing
Accessible by motorhomes and 5th-wheels

Continuing north on Augier FS road, passing the turnoff to Co-op Lake campground.

4.8 km (3 mi)
Stay straight on the main road.

24 km (14.9 mi)
Reach a major junction. Turn right for Taltapin Lake. Continue left for Pinkut and Augier lakes.

Mired in the 1960's at Taltapin Lake

0 km (0 mi)
Turning right, starting northeast on Augier-Taltapin FS road, heading for Taltapin Lake.

1.9 km (1.2 mi)
Cross a small bridge, then fork right.

5 km (3 mi)
Go right at the fork.

6.1 km (3.8 mi) and **7.1 km (4.4 mi)**
Bear left.

8.2 km (5.1 mi)
Arrive at Taltapin Lake campground. Right leads 50 meters to 4 tables. Left leads 400 meters to 7 tables. A clearcut mars the view. The forest looks haggard. Other lakes in the area are more appealing.

TALTAPIN LAKE RECREATION SITE #4
Weekend / Difficult (due only to distance)
Elev: 884 m (2900 ft) / Lake: 16 km (10 mi) long, 2105 ha
5 tables around a big clearing
Accessible by motorhomes and 5th-wheels

Continuing left (northwest) on Augier FS road, passing the turnoff to Taltapin Lake campground.

34.2 km (21.2 mi)
Reach a major intersection. **Turn sharply right** to enter Pinkut Lake campground in 0.5 km (0.3 mi). **Turn left** to quickly arrive at Division Lake campground or proceed southwest to Hwy 16 and the town of Burns Lake. **Continue straight** on Augier Main FS road for Augier Lake campground (read further directions on page 216), as well as provincial parks on the north end of Pinkut Lake and south shore of Babine Lake.

PINKUT LAKE RECREATION SITE #2
Weekend / Difficult (due only to distance)
Elev: 930 m (3050 ft) / Lake: 7.5 km (4.7 mi) long, 586 ha
5 tables, good boat launch
Accessible by motorhomes and 5th-wheels

Turning left (southwest) onto Old Babine Road, from the 34.2-km (21.2-mi) junction on Augier FS road. Set your tripometer to 0.

0 km (0 mi)
Starting southwest on Old Babine Road, heading for Division Lake and Hwy 16.

2.2 km (1.4 mi)
Turn left for Division Lake campground. It's 200 meters off the main road.

DIVISION LAKE RECREATION SITE #3
Weekend / Difficult (due only to distance)
Elev: 975 m (3200 ft) / Lake: 25 ha
3 tables, 4 campsites
Accessible by motorhomes and 5th-wheels

Pinkut Lake

Continuing southwest on Old Babine Road, passing the turnoff to Division Lake campground.

17.5 km (10.9 mi)
Reach Hwy 16, at the town of Burns Lake, across from Lakes District Secondary School.

DIRECT ROUTE TO AUGIER LAKE

0 km (0 mi)
Starting north on Old Babine Road, from Hwy 16 in the town of Burns Lake, across from Lake District Secondary School. Set your tripometer to 0.

15.3 km (9.5 mi)
Turn right for **Division Lake campground**, described on page 214. It's 200 meters off the main road.

17.5 km (10.9 mi)
Reach a major intersection. Proceed straight through, then go right 0.5 km (0.3 mi) to enter **Pinkut Lake campground**,

described on page 214. Continue left (north) onto Augier Main FS road for Augier Lake campground, as well as provincial parks on the north end of Pinkut Lake and south shore of Babine Lake. Right is Augier FS road (good gravel), which you can follow southeast 34.2 km (21.2 mi) back to Hwy 16 by keeping right at main junctions.

Continuing left (north) onto Augier Main FS road, from the 17.5-km (10.9-mi) intersection on Old Babine Road, passing the turnoff to Pinkut Lake campground, heading for Augier Lake campground.

28.5 km (17.7 mi)
Turn right (east) onto Augier-Campsite FS road, near the KM 47 sign.

33.5 km (20.8 mi)
Arrive at Augier Lake campground, on the northeast shore.

AUGIER LAKE RECREATION SITE #1
Weekend / Difficult (due only to distance)
910 m (2985 ft) / Lake: 10 km (6.2 mi) long, 906 ha
15 tables, pebble beach, good boat launch
Accessible by motorhomes and 5th-wheels

~~

BURNS LAKE TO HOUSTON

These two campgrounds near Hwy 16 are handy if you're buzzing through the area. Maxan Lake, 21.8 km (13.5 mi) off pavement, is not scenic. But Sunset Lake is. Ringed by low hills, adorned with quaking aspen and sun-licking lime grass, it has a soothing charm. And it's just 5.3 km (3.3 mi) from the highway. Both are accessible by motorhomes and 5th-wheels.

If you're heading northeast on Hwy 16 from Houston

From midway across the Bulkley River bridge, on the northeast side of Houston, drive 29.2 km (18.1 mi) to the hamlet of Topley. Set your tripometer to 0.

Camp in a grove of quaking aspen at Sunset Lake.

For Sunset Lake, turn right (south) onto Sunset Road.

For Maxan Lake, continue southeast on Hwy 16. After a major hill, pass a yellow sign: TRUCKS TURNING. Slow down. At 15.2 km (9.4 mi), turn right (south) onto Forestdale Canyon Road. Reset your tripometer to 0.

If you're heading northwest on Hwy 16 from the town of Burns Lake

Drive 36 km (22.3 mi) to where the paved Broman Lake Frontage Road parallels the highway. Set your tripometer to 0.

For Maxan Lake, turn left (south) onto Forestdale Canyon Road.

For Sunset Lake, continue 14 km (8.7 mi) northwest on Hwy 16 to the hamlet of Topley. Turn left (south) onto Sunset Road. Reset your tripometer to 0.

For SUNSET LAKE, now follow the directions below

0 km (0 mi)
Turning south onto Sunset Road.

0.4 km (0.25 mi)
Cross railroad tracks and bear right on pavement.

2 km (1.2 mi)
Pavement ends. Continue straight.

4 km (2.5 mi)
Turn right onto Rondeau Road.

5.3 km (3.3 mi)
Turn right for Sunset Lake campground.

> Proceed straight, past the sign, through the barbed-wire fence. Turn left for the day-use area, right for campsites. Expect to hear cows bellowing across the small lake. If it's breezy, the rustle of quaking aspen will improve the concert.

SUNSET LAKE RECREATION SITE #15
Weekend / Easy
Elev: 866 m (2840 ft) / Lake: 2.5 km (1.6 mi) long, 125.5 ha
6 tables, 5 campsites, good boat launch, dock
Accessible by motorhomes and 5th-wheels

For MAXAN LAKE, now follow the directions below

0 km (0 mi)
Turning south onto Forestdale Canyon Road—broad, well-graded gravel. It winds as it descends.

3.1 km (1.9 mi)
Reach a T-junction. Turn right onto Rose Lake Cutoff Road.

4.6 km (2.9 mi)
Bear left and cross railroad tracks.

4.9 km (3 mi)
Cross the Bulkley River (now quite small) and head south.

6.4 km (4 mi)
Stay straight where Day Lake Road forks right.

9.4 km (5.8 mi)
Reach a signed junction. Bear left on Maxan Creek FS road.

10.7 km (6.6 mi)
Bear right, on the main road.

18.3 km (11.3 mi)
Stay straight where a wide road forks left.

19.5 km (12.1 mi)
Cross a bridged creek.

19.8 km (12.3 mi)
Bear right, on the main road.

21.2 km (13.1 mi)
Turn left and descend.

21.8 km (13.5 mi)
Arrive at Maxan Lake campground.

They decimated the trees to create the campground. It's ugly, the atmosphere desolate. Fisherfolk in boats can ignore this and enjoy the medium-size lake surrounded by low, forested hills. But the site itself is not conducive to family frolic.

MAXAN LAKE RECREATION SITE #5
Weekend / Moderate
Elev: 762 m (2500 ft) / Lake: 5.6 km (3.5 mi) long, 643 ha
12 tables, easy boat launch
Accessible by motorhomes and 5th-wheels

Maxan Lake is appealing, even if the campground's not.

MORICE RIVER and FRANCOIS LAKE

Big, beautiful, weekend-worthy campgrounds await you south of Houston. Several smaller ones allow pleasant overnight stops on deeper forays. Aspen is just 18 km (11 mi) from Hwy 16. Owen Lake is farther (40 km / 25 mi) but worth it; the drive is easy, on a broad, well-maintained road. Both are provincial-park quality, and Owen is rated Destination.

For an enjoyable backroads tour, leave Hwy 16 near Houston. Head south on Morice River and Morice-Owen FS roads. Drive Colleymount Road along the north shore of Francois Lake, passing several campgrounds at the west end. Then loop back up to Hwy 16 and Burns Lake. Just be wary of industrial traffic; these roads are not lonely. At day's end, pub-bound loggers sometimes blast along at 90 kph.

If you're heading west on Hwy 16 through Houston

From the sign WELCOME TO HOUSTON just east of town, drive 7 km (4.3 mi) through the business district to the west side of town. Turn left (south) at the large signs described below. Set your tripometer to 0.

If you're heading southeast on Hwy 16 from Smithers

Drive almost to Houston. Immediately after the railroad over-pass just west of town, turn right (south) at the large signs described below. Set your tripometer to 0.

For either approach above, now follow the directions below

0 km (0 mi)
Turning south on the prominently-signed paved road. You'll see a large, brown, wood sign with white letters: NORTHWOOD - HOUSTON DIVISION. Another sign announces: HOUSTON FOREST PRODUCTS COMPANY. Small road signs point south: FRANCOIS LK 64, MORICE LAKE 82, OWEN LAKE 40.

1.5 km (0.9 mi)
Pass the mill. Pavement ends. You're now on well-maintained Morice River FS road.

17.8 km (11 mi)
Turn right for Aspen campground.

> Arrive at the campground in 0.4 km (0.25 mi). It's lovely, beside broad, fast-flowing, quiet Morice River. An accommodating layout enables large RVs to park and turn around in an initial spacious clearing. Beyond are individual campsites separated by fir, spruce, aspen, and berry bushes.

ASPEN RECREATION SITE #1
Weekend / Easy
8 sites with tables, exceptionally well-designed campground
Accessible by motorhomes and 5th-wheels

Continuing south on Morice River FS road, passing the turnoff to Aspen campground.

27.8 km (17.2 mi)
Reach a signed junction. Set your tripometer to 0 before turning either way. Left leads southeast to campgrounds on Francois and Ootsa lakes; for directions continue reading on page 225. Right soon reaches the Owen Flats campgrounds then proceeds southwest about 55 km (34 mi) to Morice Lake campground.

Aspen campground, on Morice River, is provincial-park quality.

Turning right (west) at the 27.8-km (17.2-mi) junction on Morice River FS road.

0 km (0 mi)
Turning right (west), still on Morice River FS road.

0.7 km (0.4 mi)
Cross a bridge. Immediately after, on the right, is the first of three roadside tables comprising Owen Flats "A" campground. The other tables are at 0.8 km (0.5 mi) and 0.9 km (0.6 mi).

OWEN FLATS "A" RECREATION SITE #3
Overnight / Moderate
3 tables between the road and Morice River
Accessible by small motorhomes and trailers

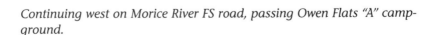

Continuing west on Morice River FS road, passing Owen Flats "A" campground.

1.9 km (1.2 mi)
Stay straight where Chisholm FS road forks right, near the KM 29 sign.

2.3 km (1.4 mi)
Turn right for Owen Flats "B" campground.

Small motorhomes and trailers can make it, although your paint job might suffer. In 200 meters fork left. Arrive in another 150 meters. The narrow road loops back to the entrance. The campsites offer limited views. Across the Morice River is a stand of dead trees. Aspen campground is better.

OWEN FLATS "B" RECREATION SITE #4
Weekend / Moderate
8 riverbank tables, room for only 4 vehicles
Accessible by small motorhomes and trailers

Continuing west on Morice River FS road, passing the turnoff to Owen Flats "B" campground.

3 km (1.9 mi)
Stay straight.

14.7 km (9.1 mi)
Bear right, continuing level on the main road. Pimpernel FS road ascends left.

17 km (10.5 mi)
Turn right (just before the bridge) for Lamprey Creek campground.

In 150 meters arrive at the campground, on the confluence of Morice River and Lamprey Creek. Trees block views of water from the campsites.

LAMPREY CREEK RECREATION SITE #5
Weekend / Moderate
3 tables, comfortably spaced campsites
Accessible by small motorhomes and trailers

Continuing west on Morice River FS road, passing the turnoff to Lamprey Creek campground.

17.2 km (10.7 mi)
Reach a major junction. Right is Morice West FS road; there are no more campgrounds that way. Turn left to continue southwest on Morice River FS road. In about 38 km (23.6 mi) it ends at the northeast corner of impressively large and scenic Morice Lake.

55.2 km (34.2 mi)
Arrive at Morice Lake campground.

MORICE LAKE RECREATION SITE #6
Destination / Difficult (due only to distance)
Elev: 797 m (2615 ft) / Lake: 40.5 km (25 mi) long, 9708 ha
18 tables, boat launch, glacier views, provincial-park quality
Accessible by motorhomes and 5th wheels

Turning left (southeast) at the 27.8-km (17.2-mi) junction (page 221) on Morice River FS road. Set your tripometer to 0.

Inviting expanse of grass at Owen Lake campground

0 km (0 mi)
Starting on Morice-Owen FS road, heading southeast toward Francois and Ootsa lakes.

12.6 km (7.8 mi)
Turn right for Owen Lake campground.

In 300 meters arrive at the campground—a big, open, very inviting grassy area scattered with tables. Owen Creek is nearby. The only secluded campsite is right of the dock. You'll find a little privacy farther west, away from the lake. All sites have views. Logging trucks are audible, but the road is obscured. A 10-km (6.2-mi) trail ascends to treeline on 2124-m (6967-ft) Nadina Mountain, visible west. For permission to hike, ask at Nadina Mountain Lodge, 1.5 km (0.9 mi) down the road.

OWEN LAKE RECREATION SITE #2
Destination / Moderate
Elev: 762 m (2500 ft) / Lake: 7.5 km (4.7 mi) long, 296 ha
14 tables, dock, good boat launch, provincial-park quality
Accessible by motorhomes and 5th-wheels

Continuing southeast on Morice-Owen FS road, passing the turnoff to Owen Lake campground.

21 km (13 mi)
Bear left for Francois and Ootsa lakes. (Right is Morice-Tahtsa FS road leading southwest. It passes tiny **Nadina Pool Recreation Site #8** on Nadina River in about 11 km / 6.8 mi. It accesses **Nadina Lake Recreation Site #9** in about 25 km / 15.5 mi, where you'll find 6 tables, a pebble beach, and a view of the Sibola Mtns. The 930-hectare lake is 10 km / 6.2 mi long.)

24.2 km (15 mi)
Bear right on the wide, main road.

26 km (16.1 mi)
Reach a major junction. For Francois and Ootsa lakes, turn left (east) onto Owen East FS road. Ignore the two right forks here.

38.8 km (24.1 mi)
Reach a major junction. It's signed for various points including Wisteria (right, 21 km, en route to Ootsa Lake), and Burns Lake (left, 77 km, on Hwy 16). Right leads southeast to Ootsa Lake and accesses the Francois Lake ferry at Southbank; for directions continue reading on page 230. Left (east) follows the north shore of Francois Lake and is the direct route to Hwy 16. Set your tripometer to 0 before turning either way.

Turning left (east) onto Colleymount Road, from the 38.8-km (24.1-mi) junction on Owen East FS road. Set your tripometer to 0.

0 km (0 mi)
Starting on Colleymount Road, heading east along Francois Lake's north shore.

3.4 km (2.1 mi)
Turn right for Noralee West campground, beside the road.

NORALEE WEST RECREATION SITE #13
Overnight / Difficult (due only to distance)
4 tables, good boat launch, small pebble beach
Accessible by motorhomes and 5th-wheels

Continuing east on Colleymount Road, passing the turnoff to Noralee West campground.

5 km (3 mi)
Pass Noralee store. There's a private campground, cabins and laundromat here.

6.8 km (4.2 mi)
Turn right for Noralee East campground, a large open area on a short peninsula.

NORALEE EAST RECREATION SITE #14
Overnight / Difficult (due only to distance)
4 tables, boat launch, small pebble beach
Accessible by motorhomes and 5th-wheels

Continuing east on Colleymount Road, passing the turnoff to Noralee East campground.

15.6 km (9.7 mi)
Cross bridged Trout Creek.

20.4 km (12.6 mi)
Pass Lake Terrace Drive on the left.

22 km (13.6 mi)
Turn right for Colleymount campground. It's a large open area and has a cooking shelter with a woodstove.

COLLEYMOUNT RECREATION SITE #15
Weekend / Difficult (due only to distance)
5 tables, 2 lakeshore campsites, gravel beach, good boat launch
Accessible by motorhomes and 5th-wheels

Continuing east on Colleymount Road, passing the turnoff to Colleymount campground.

It's about another 30 km (18.5 mi) to the community of Francois Lake and the north-shore ferry landing. From there, paved Hwy 35 leads north about 25 km (15.5 mi) to Hwy 16 and the town of Burns Lake. The free ferry across Francois Lake departs hourly, on the half hour, 5:30 a.m. to 12:30 a.m., every day. The south-shore landing is at the community of Southbank.

Turning right at the 38.8-km (24.1-mi) junction (page 226) on Owen East FS road. Set your tripometer to 0.

0 km (0 mi)
Starting on Ootsa-Nadina FS road, rounding the west end of Francois Lake en route to Ootsa Lake.

1.1 km (0.7 mi)
Cross a bridge over Nadina River.

3.5 km (2.2 mi)
Turn left for West Francois Lake campground.

Descend to enter the campground in 150 meters. It's a grassy clearing on the lakeshore, just below the main road.

WEST FRANCOIS LAKE RECREATION SITE #12
Overnight / Difficult (due only to distance)
3 tables, 2 campsites, good boat launch
Inaccessible by motorhomes and trailers

Continuing southeast on Ootsa-Nadina FS road, passing the turnoff to West Francois Lake campground.

7.9 km (4.9 mi)
Stay straight at the 4-way junction. West Francois Main FS road is left.

15.8 km (9.8 mi)
The mountainous northern reaches of Tweedsmuir Park are visible south, across Ootsa Lake.

16.5 km (10.2 mi)
Spicer Road forks left.

18.1 km (11.2 mi)
Turn left for Lund Lake campground.

In 0.5 km (0.3 mi) bear left to reach the campground in another 200 meters. The lake is tiny, but the setting is attractive: a treed, grassy, pastoral bowl.

LUND LAKE RECREATION SITE #19
Overnight / Difficult (due only to distance)
2 tables, rough boat launch
Accessible by small motorhomes and trailers

Continuing southeast on Ootsa-Nadina FS road, passing the turnoff to Lund Lake campground.

Quest for Adventure

When you seek adventure outdoors, it might be that deep inside you feel the need to embark on the mythic hero's journey. Joseph Campbell, author of The Power of Myth, *explains: "The hero feels there's something lacking in the normal experiences available or permitted to the members of his society. This person then takes off on a series of adventures beyond the ordinary, either to recover what has been lost or to discover some life-giving elixir."*

18.7 km (11.6 mi)
Reach a junction. Bear left to continue southeast to Ootsa Lake. Go right (southwest) to quickly reach Eastern Lake campground. Set your tripometer to 0 before turning either way.

Turning right (southwest) at the 18.7-km (11.6-mi) junction, onto Wisteria Main FS road. Set your tripometer to 0.

0 km (0 mi)
Starting on Wisteria Main FS road, signed for Andrews Bay Provincial Park (22 km).

1.3 km (0.8 mi)
Turn left off the main road.

2.2 km (1.4 mi)
Arrive at Eastern Lake campground. The campsites are well spaced. Each has its own area of grass and trees.

EASTERN LAKE RECREATION SITE #18
Overnight / Difficult (due only to distance)
3 tables, good boat launch
Accessible by small motorhomes and trailers

Bearing left (continuing southeast) at the 18.7-km (11.6-mi) junction on Ootsa-Nadina FS road. Set your tripometer to 0.

Don't be confused by the barrage of signs at some major backroad junctions.

0 km (0 mi)
On Ootsa-Nadina FS road, proceeding southeast to Ootsa Lake.

5.5 km (3.4 mi)
Reach a junction. Bear right (southeast) on Ootsa-Nadina FS road, also called Wisteria Road. Carroll Road forks north.

9.3 km (5.8 mi)
Pass Wisteria Community Hall and baseball field on the left.

24.2 km (15 mi)
Turn right (just before where the road is sealcoated) for Ootsa Lake campground.

It's in a grassy aspen grove, on a north-shore bay of this giant lake. The view is south into the mountains of Tweedsmuir Park. The lake's south shore is the park's north boundary.

OOTSA LAKE RECREATION SITE #25
Overnight / Difficult (due only to distance)
Elev: 854 m (2800 ft) / Lake: 260 km (160 mi) long, 47,453 ha
3 tables, gravel beach, good boat launch
Accessible by small motorhomes and trailers

Continuing southeast on Wisteria Road, passing the turnoff to Ootsa Lake campground.

25.2 km (15.6 mi)
Stay straight on the main road. Pass Ootsa Lake Bible Camp cabins.

26.3 km (16.3 mi)
Reach a junction. Turn left (northeast) onto Ootsa-Nadina Jct. FS road for Southbank, the Francois Lake ferry, Hwy 16 and Burns Lake. A green sign states Southbank is 39 km, Burns Lake 63 km. (Straight continues following the north shore of Ootsa Lake, where there are no more campgrounds.)

37 km (23 mi)
Pavement begins.

45.6 km (28.3 mi)
Reach a T-junction at Hwy 35. Turn left (north) to reach Southbank in 18.4 km (11.4 mi); for directions continue reading on page 232. Turn right (south) for Takysie Lake campground.

Turning right (south) onto Hwy 35, from the 45.6-km (28.3-km) junction. Set your tripometer to 0.

0 km (0 mi)
Starting on Hwy 35, heading south to Takysie Lake.

3 km (1.9 mi)
Turn left on Takysie Pit Road, just before Takysie Creek bridge.

3.1 km (1.9 mi)
Arrive at Takysie Lake campground's first section—7 tables clustered around grassy hills near a cove.

3.7 km (2.3 mi)
Turn right, toward the lake, for 2 more campsites. Even here, noise from the paved road and nearby private cabins is audible, creating a city-park atmosphere.

TAKYSIE LAKE RECREATION SITE #20
Overnight / Difficult (due only to distance)
Elev: 825 m (2706 ft) / Lake: 5.5 km (3.4 mi) long, 507 ha
7 tables, boat launch
Accessible by small motorhomes and trailers

Turning left (north) onto Hwy 35, from the 45.6-km (28.3-mi) junction.

51.3 km (31.8 mi)
Drive through the aptly-named community of Grassy Plains.

64 km (40 mi)
Reach the ferry landing in the community of **Southbank**, on the south shore of Francois Lake. The ferry is free. It departs hourly, on the hour, 5 a.m. to 12 a.m., every day. The north-shore ferry landing is at the community of Francois Lake. From there, paved Hwy 35 leads 25 km (15.5 mi) north to the town of Burns Lake on Hwy 16. You can also turn left (west) onto dirt Colleymount Road, which follows the north shore of Francois Lake (page 209).

To reach Hwy 16 and the town of Fraser Lake, via the east end of Francois Lake, turn right at the Southbank ferry landing and set your tripometer to 0.

0 km (0 mi)
Turning right (east), from the Southbank ferry landing, onto Ancha Lake Road (still paved).

2.4 km (1.5 mi)
Turn left for Indian Bay campground. It's on Francois Lake, 1.2 km (0.7 mi) from the main road.

INDIAN BAY RECREATION SITE #16
5 tables, more campsites, convenient to Francois Lake ferry
Inaccessible by large motorhomes and trailers

Continuing southeast on Ancha Lake Road, passing the turnoff to Indian Bay campground.

6.3 km (3.9 mi)
Pavement ends.

12 km (7.4 mi)
Reach a signed junction. Go right on Campbell Road for Uncha and Binta lakes, the east end of Francois Lake, and Hwy 16.

13.6 km (8.4 mi)
Go right at the junction, on Binta FS road.

16.3 km (10.1 mi)
Bear left.

21 km (13 mi)
Stay left, following a sign for Uncha, Binta and Knapp lakes. Ignore the right fork.

26 km (16.1 mi)
Turn left for Uncha Lake campground.

Arrive at the campground in 1 km (0.6 mi). It's confined, and most sites are not on the lake.

UNCHA LAKE RECREATION SITE #21
Weekend / Difficult
Elev: 786 m (2578 ft) / 13.5 km (8.4 mi) long, 1340 ha
7 tables, boat launch
Inaccessible by large motorhomes and trailers

Continuing southeast on Binta FS road, passing the turnoff to Uncha Lake campground.

27.1 km (16.8 mi)
Stay right, on the main road.

27.5 km (17.1 mi)
Turn left for Binta North campground.

In 1.7 km (1.1 mi) fork left to 7 tables with lake views, or right to 2 more tables.

BINTA NORTH RECREATION SITE #22
Weekend / Difficult (due only to distance)
Elev: 820 m (2690 ft) / Lake: 8.7 km (5.4 mi) long, 833 ha
9 tables, boat launch
Inaccessible by large motorhomes and trailers

Continuing southeast on Binta FS road, passing the turnoff to Binta North campground.

29 km (18 mi)
Stay straight.

35.6 km (22.1 mi)
The road abruptly curves left.

39.4 km (24.4 mi)
Go left at the signed fork to reach South Binta Lake, Trout Lake, the east end of Francois Lake, and Hwy 16. Right is a narrow, rough, winding road to small campgrounds (suitable for tenting only) on Knapp and Moose lakes.

41 km (25.4 mi)
Turn left for Binta South campground.

> Arrive at the campground in 0.5 km (0.3 mi). The campsites ring a clearing on the southeast end of Binta Lake. The sunset view northwest up the lake is a treat.

BINTA SOUTH RECREATION SITE #23
Weekend / Difficult (due only to distance)
Elev: 820 m (2690 ft) / Lake: 8.7 km (5.4 mi) long, 833 ha
7 tables, beach, boat launch
Inaccessible by large motorhomes and trailers

Continuing northeast on Binta FS road, passing the turnoff to Binta South campground.

43.1 km (26.7 mi)
Stay straight on Binta FS road and set your tripometer to 0. Binta North FS road forks left.

0 km (0 mi)
Continuing straight (northeast) on Binta FS road.

6.1 km (3.8 mi)
Stay straight.

8.7 km (5.4 mi)
Turn right for tiny **Trout Lake Recreation Site #24**. Reach the lone campsite by driving 200 meters along the access road that parallels the main road.

10 km (6.2 mi)
Enter Vanderhoof FS District.

15 km (9.3 mi)
Turn left for Meuoon Lake campground.

> The lone table is 40 meters off the main road. Faint tracks continue right to a possible second campsite.

MEUOON LAKE RECREATION SITE #9
Overnight / Difficult (due only to distance)
1 table, marshy 9-hectare pond
Inaccessible by motorhomes and trailers

Continuing northeast on Binta FS road, passing the turnoff to Meuoon Lake campground.

21.4 km (13.3 mi)
Turn right for **Anzus Lake Recreation Site #11**. It has 3 campsites and offers no privacy from the main road. This 304-hectare lake is at 868 m (2847 ft) elevation.

24.3 km (15.1 mi)
Reach a junction. Set your tripometer to 0 before going either way. Left (northeast) on Holy Cross-Francois FS road leads to the east end of Francois Lake and Hwy 16. Straight (east) reaches Burner Bay campground on Borel Lake in 5 minutes.

0 km (0 mi)
Proceeding straight (east) from the 24.3-km (15.1-mi) junction, heading to Borel Lake.

1.5 km (0.9 mi)
Stay straight on the main road.

2.5 km (1.6 mi)
Pass a large **overnight pullout** above the west end of Borel Lake.

4 km (2.5 mi)
Reach Burner Bay campground on the right. It's beside the road, on Borel Lake. Numerous clearcuts mar the view. Shade is limited.

BURNER BAY RECREATION SITE #39
Weekend / Moderate
Elev: 865 m (2837 ft) / Lake: 4 km (2.5 mi) long, 203 ha
3 tables, rough boat launch
Accessible by motorhomes and 5th-wheels

0 km (0 mi)
Starting northeast on Holy Cross-Francois FS road, from the 24.3-km (15.1-mi) junction, heading to the east end of Francois Lake and Hwy 16.

2.3 km (1.4 mi)
Bear left on Francois Lake East road, heading northeast.

6.1 km (3.8 mi)
The signed **Black Point trail** is on the left. It descends to a campsite on Francois Lake.

8.3 km (5.1 mi)
Pass the first house on this end of Francois Lake.

9.3 km (5.8 mi)
Watch carefully for the small, obscure, left fork dropping steeply to Sawmill Point campground.

Directly below the main road is a table tucked into the trees; another is within one meter of the shore. The hills across the lake were denuded by the Endako molybdenum mine.

SAWMILL POINT RECREATION SITE #8
Weekend / Moderate
2 tables, boat launch
Accessible by motorhomes and 5th-wheels

~

Continuing northeast, passing the turnoff to Sawmill Point campground.

13.6 km (8.4 mi)
Turn left at the T-junction.

15.6 km (9.7 mi)
Go right onto the sealcoated road.

23 km (14.3 mi)
Reach Hwy 16 and the town of Fraser Lake.

~

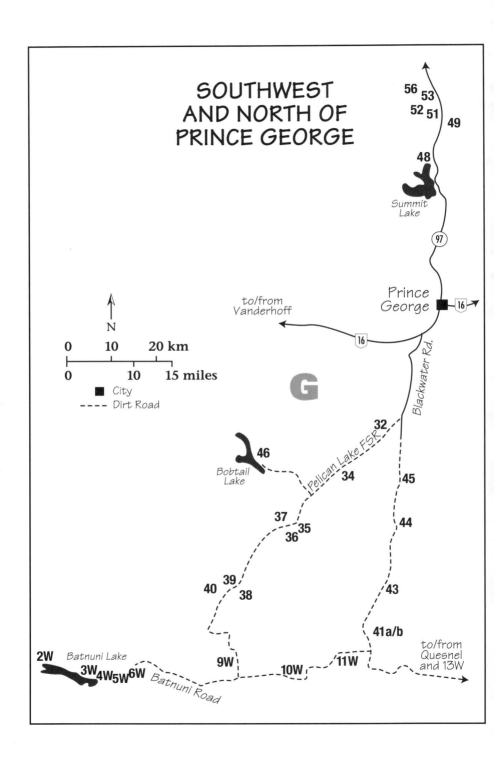

SOUTHWEST AND NORTH OF PRINCE GEORGE

56 53
52 51
49

48

Summit
Lake

97

Prince
George

to/from
Vanderhoff

16

16

Blackwater Rd.

N

| 0 | 10 | 20 km |

| 0 | 10 | 15 miles |

■ City
- - - Dirt Road

32

46

Bobtail
Lake

Pelican Lake FSR

34

45

37
35
36

44

39
40
38

43

41a/b

to/from
Quesnel
and 13W

2W   Batnuni Lake

3W
4W 5W 6W

9W

10W

11W

Batnuni Road

G

G: Southwest and North of Prince George

Most of these campgrounds are in **Prince George FS District**. **W** stands for **West Cariboo FS Region**.

2 W	Batnuni Lake West	38	Meadow Lake
3 W	Batnuni Lake East	39	Lintz Lake
4 W	Snag Lake	40	Tagai Lake
5 W	Hanham Lake	41	Blackwater Crossing
6 W	Boat Lake	43	Cleswuncut Lake
9 W	Pelican Lake	44	Punchaw Lake
10 W	Kilometre 64	45	MacKenzie Lakes
11 W	Boot Lake	46	Bobtail Lake
13 W	Twin Lakes	48	Summit Lake
32	Shesta Lake	49	Crystal Lake
34	Chilako Bridge	51	100 Road Bridge
35	Chilako River	52	Dominion Lake
36	Barton Lake	53	Caines Bridge
37	Tory Lake	56	Davie Lake South

Southwest and North of Prince George

Circling the wagons at a typical Prince George region campground

SOUTHWEST OF PRINCE GEORGE

Many rivers southwest of Prince George are the colour of dark beer or strong tea, which is how the main backcountry artery got its name: Blackwater-Mud River FS road. But little else distinguishes this region from the rest of central B.C. The terrain is nondescript, flat to gently undulating. The forest is typical of second- and third-growth forests everywhere: a little sad.

But campers won't be entirely displeased with the region. Many of the roads are broad and smooth, allowing you to safely drive 80 kph (50 mph). That includes Quesnel-Blackwater FS road, from northwest of Bouchie Lake nearly all the way to Prince George. You'll also find some attractive, quiet campgrounds here. Pelican Lake, for example, is exceptionally pretty for a plateau-country lake, and the campground is provincial-park quality. Blackwater River campground, north of Batnuni-Blackwater junction, is another inviting hideaway.

Heading northwest from Quesnel

Follow signs for West Quesnel. Set your tripometer to 0 as you begin crossing the Fraser River bridge.

0 km (0 mi)
In Quesnel, starting across the Fraser River bridge. Just after the bridge, turn right (northwest) toward Bouchie Lake.

1 km (0.6 mi)
Turn left onto North Fraser Drive. Continue ascending the main road.

9.3 km (5.8 mi)
Just before cresting the hill, pass the public laundromat and showers on the right.

10.1 km (6.2 mi)
In the village of Bouchie Lake, turn right onto Quesnel-Blackwater Road.

36 km (22.3 mi)
Pass Bouchie Lake.

38 km (23.6 mi)
Pass a gravel pit and a possible **overnight pullout** on the right.

45.4 km (28.1 mi)
Reach the insignificant campground at Twin Lakes.

TWIN LAKES RECREATION SITE #2
Overnight / Difficult (due only to distance)
small campsite on a steep sided pond
Accessible by motorhomes and 5th-wheels

Continuing northwest on Quesnel-Blackwater Road, passing Twin Lakes campground.

56 km (34.7 mi)
Pantage Lake is visible on the left.

61.6 km (38.3 mi)
Pass Blackwater-Spruce Road on the left.

67.6 km (42 mi)
Cross Pantage Creek and arrive at a major junction. Set your tripometer to 0 before proceeding either way. Right (north) is Blackwater-Mud River FS road. It leads directly to Hwy 16 at the southwest edge of Prince George in about 68 km (42 mi). Left (west) leads 71 km (44 mi) to Batnuni Lake; for directions continue reading on page 245.

BLACKWATER-MUD RIVER FS ROAD

0 km (0 mi)
Starting north on Blackwater-Mud River FS road, from the 67.6-km (42-mi) junction on Quesnel-Blackwater Road. A sign warns the road is narrow and winding.

3.4 km (2.1 mi)
Cross a bridge over Blackwater River. Just after is a small campground on the left. It's beside the road, girdled by trees, on an escarpment 7 meters above the river, which is audible.

Blackwater Crossing

BLACKWATER CROSSING RECREATION SITE #41a
Weekend / Difficult (due only to distance)
2 tables, 3 campsites
Accessible by motorhomes and 5th-wheels

Continuing north on Blackwater-Mud River FS road, passing Blackwater Crossing campground.

3.6 km (2.2 mi)
Turn right to reach Blackwater River campground in 200 meters.

BLACKWATER RIVER RECREATION SITE #41b
Weekend / Difficult (due only to distance)
7 tables near riverbank, some with views
Accessible by motorhomes and 5th-wheels

Continuing north on Blackwater-Mud River FS road, passing the turnoff to Blackwater River campground.

Cleswuncut Lake

10.5 km (6.5 mi)
Bear left at the fork.

12 km (7.4 mi)
Turn right for Cleswuncut Lake campground. The sign parallels the road, so it's difficult to see. The small, marshy lake is pretty.

CLESWUNCUT LAKE RECREATION SITE #43
Weekend / Difficult (due only to distance)
Elev: 720 m (2360 ft) / Lake: 34 ha
a couple campsites
Inaccessible by motorhomes and 5th-wheels

Continuing north on Blackwater-Mud River FS road, pass **Punchaw Lake Recreation Site #44** at about 20 km (12.4 mi) and **Mackenzie Lake Recreation Site #45** at about 36 km (22.3 mi). Both campgrounds are quite small. Punchaw (246 hectares) is the larger of the two lakes and has a boat launch. Reach paved Blackwater Road at about 44 km (27.3 mi). Intersect Hwy 16, on the southwest edge of Prince George, at about 71 km (44 mi).

BATNUNI ROAD TO PELICAN LAKE

0 km (0 mi)
Starting west on Batnuni Road (also called Nazco Road), from the 67.6-km (42-mi) junction on Quesnel-Blackwater Road.

11.7 km (7.3 mi)
Turn left and descend to reach Boot Lake campground in 100 meters. The lake is small. The campsites are on the shore. A clearcut is visible across the water.

BOOT LAKE RECREATION SITE #11
Weekend / Difficult (due only to distance)
4 tables
Inaccessible by motorhomes and 5th-wheels

Continuing west on Batnuni Road, passing the turnoff to Boot Lake campground.

24.6 km (15.3 mi)
Cross a bridge over the broad Blackwater River. Just after is an **overnight pullout** on the right. Any vehicle that passes will be audible as it rattles over the loose bridge-beams, but there's little traffic here.

30 km (18.7 mi)
Proceed straight (northwest) on Batnuni Road. Nazco Road forks left (south), reaching a gas station in about 40 km (25 mi).

33.6 km (20.8 mi)
Pass **Kilometre 64 campsite** on the right. It's unpleasant, beside the road, useful only for a brief overnight stay.

39.2 km (24.3 mi)
Reach a major junction. Set your tripometer to 0 before proceeding either way.

Bear left (west) on Batnuni Road to reach Batnuni Lake in 30 km (18.6 mi), passing several campgrounds en route. Turn right (north) onto Pelican Lake FS road to reach large, provincial-park quality Pelican Lake campground in 3.3 km (2 mi).

Pelican Lake FS road continues generally northeast to paved Blackwater Road, which leads to Hwy 16 at the southwest edge of Prince George. Read further directions on page 247.

WEST TO BATNUNI LAKE

You'll find three small campgrounds at tiny lakes just before reaching larger Batnuni Lake, which has campgrounds near its east and west ends. They're close enough together that you can check them all out, then settle in at your favourite for a weekend of canoeing, fishing, reading, or intensive supine therapy (sleeping). The lakes are at an elevation of about 875 m (2870 ft). They range in size from 23 to 54 hectares. The surrounding forests are primarily willow, aspen, spruce and pine. Batnuni is 8.5 km (5.3 mi) long and covers 514 hectares. The following distances are approximate. Brown FS signposts indicate the campground turnoffs.

0 km (0 mi)
Continuing west on Batnuni Road, from the 39.2-km (24.3-mi) junction with Pelican Lake FS road.

21 km (13 mi)
Turn left for **Boat Lake Recreation Site #6.**

24 km (14.9 mi)
Turn left for **Hanham Lake Recreation Site #5**, at the east end of the lake. The steep shore makes it difficult to swim or launch a boat.

28 km (17.4 mi)
Turn left onto Swede Lake road for **Snag Lake Recreation Site #4**. Cross the Euchiniko River bridge, then turn right to enter the campground.

30 km (18.6 mi)
Turn left for **Batnuni Lake East Recreation Site #3**. It has a boat launch.

Near 37.5 km (23.3 mi)
Turn left for **Batnuni Lake West Recreation Site #2**. Rough access prohibits big RVs.

Pelican Lake

PELICAN LAKE TO PRINCE GEORGE

0 km (0 mi)
Starting north on Pelican Lake FS road, from the 39.2-km (24.3-mi) junction on Batnuni Road.

3.3 km (2 mi)
Turn left for Pelican Lake campground. Just off the main road, a spur road right leads to two secluded campsites, then continues onto private property. Go left or straight for the rest of the campsites scattered along two loop roads. Most are treed. Only two are on the shore.

PELICAN LAKE RECREATION SITE #9
Destination / Difficult (due only to distance)
Elev: 810 m (2657 ft) / Lake: 3.2 km (2 mi) long, 392 ha
13 tables, provincial-park quality
Accessible by motorhomes and 5th-wheels

Continuing north on Pelican Lake FS road, passing the turnoff to Pelican Lake campground.

13.5 km (8.4 mi)
Bear right where rough 50 FS road forks left to Clear Lake.

18.3 km (11.3 mi)
Enter Prince George Forest District.

19.3 km (12 mi)
Turn sharply left for Tagai Lake campground.

> Drive 1.1 km (0.7 mi) off the main road, then turn right. Reach the brown lake at 2.3 km (1.4 mi).

TAGAI LAKE RECREATION SITE #40
Weekend / Difficult (due only to distance)
Elev: 830 m (2722 ft) / Lake: 3.7 km (2.3 mi) long, 249 ha
10 tables, comfortably spaced campsites
Accessible by motorhomes and 5th-wheels

Continuing northeast on Pelican Lake FS road, passing the turnoff to Tagai Lake campground.

24 km (14.9 mi)
Turn right for Lintz Lake campground. It's beside the main road.

The setting is exposed, the scenery uninspiring. Though Tagai and Pelican are superior, Lintz seems to be more popular, perhaps because motorboats are allowed.

LINTZ LAKE RECREATION SITE #39
Weekend / Difficult (due only to distance)
Lake: 2.4 km (1.5 mi) long
11 tables, good boat launch
Accessible by motorhomes and 5th-wheels

Continuing northeast on Pelican Lake FS road, passing the turnoff to Lintz Lake campground.

26.5 km (16.4 mi)
Turn right for Meadow Lake campground.

Follow the narrow, winding spur road 2 km (1.2 mi) southeast to the lake.

MEADOW LAKE RECREATION SITE #38
Weekend / Difficult (due only to distance)
Lake: 1.2 km (0.7 mi) long
11 tables, good boat launch
Inaccessible by motorhomes and 5th-wheels

Continuing northeast on Pelican Lake FS road, passing the turnoff to Meadow Lake campground.

32 km (20 mi)
Proceed straight at the junction. Left leads to Tatuk Lake.

39.3 km (24.4 mi)
Reach Tory Lake campground. It's beside the road, useful only for a brief overnight stay. A short path drops steeply to the lake.

TORY LAKE RECREATION SITE #37
Overnight / Difficult (due only to distance)
2 tables, 3 campsites
Accessible by motorhomes and 5th-wheels

Continuing east on Pelican Lake FS road, passing Tory Lake campground.

39.6 km (24.6 mi)
Turn right for Barton Lake campground.

Follow Pelican-Barton FS road 3.2 km (2 mi), then turn right to reach the lake in 100 meters.

Low-tech inter-camper communication system.

BARTON LAKE RECREATION SITE #36
Weekend / Difficult (due only to distance)
Elev: 777 m (2550 ft) / Lake: 1 km (0.6 mi) long, 64.5 ha
5 tables, 3 campsites, rough boat launch
Accessible by motorhomes and 5th-wheels

Continuing east on Pelican Lake FS road, passing the turnoff to Barton Lake campground.

41 km (25.4 mi)
Reach Chilako River campground on the right. It's unappealing, beside the road, next to the brown, slow-moving river.

CHILAKO RIVER RECREATION SITE #35
Overnight / Difficult (due only to distance)
2 tables
Accessible by motorhomes and 5th-wheels

Continuing northeast on Pelican Lake FS road, passing Chilako River campground.

46.8 km (29 mi)

Reach a major junction. Proceed straight (northeast) for Prince George. Turn left (northwest) onto Telegraph Road for Bobtail Lake campground. Set your tripometer to 0 before going either way.

0 km (0 mi)

Starting northwest on Telegraph Road. It's labeled Blackwater FS road on the Vanderhoof FS district map.

13 km (8.1 mi)

Reach the south end of Bobtail Lake.

17.5 km (10.9 mi)

Turn left to reach the campground in about 150 meters. It has 3 sections, each with a couple campsites.

BOBTAIL LAKE RECREATION SITE #46

Weekend / Difficult (due only to distance)
Elev: 815 m (2282 ft) / Lake: 9.3 km (5.7 mi) long, 850 ha
5 tables, 6 campsites, rough boat launch
Accessible by motorhomes and 5th-wheels

0 km (0 mi)

Resuming northeast on Pelican Lake FS road, from the 46.8-km (29-mi) junction with Telegraph Road. Set your tripometer to 0.

12.2 km (7.6 mi)

Reach Chilako Bridge campground.

Shadeless campsites are on both sides of the Blackwater River. The tables were hacked for firewood, but maybe the idiot's damage has since been repaired.

CHILAKO BRIDGE RECREATION SITE #34
Overnight / Difficult (due only to distance)
2 tables, grassy clearing
Accessible by motorhomes and 5th-wheels

Continuing northeast on Pelican Lake FS road, passing Chilako Bridge campground.

21.8 km (13.5 mi)
Bear left. Pelican-Chehischic FS road forks right.

27.8 km (17.2 mi)
Reach **Shesta Lake Recreation Site #33** on the left. There are 2 tables, intended for day use, at the scummy south end of the lake. You'll be dusted by every passing vehicle; don't bother stopping.

29.5 km (18.3 mi)
Reach **Shesta Lake Recreation Site #32** on the left. A former mill site, this small campground is beside the road. It has no tables and no shade. There's a good boat launch here, but the lake is tiny. Just beyond, a left fork quickly leads to **Clear Lake Recreation Site #31**, accessible by motorhomes and 5th-wheels. It's another minimal campground on a tiny, minor lake with a boat launch.

32.7 km (20.3 mi)
Bear right to proceed northeast on Pelican FS road.

35.3 km (21.9 mi)
Reach a junction with paved Blackwater Road. Turn left for Prince George.

36.4 km (22.6 mi)
Pass Clear Lake Division Road on the left. It's the north access to Clear Lake campground.

45.5 km (28.2 mi)
Pass the turnoff to West Lake Provincial Park on the right.

57 km (35.3 mi)
Blackwater Road intersects Hwy 16. Turn right to drive northeast into Prince George.

HWY 97 NORTH OF PRINCE GEORGE

Northbound travellers will find several handy campgrounds within an hour of leaving Prince George. This book covers Hwy 97 as far as Davie Lake South, 78.6 km (48.7 mi) north of the city.

The ragged shoreline of Summit Lake is pretty. Summer sunsets are a soothing sight here. The campground is comfortably spacious, with two distinct sections. A potential drawback, however, is noise. The nearby city occasionally regurgitates urban dissonance in the form of headbanging partiers. They destroy the atmosphere that campers come here to appreciate. Vandalism has also been a problem. So don't be surprised if you're charged a camping fee at Summit Lake, to help pay for extra patrols and maintenance.

Crystal Lake campground is as attractive as it is convenient. The well-spaced campsites are in a subtle variety of forested settings including lakeshore, secluded niche, and atop a small knoll. But like Summit Lake, Crystal is subject to heavy use and is sometimes the victim of abuse, due to its proximity to the city. So it's likely you'll have to pay a modest camping fee here too. The money will fund services that keep the campground open and improve the quality of your camping experience.

0 km (0 mi)
In Prince George, at the junction of Hwys 97 and 16, heading north on Hwy 97.

28 km (17.4 mi)
Cross the Salmon River bridge (blue metal).

50.4 km (31.2 mi) and **54.5 km (33.8 mi)**
Ignore Summit Lake Road turnoffs on the left. They don't access the campground.

56 km (34.7 mi)
Turn left onto Tallus Road for Summit Lake campground.

    0 km (0 mi)
Starting west on Tallus Road.

0.9 km (0.5 mi)
Turn right onto Caine Creek FS road.

1.8 km (1.1 mi)
The lake is visible. Turn left to enter the cleared section of the campground. Continue right to enter the treed section.

2 km (1.2 mi)
Arrive at the cleared section of Summit Lake campground.

SUMMIT LAKE RECREATION SITE #48a
Weekend / Easy
Elev: 706 m (2315 ft)
Lake: 7 km (4.3 mi) long, 5.6 km (3.5 mi) wide, 314 ha
11 tables, more campsites
Accessible by motorhomes and 5th-wheels

Continuing to the treed section of the campground, from the 1.8-km (1.1-mi) junction on the access road.

In another 0.6 km (0.4 mi), reach the entrance. Turn left to arrive in 350 meters. This section feels more intimate because trees border the lakeshore and shelter the large grassy clearing. The old cement foundation here serves as a level campsite.

SUMMIT LAKE RECREATION SITE #48b
Weekend / Easy
7 tables, more campsites
Accessible by motorhomes and 5th-wheels

Continuing north on Hwy 97, passing the turnoff to Summit Lake campground.

69 km (42.8 mi)
Turn right for Crystal Lake campground.

0 km (0 mi)
Starting east on a broad, rocky road.

0.5 km (0.3 mi)
Bear left.

0.8 km (0.5 mi)
Cross an oil pipeline swath.

2.3 km (1.4 mi)
Pass the first entrance.

2.4 km (1.5 mi)
Reach the main entrance to Crystal Lake campground. It's a small lake in the hills, ringed by lodgepole pine forest. Many spacious campsites are scattered around it. Don't drive or camp on the mossy, grassy groundcover, or it will soon be gone. You'll find plenty of bare ground to pitch your tent or park your vehicle on.

CRYSTAL LAKE RECREATION SITE #49
Weekend / Easy
Elev: 724 m (2375 ft) / Lake: 36 ha
20 tables, rough boat launch
Accessible by motorhomes and 5th-wheels

Continuing north on Hwy 97, passing the turnoff to Crystal Lake campground.

70.3 km (43.6 mi)
Turn left onto Davie Lake FS road for two nearby campgrounds.

0 km (0 mi)
Starting west on Davie Lake FS road.

1.3 km (0.8 mi)
A spur road descends to a lone **campsite** on the Crooked River.

1.7 km (1.1 mi)
Turn right to enter 100 Road Bridge campground. The Crooked River is clear and slow-moving here. The bottom is rocky, the bank reedy. It's ideal for canoeing.

100 ROAD BRIDGE RECREATION SITE #51
Overnight / Easy
3 tables, 4 riverside campsites
Accessible by motorhomes and 5th-wheels

Continuing on Davie Lake FS road, passing the turnoff to 100 Road Bridge campground.

4.4 km (2.7 mi)
Turn left to enter Dominion Lake campground in 200 meters. It's on a treed bench, so reaching the shore or seeing the lake is awkward. Other campgrounds in the area are superior.

DOMINION LAKE RECREATION SITE #52
Overnight / Easy
Elev: 700 m (2296 ft) / Lake: 1.6 km (1 mi) long, 67 ha
2 tables, 4 campsites
Inaccessible by motorhomes and 5th-wheels

~

Continuing north on Hwy 97, passing the turnoff to 100 Road Bridge and Dominion Lake campgrounds.

76 km (47 mi)
Pass the turnoff to Crooked River Provincial Park.

77.6 km (48.1 mi)
Pass Grizzly Avenue in the community of Bear Lake. You can buy gas and food here.

78.4 km (48.6 mi)
Turn left (west) onto Davie-Muskeg FS road for an easy-to-access campsite at Caines Bridge. It's inaccessible by large motorhomes and trailers

At 4.3 km (2.7 mi) you'll cross a bridge. At 4.6 km (2.9 mi), turn left to reach **Caines Bridge Recreation Site #53** in 100 meters. It's on a bend in the mossy-bottomed river and has only a single, unattractive campsite with a table.

~

Continuing north on Hwy 97, passing the turnoff to Caines Bridge campground.

Close-range sightings are usually brief because moose are shy, so keep your camera handy.

78.6 km (48.7 mi)
Turn left for Davie Lake South campground. Big RVs will find the access rough but passable.

> Drive 3.2 km (2 mi) off the highway. Fork left and descend to arrive in another 200 meters. There's a large grassy clearing. The campground is surrounded by bushy trees.

DAVIE LAKE SOUTH RECREATION SITE #56
Overnight / Easy
Elev: 683 m (2240 ft) / Lake: 6.5 km (4 mi) long, 938 ha
6 tables, good boat launch
Accessible by motorhomes and 5th-wheels

HWY 97 SOUTH TO PRINCE GEORGE

0 km (0 mi)
Passing the turnoff to Crooked River Provincial Park. It's just south of the Bear Lake community.

5.5 km (3.4 mi)
Cross a second set of railroad tracks.

5.7 km (3.5 mi)
Turn right onto Davie Lake FS road for **100 Road Bridge and Dominion Lake campgrounds**; read further directions on page 255.

7 km (4.3 mi)
After passing a power substation, turn left onto a wide, rocky road for **Crystal Lake campground**; read further directions on page 254.

20 km (12.4 mi)
Turn right onto Tallus Road for **Summit Lake campground**; read further directions on page 254.

21.5 km (13.3 mi) and **25.7 km (15.9 mi)**
Ignore Summit Lake Road turnoffs on the right. They don't access the campground.

29.8 km (18.5 mi)
Pass beneath three sets of powerlines.

48 km (30 mi)
Cross the Salmon River bridge (blue metal).

76 km (47 mi)
Arrive at the junction of Hwys 97 and 16 in Prince George.

PRINCE GEORGE TO PELICAN AND BATNUNI LAKES

From the junction of Hwys 97 and 16 in Prince George, drive west on Hwy 16. In 9 km (5.6 mi) turn left (southwest) onto Blackwater FS road, signed for West Lake Provincial Park. This turn is near the top of the hill, as you're leaving Prince George and the Fraser River valley. Set your tripometer to 0.

0 km (0 mi)
Starting south on Blackwater FS road, departing Hwy 16.

11.5 km (7.1 mi)
Pass the turnoff to West Lake Provincial Park on the left.

21.7 km (13.5 mi)
Turn right onto Pelican Lake FS road. Pavement ends.

24.3 km (15.1 mi)
Bear left to proceed southwest on Pelican Lake FS road.

27.5 km (17 mi)
Reach **Shesta Lake campground** on the right. Read page 252 for details.

35.2 km (21.8 mi)
Bear right. Pelican-Chehischic FS road forks left.

44.8 km (27.8 mi)
Reach **Chilako Bridge campground**. Read page 252 for details.

57 km (35.3 mi)
Reach a major junction. Turn right (northwest) onto Telegraph Road for **Bobtail Lake campground**; read further directions on page 251. Proceed straight (southwest) on Pelican Lake FS road for Pelican and Batnuni lakes. Set your tripometer to 0 before going ether way.

～

0 km (0 mi)
Resuming southwest on Pelican Lake FS road, from the 57-km (35.3-mi) junction with Telegraph Road. Set your tripometer to 0.

5.8 km (3.6 mi)
Reach **Chilako River campground** on the left. Read page 250 for details.

7.2 km (4.5 mi)
Turn left onto Pelican-Barton FS road for **Barton Lake campground**. Read further directions on page 249, from the 39.6-km point.

7.5 km (4.7 mi)
Reach **Tory Lake campground**. It's beside the road, useful only for a brief overnight stay. Read page 249 for details.

14.8 km (9.2 mi)
Bear left (southwest) on Pelican Lake FS road. Right leads to Tatuk Lake.

20.3 km (12.6 mi)
Turn left for **Meadow Lake campground**. Read further directions on page 249.

22.8 km (14.1 mi)
Reach **Lintz Lake campground** on the left. Read the bottom of page 248 for details.

27.5 km (17.1 mi)
Turn right for **Tagai Lake campground**. Read further directions on page 248.

33.3 km (20.6 mi)
Bear left where 50 FS road forks right to Clear Lake.

43.5 km (27 mi)
Turn right for **Pelican Lake campground**. For details read page 247, from the 3.3-km point.

46.8 km (29 mi)
Reach a T-junction with Batnuni Road. Set your tripometer to 0 before turning either way. Right (west) leads to **Batnuni Lake** in 30 km (18.6 mi). It has two campgrounds. En route you'll pass three others at tiny lakes. Read further directions on page 246. Turn left (southeast), following directions immediately below, for several small campgrounds en route to Quesnel.

BATNUNI ROAD TO QUESNEL

0 km (0 mi)
Starting southeast on Batnuni Road, from the 46.8-km (29-mi) junction with Pelican Lake FS road, heading for Quesnel.

5.6 km (3.5 mi)
Pass **Kilometre 64 campsite** on the left. It's unpleasant, beside the road, useful only for a brief overnight stay.

9.2 km (5.7 mi)
Proceed straight (southeast) on Batnuni Road. Nazco Road forks right (south), reaching a gas station in about 40 km (25 mi).

14.6 km (9.1 mi)
Pass an **overnight pullout** on the left, just before crossing a bridge over the broad Blackwater River. Proceed generally east.

27.5 km (17.1 mi)
Turn right and descend to reach **Boot Lake campground** in 100 meters. Read page 245 for details.

39.2 km (24.3 mi)
Reach a major junction. Left (north) is Blackwater-Mud River FS road. It leads to Hwy 16 at the southwest edge of Prince George in about 68 km (42 mi), passing pleasant **Blackwater River campgrounds** en route. Read page 242 for further directions and set your tripometer to 0. Turn right (south), continuing with the same tripometer reading, for Bouchie Lake and Quesnel.

45.2 km (28 mi)
Pass Blackwater-Spruce Road on the right.

50.8 km (31.5 mi)
Pantage Lake is visible on the right.

61.4 km (38.1 mi)
Reach insignificant **Twin Lakes campground.** Read page 242 for details.

96.7 km (60 mi)
Reach the village of Bouchie Lake. Bear left for Quesnel.

97.5 km (60.5 mi)
Pass the public laundromat and showers on the left.

106 km (65.6 mi)
Bear right.

106.8 km (66.2 mi)
Arrive in Quesnel. Cross the Fraser River bridge to enter downtown.

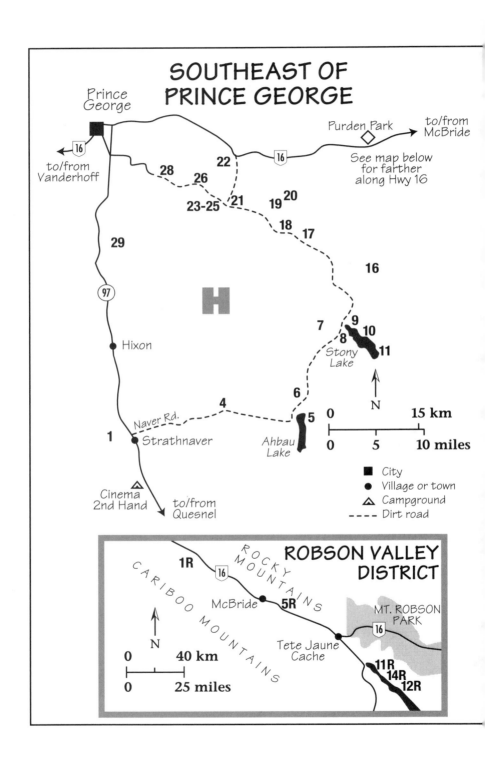

SOUTHEAST OF PRINCE GEORGE

Prince George

to/from Vanderhoff

16

28

26

22

23-25

21

29

97

Hixon

Naver Rd.

4

1

Strathnaver

Cinema 2nd Hand

to/from Quesnel

Purden Park

to/from McBride

16

See map below for farther along Hwy 16

19 20

18

17

16

7

9

8

10

11

Stony Lake

6

5

Ahbau Lake

0   5   15 km

N

0   5   10 miles

■ City
● Village or town
⌂ Campground
---- Dirt road

ROBSON VALLEY DISTRICT

ROCKY MOUNTAINS

CARIBOO MOUNTAINS

1R

16

McBride

5R

MT. ROBSON PARK

16

Tete Jaune Cache

11R

14R

12R

N

0   40 km

0   25 miles

H: Southeast of Prince George

Most of these campgrounds are in **Prince George FS District**. **R** stands for **Robson Valley FS District**.

1	Chubb Lake	16	Narrow Lake
1R	LaSalle Lakes	17	Pitoney Lake
4	Naver Creek	18	Ispah Lake
5	Ahbau Lake	19	Grizzly Lake
5R	Holmes (Beaver) River	20	Wansa Lake
6	Hay Lake	21	Willow Bend
7	Teapot Lake	22	Willow North
8	Stony Lake South	23	Opatcho Lake
9	Stony Lake West	24	Ste. Marie Lake East
10	Stony Lake North	25	Ste. Marie Lake
11	Stony Lake East	26	Francis Lake
11R	Yellowjacket Creek	28	Buckhorn Lake
12R	Canoe Reach Marina	29	Camp Lake
14R	Horse Creek		

Southeast of Prince George

Kinbasket Lake

SOUTHEAST OF PRINCE GEORGE VIA HWY 97, page 265
SHORTEST ROUTE TO AHBAU AND STONY LAKES, page 283
PRINCE GEORGE TO MCBRIDE, page 286
SOUTHEAST OF MCBRIDE, page 290
KINBASKET LAKE, page 292

SOUTHEAST OF PRINCE GEORGE VIA HWY 97

B.C. is a land of lakes. In that regard, southeast of Prince George ("P.G." as it's known locally) is typical of the province. But the lakes here, even the bigger ones, are small compared to the great blue swaths—like Babine, Francois or Quesnel lakes—that streak the B.C. map. And the campgrounds on many of these tiny lakes are sad. They're just token scraps thoughtlessly tossed at the public. Also, P.G. is a sizable city, so the most convenient campgrounds—Francis and Opatcho lakes, for example—can siphon off groups of teenagers, for whom camping is synonymous with partying.

What's good about the area? Venture well off the pavement and you'll see. Stony and Ahbau are beautiful, healthy-sized lakes graced with large campgrounds. Stony's campsites are mostly in the open, Ahbau's are treed. Stony has an especially wild, remote atmosphere despite visible clearcuts across the lake.

If you're heading south on Hwy 97 from Prince George

0 km (0 mi)
In Prince George, at the junction of Hwys 16 and 97, starting south on Hwy 97 (signed for Airport and Vancouver). Set your tripometer to 0. Follow signs for Quesnel.

12 km (7.4 mi)
Stay right, passing a turnoff for Giscome and Jasper.

15 km (9.3 mi)
For **most of the campgrounds**, turn left (east) beneath overhead highway lights, onto paved Buckhorn Lake Road. Continue reading directions on page 268.

35.5 km (22 mi)
For **Camp Lake campground**, turn left (east) onto Stone Creek FS road. Continue reading directions on page 281. (Camp Lake is not recommended, except as a convenient overnight pullout for one vehicle only.)

60 km (37.2 mi)
Cross the bridge (just past Husky gas station) in the community of Hixon.

69.5 km (43.1 mi)
For **Chubb Lake campground**, turn right (west) onto Plett Road. Continue reading directions on page 281. (Chubb Lake is not recommended, except as a convenient overnight pullout.)

77.1 km (47.8 mi)
For the **shortest route to Ahbau and Stony lakes campgrounds**, turn left (east) onto Naver FS road. Continue reading directions on page 283.

78.7 (48.8 mi)
Pass Dunkley Lumber Mill on the left (indicated as Strathnaver on maps).

83.8 km (52 mi)
For **Cinema campground**, turn right (west) into the parking lot. Read page 286 for details.

91.5 km (56.7 mi)
Enter Quesnel FS District.

120.5 km (74.7 mi)
Arrive in Quesnel.

If you're heading north on Hwy 97 from Quesnel

0 km (0 mi)
Set your tripometer to 0 at the sign ENTERING PRINCE GEORGE FOREST SERVICE DISTRICT. Watch for it on your right, after descending a long hill, about 29 km (18 mi) north of Quesnel.

0.7 km (0.4 mi)
Cross a bridge over railroad tracks.

5.6 km (3.5 mi)
Cross Ahbau Creek bridge, at the bottom of a hill.

7.7 km (4.8 mi)
For **Cinema campground**, turn left (west) into the parking lot.
Read page 286 for details.

12.8 km (7.9 mi)
Pass Dunkley Lumber Mill on the right (indicated as
Strathnaver on maps).

14.4 km (8.9 mi)
For the **shortest route to Ahbau and Stony lakes campgrounds**, turn right (east) onto Naver FS road. Continue
reading directions on page 283.

15.5 km (9.6 mi)
For **Chubb Lake campground**, turn left (west) onto Meadow
Creek Road. Continue reading directions on page 281.(Chubb Lake
is not recommended, except as a convenient overnight pullout.)

31.5 km (19.5 mi)
Cross the bridge (just before Husky gas station) in the community
of Hixon.

56 km (34.7 mi)
For **Camp Lake campground**, turn right (east) onto Stone
Creek FS road. Continue reading directions on page 281. (Camp
Lake is not recommended, except as a convenient overnight
pullout for one vehicle only.)

76.5 km (47.4 mi)
For **most of the campgrounds**, turn right (east) beneath
overhead highway lights, onto paved Buckhorn Lake Road.
Continue reading directions on page 268.

91.5 km (56.7 mi)
Reach the junction of Hwys 97 and 16, in Prince George.

~

For MOST OF THE CAMPGROUNDS, follow the directions below

0 km (0 mi)
Turning east onto paved Buckhorn Lake Road. Set your tripometer to 0.

11.4 km (7.1 mi)
Reach a stop sign. Bear left onto Willow FS road (gravel). Soon cross a creek.

12.7 km (7.9 mi)
Buckhorn Lake is visible on the right.

13 km (8.1 mi)
Turn right for Buckhorn Lake campground.

It's just off the main road. It's probably still trashed, so watch out for broken glass.

BUCKHORN LAKE RECREATION SITE #28
Overnight / Easy
Elev: 692 m (2270 ft) / Lake: 73 ha
2 tables, 3 campsites
Inaccessible by motorhomes and 5th-wheels

Continuing east on Willow FS road, passing the turnoff to Buckhorn Lake campground.

16.2 km (10 mi)
Bear left. Expect the road to be severely washboarded.

24.4 km (15.1 mi)
Turn left (just before the KM 134 sign) for Francis Lake campground. It's 0.4 km (0.25 mi) off the main road.

FRANCIS LAKE RECREATION SITE #26
Overnight / Easy
Elev: 808 m (2650 ft) / Lake: 19 ha
several tables, more campsites, boat launch
Inaccessible by large motorhomes and 5th-wheels

Continuing east on Willow FS road, passing the turnoff to Francis Lake campground.

26 km (16.1 mi)

Turn right for Ste. Marie Lake campground.

> The access road is narrow, winding, rough. The left fork leads 0.4 km (0.25 mi) to 6 campsites. Right leads 100 meters to 3 campsites. The view—pretty for this region—is of nearby hills.

STE. MARIE LAKE RECREATION SITE #25
Weekend / Easy
Elev: 808 m (2650 ft) / Lake: 1.6 km (0.9 mi) long, 49 ha
9 tables, heavily-used campground
Inaccessible by large motorhomes and 5th-wheels

Continuing east on Willow FS road, passing the turnoff to Ste. Marie Lake campground.

29.7 km (18.4 mi)

Turn right for Ste. Marie Lake East campground.

> In 200 meters fork left or right. Spur roads squirm in all directions. It's chaotic—more roads than campsites. But it's farther from the main road and therefore quieter than the other Ste. Marie campground. Ignore the gravel road veering right immediately to the east.

STE. MARIE LAKE EAST RECREATION SITE #24
Weekend / Easy
6 campsites wedged between trees, a few tables
Inaccessible by large motorhomes and 5th-wheels

Continuing east on Willow FS road, passing the turnoff to Ste. Marie Lake East campground.

31.7 km (19.7 mi)

Turn left for Opatcho Lake campground.

0 km (0 mi)
Starting on the access road.

0.6 km (0.4 mi)
Bear right.

0.8 km (0.5 mi)
Bear right.

2.1 km (1.3 mi)
Turn left onto a narrow road.

2.4 km (1.5 mi)
Arrive at the campground. The sites are well spaced among sheltering trees. One site is on the shore. Views are restricted. Appreciating the lake requires a boat.

OPATCHO LAKE RECREATION SITE #23
Weekend / Moderate
Elev: 777 m (2550 ft) / Lake: 37.5 ha
4 tables, rough boat launch
Inaccessible by large motorhomes and 5th-wheels

Continuing southeast on Willow FS road, passing the turnoff to Opatcho Lake campground.

32.4 km (20 mi)
Reach a signed junction with Willow-Coalmine FS road. Set your tripometer to 0 before turning either way. Right proceeds southeast to Ispah, Pitoney and Narrow lakes campgrounds, and others beyond; for directions continue reading on page 273. Turn left to quickly reach the first Willow Bend campground, proceed north to the second Willow Bend campground, or head northeast to Grizzly and Wansa lakes campgrounds. (Heavy rain and muddy roads might necessitate 4WD for Grizzly and Wansa.)

Turning left (north) at the 32.4-km (20-mi) junction on Willow FS road. Set your tripometer to 0.

0 km (0 mi)
Starting on Willow-Coalmine FS road, heading north. Immediately cross the Willow River bridge.

0.2 km (0.1 mi)
Willow Bend Recreation Site #21 is on the left, beside the Willow River. It's a tiny campground (1 table, room for only 2 vehicles) often used as a put-in for rafters and kayakers.

0.7 km (0.4 mi)
Reach a junction. Turn right for Grizzly and Wansa lakes. (Left on Willow-North FS road leads north about 19 km / 11.8 mi to Hwy 16. Just 200 meters before the highway, turn left and descend to arrive at **Willow North Recreation Site #22** in another 400 meters. It's a big, flat gravel area with 3 tables and 1 tent pad on the Willow River.)

5.5 km (3.3 mi)
For Grizzly Lake, turn right (southeast) onto Willow-Grizzly FS road—severely potholed. For Wansa Lake, stay left (northeast).

Turning right (southeast) at 5.5 km (3.3 mi), heading for Grizzly Lake.

10.3 km (6.4 mi)
Stay left.

11.2 km (6.9 mi)
Go either way to reach Grizzly Lake campground in 100 meters. There's little shade but lots of dirt, possibly mud, at this abandoned mill site.

GRIZZLY LAKE RECREATION SITE #19
Weekend / Moderate
Elev: 965 m (3165 ft) / 1.2 km (0.7 mi) long, 69 ha
6 tables, 3 more campsites, gravel boat launch
Accessible by motorhomes and 5th-wheels

Staying left at 5.5 km (3.3 mi), passing the turnoff to Grizzly Lake, heading for Wansa Lake.

8 km (5 mi)
Turn right (east) onto Willow-Wansa FS road.

12 km (7.4 mi)
Arrive at Wansa Lake campground, near the 454 KM sign.

WANSA LAKE RECREATION SITE #20
Weekend / Moderate
Elev: 845 m (2770 ft) / Lake: 37.5 ha
small open area, rough boat launch
Accessible by motorhomes and 5th-wheels

Take Your Brain For A Walk

We all seek relaxation when we go camping. For some, that means plunking down and moving as little as possible. But that's actually not very relaxing. Here's why.

Relaxation has two components: physical and mental. Your body relaxes most deeply after physical exertion. Everyone knows that. What few realize is that the mind also relaxes most deeply after physical exertion.

Even the simple act of walking "pumps up" your brain, as well as your blood vessels and denser nerve connections. It gives your brain a workout and keeps it in shape. Afterward, your thoughts settle and soften, just as your muscles do. The brain is, of course, just a big, complex muscle.

Walking is especially relaxing because it's a cross-patterned movement. Opposite limbs—the arm on one side, the leg on the other—are synchronized. This generates harmonizing electrical activity in your central nervous system. It also tones your nervous and immune systems, reduces stress, increases the flow of oxygen throughout the body, and gives you a sense of strength and well-being.

Definitely bring your lawn chair to the campground. But before you take a load off, take your brain for a walk. Lightweight, high-quality hiking boots are best. Keep a brisk pace. About 45 minutes (4 km / 2.5 mi) a day will ensure you enjoy all the relaxation you came for.

Turning right (southeast) at the 32.4-km (20-mi) junction on Willow FS road. Set your tripometer to 0.

0 km (0 mi)
Continuing on Willow FS road, heading southeast to Ispah, Pitoney and Narrow lakes campgrounds, and others beyond.

3.6 km (2.2 mi)
Bear left on the main road.

4.4 km (2.7 mi)
Cross a small bridge near the KM 146 sign.

6 km (3.7 mi)
Pass an **overnight pullout** on the left, next to a creek, immediately before a bridge.

8.8 km (5.5 mi)
Reach a junction. Stay left on Willow FS road, signed for Ispah, Narrow, Stony and Ahbau lakes.

9.9 km (6.1 mi)
Cross the broad Willow River on an old, impressive wooden bridge.

11.8 km (7.3 mi)
Turn left for Ispah Lake campground.

> Arrive at the lone table in 350 meters. This small, unscenic clearing in the forest is simply a secluded, individual campsite. If you're here to canoe or fish from a boat, and nobody else barges in, it could be enjoyable. Motors are prohibited on the lake.

ISPAH LAKE RECREATION SITE #18
Weekend / Moderate
Elev: 846 m (2775 ft) / Lake: 1.2 km (0.7 mi) long, 39 ha
1 table, boat launch
Inaccessible by motorhomes and 5th-wheels

Continuing southeast on Willow FS road, passing the turnoff to Ispah Lake campground.

16.4 km (10.2 mi)
Stay straight on the main road.

22.2 km (13.8 mi)
Reach a signed junction. For Pitoney Lake campground, turn left (north) onto Willow-Wansa FS road.

Arrive at this tiny, derelict campground in 0.9 km (0.5 mi). Beside the main road, it offers no buffer from industrial traffic.

PITONEY LAKE RECREATION SITE #17
Overnight / Moderate
Elev: 930 m (3050 ft) / Lake: 2.5 km (1.6 mi) long, 170 ha
2 tables, boat launch
Accessible by motorhomes, but not 5th-wheels.

Continuing southeast on Willow FS road, passing the turnoff to Pitoney Lake campground.

29.3 km (18.2 mi)
Reach a signed junction. For Narrow Lake campground, turn left (east) onto Narrow FS road.

Arrive at the campground, on the east end of this long, slim lake, in about 5 km (3 mi).

NARROW LAKE RECREATION SITE #16
Weekend / Difficult (due only to distance)
Elev: 943 m (3093 ft) / Lake: 8 km (5 mi) long, 352 ha
small open area, gravel boat launch
Accessible by motorhomes and 5th-wheels

Continuing south on Willow FS road, passing the turnoff to Narrow Lake campground.

31.8 km (19.7 mi)
Follow either of the two ascending roads. They soon rejoin.

45.8 km (28.4 mi)
Reach a junction. Set your tripometer to 0 before turning either way. Right leads southwest to Ahbau Lake, then west to Hwy 97; for directions continue reading on page 277. Left leads southeast to excellent campgrounds on Stony Lake's northeast shore.

Turning left (southeast) at the 45.8-km (28.4-mi) junction on Willow FS road.

0 km (0 mi)
Continuing on Willow FS road, heading southeast along Stony Lake's northeast shore.

4.5 km (2.8 mi)
Turn right for Stony Lake West campground.

In 50 meters reach the campground—a large, flat open area. It's excellent for swimming, sunning, or just enjoying the scenery. A campsite on the rocky beach is the only one with a lake view.

STONY LAKE WEST RECREATION SITE #9
Weekend / Difficult (due only to distance)
Elev: 992 m (3254 ft) / Lake: 8.7 km (5.4 mi) long, 876.5 ha
2 tables, 4 campsites, good boat launch
Accessible by motorhomes and 5th-wheels

Stony Lake

Continuing southeast on Willow FS road, passing the turnoff to Stony Lake West campground.

5.5 km (3.4 mi)
A narrow road forks right, leading 0.5 km (0.3 mi) to an **unofficial campsite** accessible by small motorhomes and trailers. It's a big, open clearing on the lake, with room for two vehicles. You'll find no outhouse or tables. Read page 26 under *Practical Stuff* to ensure you leave no trace of your stay.

8 km (5 mi)
Turn right for Stony Lake North campground.

> Arrive at the campground in 450 meters. A grassy perimeter and distinctly separate campsites create a spacious feeling. Views are of surrounding forested hills. The large, gravel beach is ideal for swimming and sunning. Canoeists can explore the lake's islands.

STONY LAKE NORTH RECREATION SITE #10
Destination / Difficult (due only to distance)
Elev: 992 m (3254 ft) / Lake: 8.7 km (5.4 mi) long, 876.5 ha
3 tables, boat launch
Accessible by motorhomes and 5th-wheels

Continuing southeast on Willow FS road, passing the turnoff to Stony Lake North campground.

11.7 km (7.3 mi)
Bear right.

12.4 km (7.7 mi)
Turn right to enter Stony Lake East campground in just 200 meters. (Willow FS road bears left/northeast. In about 5 km / 3 mi, after fording a minor creek, it reaches 2.5-km / 1.6-mi long **Slender Lake** with its small, treed campground and rough boat launch.)

STONY LAKE EAST RECREATION SITE #11
Destination / Difficult (due only to the distance)
Elev: 992 m (3254 ft) / Lake: 8.7 km (5.4 mi) long, 876.5 ha
2 tables on an open, gravel beach, good views, boat launch
Accessible by motorhomes and 5th-wheels

~~

Turning right (southwest) at the 45.8-km (28.4-mi) junction on Willow FS road. Set your tripometer to 0.

0 km (0 mi)
Starting on the connector road, heading southwest for Ahbau Lake and Hwy 97.

3.4 km (2.1 mi)
Curve left.

5 km (3 mi)
Stay right on Naver-Ahbau FS road for Ahbau Lake and Hwy 97. Stony Lake South campground is left. It's not recommended. The uninviting shore is treed and rocky. The view from this side of the lake is disappointing.

0 km (0 mi)
Turning left, for Stony Lake South campground.

0.5 km (0.3 mi)
Cross a bridge over Willow River.

1.1 km (0.7 mi)
Bear left.

2.1 km (1.3 mi)
Turn left. The lake is still far below but now visible. Access is rough and narrow.

4.4 km (2.7 mi)
Arrive at **Stony Lake South Recreation Site #8**. It has a single campsite and very rough boat launch.

~~

Continuing southwest on Naver-Ahbau FS road, passing the turnoff to Stony Lake South campground.

7.7 km (4.8 mi)
Stay straight for Ahbau Lake and Hwy 97. Turn right (north) for Teapot Lake campground.

> The final approach road to Teapot is narrow and overgrown. RVs will have trouble. Even small vehicles will get scratched. To get there, drive 1.8 km (1.1 mi) off the main road, then fork left. Reach **Teapot Lake Recreation Site #7** in about another 2 km (1.2 mi). It's a tiny campground with a rough boat launch, on a 1.3-km long, forested lake.

14.8 km (9.2 mi)
Pass an **overnight pullout** on the right, beside the road, at the north end of Lodi Lake. It's possible to launch a boat here.

19 km (11.8 mi)
Turn right for Hay Lake campground.

> Descend from the main road to reach **Hay Lake Recreation Site #6** in about 75 meters. You'll find just one table at this beautiful, individual campsite. It's accessible by motorhomes and 5th-wheels, but only if unoccupied; walk in and check before driving.

19.8 km (12.3 mi)
Stay straight.

22.3 km (13.8 mi)
Reach a signed junction. Set your tripometer to 0 before turning either way. Bear right (southwest) for Hwy 97. Turn left (south) for provincial-park quality Ahbau Lake campground

> ### 0 km (0 mi)
> Starting on FS road 1000, heading south to Ahbau Lake.

> ### 2.7 km (1.7 mi)
> Go right.

Ahbau Lake

3.1 km (1.9 mi)
Reach a fork. Enter the campground either way. Right leads 300 meters to 6 campsites with flat space for tents, plus a secluded site at the end. A connector road linking the forks has 7 sites, 2 with tables. Along the lakeshore are 7 tables; another 3 are across the road. All sites are treed, most are level. The treed shore allows little room to play or relax.

AHBAU LAKE RECREATION SITE #5
Destination / Difficult (due only to distance)
Elev: 900 m (2952 ft) / Lake: 8.7 km (5.4 mi) long, 813 ha
24 well-spaced campsites, 15 tables, cement boat launch
Accessible by motorhomes and 5th-wheels

Continuing southwest at the 22.3-km (13.8-mi) junction on Naver-Ahbau FS road, from the turnoff to Ahbau Lake campground. Set your tripometer to 0.

0 km (0 mi)
On Naver-Ahbau FS road, heading southwest to Hwy 97. Cross Ahbau Creek bridge in 400 meters.

17.2 km (10.7 mi)
Reach a major three-way junction. Bear left for Hwy 97. Turn right for Naver Creek campground.

> **0 km (0 mi)**
> Turning right (north) on Naver FS road.
>
> **0.2 km (0.1 mi)**
> On the right, just before the bridge, is an **unofficial camping area**—a huge, partially-treed clearing where you can park well off the main roads. It's acceptable for a brief overnight stay.
>
> **0.3 km (0.2 mi)**
> Just after the bridge arrive at Naver Creek campground. Turn right or left for campsites. Right is beside the creek. Left is away from the creek but has more shade and useful old cement foundations.
>
> **NAVER CREEK RECREATION SITE #4**
> Overnight / Easy
> 4 tables, very convenient to Hwy 97
> Accessible by motorhomes and 5th-wheels

Continuing west from the 17.2-km (10.7-mi) junction on Naver-Ahbau FS road, starting on Naver FS road, passing the turnoff to Naver Creek campground.

24.6 km (15.3 mi)
Pass an **overnight pullout** beside the road, on Hudson Lake.

32.3 km (20 mi)
Bear right.

36.5 km (22.6 mi)
Reach Hwy 97. Turn right (north) for Prince George. Turn left (south) for Quesnel.

For CAMP LAKE CAMPGROUND, follow the directions below

0 km (0 mi)
Turning east onto Stone Creek FS road, from Hwy 97. It's 20.5 km (12.7 mi) south of Buckhorn Lake Road, or 24.5 km (15.2 mi) north of Hixon.

2 km (1.2 mi)
Bear right and proceed through clearcuts.

10 km (6.2 mi)
Arrive at **Camp Lake Recreation Site #29**, on the right. It's a miserly pullout with a single table, between the road and a pond. Industrial traffic is heavy; expect passing trucks to awaken you by 6 a.m. The idea of actually camping here is ridiculous. But it's quiet after dark and convenient to the highway, so it's a reasonable overnight pullout—for one vehicle only. A motorhome might manage to squeeze in, but not a 5th-wheel.

For CHUBB LAKE CAMPGROUND, follow the directions below

Heading south on Hwy 97 from Prince George

0 km (0 mi)
Turning right (west) onto Plett Road, 9.5 km (5.9 mi) south of Hixon.

0.2 km (0.1 mi)
Turn left onto Quesnel-Hixon Road. Pavement ends, but the road is graded gravel.

1.9 km (1.2 mi)
Stay straight on the main road.

2.8 km (1.7 mi)
Bear right on the main road.

6.8 km (4.2 mi)
Turn right, off the main road, and descend. This fork is signed on the left for Chubb Lake, on the right for Cariboo Pentacostal Camp.

7.7 km (4.8 mi)
Arrive at **Chubb Lake Recreation Site #1**, on the left. Or continue 100 meters to an overnight pullout on the right. A small motorhome might manage to squeeze in, but not a 5th wheel. The tiny campground has 2 tables. Expect nothing more than a convenient place to sleep near Hwy 97.

Heading north on Hwy 97 from Quesnel.

0 km (0 mi)
Turning left (west) onto Meadow Creek Road, 7.8 km (4.8 mi) north of Cinema campground.

100 meters / yards
Bear right.

1.8 km (1.1 mi)
Turn right, across from a barn.

4 km (2.5 mi)
The road dips dramatically. Expect mud if it's been raining.

4.1 km (2.5 mi)
Reach a T-junction in front of powerlines. Turn right onto a wider, smoother road.

6.1 km (3.8 mi)
Turn sharply left, off the main road, and descend. This fork is signed on the right for Chubb Lake, on the left for Cariboo Pentacostal Camp.

7 km (4.3 mi)
Arrive at **Chubb Lake Recreation Site #1**, on the left. Or continue 100 meters to an overnight pullout on the right. A small motorhome might manage to squeeze in, but not a 5th wheel. The tiny campground has 2 tables. Expect nothing more than a convenient place to sleep near Hwy 97.

SHORTEST ROUTE TO AHBAU AND STONY LAKES

0 km (0 mi)
Turning east onto Naver FS road, from Hwy 97. It's 17.1 km (10.6 mi) south of Hixon, or 6.7 km (4.2 mi) north of Cinema campground.

4.2 km (2.6 mi)
Stay straight.

12 km (7.4 mi)
Pass an **overnight pullout** beside the road, on Hudson Lake.

19.3 km (12 mi)
Reach a major three-way junction. Bear right for Ahbau and Stony lakes. Turn left for Naver Creek campground.

> **0 km (0 mi)**
> Turning left (north) on Naver FS road.
>
> **0.2 km (0.1 mi)**
> On the right, just before the bridge, is an **unofficial camping area**—a huge, partially-treed clearing where you can park well off the main roads. It's acceptable for a brief overnight stay.
>
> **0.3 km (0.2 mi)**
> Just after the bridge arrive at Naver Creek campground. Turn right or left for campsites. Right is beside the creek. Left is away from the creek but has more shade and useful old cement foundations.
>
> ### NAVER CREEK RECREATION SITE #4
> Overnight / Easy
> 4 tables, very convenient to Hwy 97
> Accessible by motorhomes and 5th-wheels

Continuing southeast on Naver-Ahbau FS road, passing the turnoff to Naver Creek campground.

36 km (22.3 mi)
Cross the Ahbau Creek bridge.

36.4 km (22.6 mi)
Reach a signed junction. Set your tripometer to 0 before turning either way. Bear left (north) for Stony Lake. Turn right (south) for provincial-park quality Ahbau Lake campground.

0 km (0 mi)
Starting on FS road 1000, heading south to Ahbau Lake.

2.7 km (1.7 mi)
Go right.

3.1 km (1.9 mi)
Reach a fork. Enter the campground either way. Right leads 300 meters to 6 campsites with flat space for tents, plus a secluded site at the end. A connector road linking the forks has 7 sites, 2 with tables. Along the lakeshore are 7 tables; another 3 are across the road. All sites are treed, most are level. The treed shore allows little room to play or relax.

AHBAU LAKE RECREATION SITE #5
Destination / Moderate (via west approach)
Elev: 900 m (2952 ft) / Lake: 8.7 km (5.4 mi) long, 813 ha
24 well-spaced campsites, 15 tables, cement boat launch
Accessible by motorhomes and 5th-wheels

Continuing north from the 36.4-km (22.6-mi) junction on Naver-Ahbau FS road, passing the turnoff to Ahbau Lake campground.

0 km (0 mi)
On Naver-Ahbau FS road, at the turnoff to Ahbau Lake, heading north for Stony Lake.

2.5 km (1.6 mi)
Stay straight.

3.3 km (2 mi)
Turn left for Hay Lake campground.

Stony Lake East campground

Descend from the main road to reach **Hay Lake Recreation Site #6** in about 75 meters. You'll find just one table at this beautiful, individual campsite. It's accessible by motorhomes and 5th-wheels, but only if unoccupied; walk in and check before driving.

7.5 km (4.6 mi)
Pass an **overnight pullout** on the left, beside the road, at the north end of Lodi Lake. It's possible to launch a boat here.

14.5 km (9 mi)
Stay straight for Stony Lake. Turn left (north) for Teapot Lake campground.

The final approach road to Teapot is narrow and over-grown. RVs will have trouble. Even small vehicles will get scratched. To get there, drive 1.8 km (1.1 mi) off the main road, then fork left. Reach **Teapot Lake Recreation Site #7** in about another 2 km (1.2 mi). It's a tiny campground with a rough boat launch, on a 1.3-km long, forested lake.

17.2 km (10.7 mi)
Stay left on the main road.

18.8 km (11.7 mi)
Curve right.

22.2 km (13.8 mi)
Reach a junction with Willow FS road. Set your tripometer to 0 before turning either way. Left leads northwest (follow the page 275 directions in reverse, starting at the 45.8-km point) to many small campgrounds southeast of Prince George. Right leads southeast on Willow FS road to scenic campgrounds on Stony Lake's northeast shore; follow directions on page 275.

CINEMA CAMPGROUND

Cinema 2nd Hand Store and free campground is in a big clearing on the west side of Hwy 97. It's identified by signs and a BC Tel public phone booth. The friendly owners of this private campground, Vic and Theresa, enjoy meeting travellers from all over the world and welcome you to stay here overnight at no charge. You can also buy groceries and shop for antiques here. The spacious campground has a few treed sites back from the highway.

PRINCE GEORGE TO MCBRIDE

Want to camp along Hwy 16 between Prince George and Mt. Robson Provincial Park? You have three choices. None will disappoint, because all are well maintained, in enjoyable settings, mere minutes from pavement.

Willow North is near P.G. It's small, on the Willow River, with a sufficient buffer from the highway so you won't hear vehicles whooshing past. LaSalle Lake, northwest of McBride, is more inviting, but traffic is audible. Beaver River, southeast of McBride, is a model campground offering a rare combination of peace, beauty and convenience.

East of Purden Lake, it's as if the hills of the Interior Plateau finally begin to mature. No longer soft, innocent adolescents, they puff out their chests, flex their muscles, and swagger like aspiring young mountains. Where Hwy 16 bends southeast through the valley, the Rockies rear up to your left, the Cariboos to your right. Upon reaching McBride, you're surrounded by peaks. Trailhead turnoffs are signed along the way.

If you're heading east on Hwy 16 from Prince George

0 km (0 mi)
In Prince George, at the junction of Hwys 97 and 16.

12.6 km (7.8 mi)
Pass the turnoff for Giscome and Upper Fraser River.

29 km (18 mi)
Turn left (north) and descend to reach a secluded **rest area** in about 150 meters. It's treed, beside the Willow River. A sign states you must limit your stay to 8 hours. Fires and tents are prohibited.

29.2 km (18.1 mi)
Cross the Willow River bridge.

30.5 km (18.9 mi)
Pass a pullout with garbage cans. Just after, turn right (south) for Willow North campground.

0 km (0 mi)
Starting south on Willow North FS road.

0.2 m (0.1 mi)
Fork right and descend.

0.7 km (0.4 mi)
Pass a tent pad and fire ring on the left.

0.8 km (0.5 mi)
Arrive at Willow North campground. It's a large, flat, gravel area on the Willow River. The small river rapids enhance the atmosphere. Highway traffic is not audible.

WILLOW NORTH RECREATION SITE #22
Overnight / Easy
3 tables, 1 tent pad
Inaccessible by large motorhomes and 5th-wheels

Continuing east on Hwy 16, passing the turnoff to Willow North campground.

50.8 km (31.5 mi)
Pass **Bowron Rest Area** on the left.

53.5 km (33.2 mi)
Pass the turnoff to Purden Lake Provincial Park.

156 km (96.7 mi)
Pass the signed turnoff for Crescent Spur. Slow down for the next campground.

158.7 km (98.4 mi)
Turn right for LaSalle Lake campground. The turn is immediately north of where the southeast-bound lanes merge. The campground is just 0.4 km (0.25 mi) off the highway, so traffic is audible.

LASALLE LAKE RECREATION SITE #1
Overnight / Easy
Elev: 880 m (2886 ft) / Lake: 11 ha
9 tables, a couple secluded sites, dock, grassy perimeter
Accessible by motorhomes and 5th-wheels

LaSalle Lake

Continuing southeast on Hwy 16, passing the turnoff to LaSalle Lake campground.

165 km (102.3 mi)
Pass a **rest area** just before the Goat River bridge.

205.5 km (127.4 mi)
Enter McBride. Pass the Robson Valley Forest District office on the left.

~~

If you're heading northwest on Hwy 16 from McBride

0 km (0 mi)
On the northwest edge of McBride, at the Robson Valley Forest District office.

40.5 km (25.1 mi)
Pass a **rest area** just after the Goat River bridge.

46.8 km (29 mi)
Turn left for **LaSalle Lake campground.** Read page 288 for details.

49.5 km (30.7 mi)
Pass the signed turnoff for Crescent Spur.

154.8 km (96 mi)
Pass **Bowron Rest Area** on the right.

175 km (108.6 mi)
Turn left (south) for **Willow North campground**. Read further directions on page 287, from the 30.5-km point.

176.5 km (109.4 mi)
Turn right (north) and descend to reach a secluded **rest area** in about 150 meters. It's treed, beside the Willow River. A sign states you must limit your stay to 8 hours. Fires and tents are prohibited.

193 km (119.6 mi)
Pass the turnoff for Giscome and Upper Fraser River.

205.5 km (127.5 mi)
Arrive in Prince George at the junction of Hwys 97 and 16.

SOUTHEAST OF MCBRIDE

Near the Rockies, guarded by muscular mountains, is the tidy little town of McBride. It's small enough and has sufficient charm that it adds to, rather than detracts from, the beauty of Robson Valley. A short drive east of McBride is Beaver River campground, which has the rare distinction of being convenient (just off Hwy 16), scenic (on a pretty bend of the river), and well kept (the FS office is in the nearby town). Southeast of McBride are campgrounds—described below—on Kinbasket Lake, where the topography is so grand that first-time visitors point, exclaim, and stare. It makes you wonder if Mt. Robson Park's west boundary is too far east.

If you're heading southeast on Hwy 16 from McBride

0 km (0 mi)
Just outside McBride, midway across the Fraser River bridge. Before the bridge, pass a highway sign: ALBERTA BORDER 145, JASPER 171. (Soon after the bridge, pass a left-turn sign for a hiking trail on 2270-m / 7446-ft McBride Peak. The trailhead is reached via Rainbow Road, which is rough, narrow, extremely steep, and on the edge of a near-vertical slope. There are no warning signs, but it's dangerous. Only experienced off-roaders piloting small, powerful 4WD vehicles should attempt it.)

9.8 km (6.1 mi)
Midway across the Holmes River bridge.

10 km (6.2 mi)
Turn left (east) onto Holmes River FS road for the Beaver River campground. Set your tripometer to 0.

If you're heading northwest on Hwy 16
from Tete Jaune Cache

From the junction of Hwys 5 and 16 at Tete Jaune Cache, drive Hwy 16 northwest 52.7 km (32.7 mi). Turn right (east) onto Holmes River FS road, just before the bridge. (It's 11.3 km / 7 mi past Baker Creek Rest Area, and 11 km / 6.8 mi before McBride.) Set your tripometer to 0.

Beaver River near McBride

For either approach above, now follow the directions below

In 300 meters pass a rockslide and cross a cattle guard. Proceed along the southeast side of the river. At 1.1 km (0.7 mi) turn left through a big, brown, gated fence to arrive at the campground. A short trail leads downstream to Beaver Falls.

BEAVER RIVER RECREATION SITE #5
Weekend / Easy
6 riverside tables, some sites in trees, audible river
Accessible by motorhomes and 5th-wheels

KINBASKET LAKE

Wedged between the Columbia Mountains on the west and the Rocky Mountains on the east is Kinbasket Lake. (See photo on page 264.) It's 210 km (130 mi) long and sits at 755 m (2475 ft) elevation. The campgrounds described below are on Canoe Reach, the lake's north arm. Just 20 km (12.4 mi) of off-pavement driving can earn you a secluded campsite with spectacular scenery. Views are across the turquoise water to 2653-m (8700-ft) Mt. Thompson and other burly peaks coated with lush vegetation and draped with glaciers. The lakeshore is rocky and the water frigid, so don't plan on swimming. If you're hauling a boat, check out the excellent facilities at Canoe Reach Marina campground. That's also where you can most easily maneuver a large RV.

If you're heading south on Hwy 5 from Tete Jaune Cache

From midway across the Fraser River bridge, at the junction of Hwys 16 and 5, drive south 19.8 km (12.3 mi) to the Visitor Information Centre (on the left) in Valemount. Continue south 3.3 km (2 mi) to a large sign: SLOCAN FOREST PRODUCTS LTD. Turn left (east) here, onto Cedarside Road, also signed for Kinbasket Lake. Set your tripometer to 0.

If you're heading north on Hwy 5 toward Valemount

A couple kilometers before Valemount's business district, look for a large sign: SLOCAN FOREST PRODUCTS LTD. Turn right (east) here, onto Cedarside Road, also signed for Kinbasket Lake. Set your tripometer to 0.

For either approach above, now follow the directions below

0 km (0 mi)
Turning east off Hwy 5, toward Slocan Forest Products. Immediately turn left (staying on pavement) toward the weigh scales. Do not go straight on the dirt road into the mill.

2.6 km (1.6 mi)
Cross railroad tracks and Canoe Road. Proceed straight onto the dirt road.

10.1 km (6.3 mi)
Reach a junction. Go straight onto Canoe East FS road. Kinbasket Lake is visible in 2 km (1.2 mi). Right at the junction follows the lake's west shore.

17.4 km (10.8 mi)
Turn right (before a narrow bridge over a small, deep gorge) to descend to an **unofficial camping area**. It's on a broad, open peninsula dominated by a huge, abandoned, cement foundation. The lakeview is excellent, but ugly heaps of rusty metal give the area a creepy, apocalyptic atmosphere.

22.8 km (14.1 mi)
Turn right for Yellowjacket Creek campground.

> Descend from the main road. In 300 meters the road forks at a sign. Go right then straight to arrive at a rocky beach in 150 meters. Left leads 150 meters to campsites—the nicest on Canoe Reach. Trees provide shelter from wind and sun.

YELLOWJACKET CREEK RECREATION SITE #11
Destination / Moderate
4 tables secluded in trees, 2 more campsites, rocky beach
Accessible by small motorhomes and trailers, but not 5th-wheels

Continuing south on Canoe East FS road, passing the turnoff to Yellowjacket Creek campground.

23 km (14.3 mi)
Cross a bridge over a creek.

23.3 km (14.4 mi)
Bear right at the fork.

25.9 km (16.1 mi)
Cross bridged Horse Creek.

26 km (16.2 mi)
Turn right for Horse Creek campground.

Descend from the main road. In 50 meters fork either way to treed campsites. Some near the lakeshore have views.

HORSE CREEK RECREATION SITE #14
Destination / Moderate
3 tables, 6 more campsites, rocky beach
Accessible by small motorhomes and trailers, but not 5th-wheels

Continuing south on Canoe East FS road, passing the turnoff to Horse Creek campground.

26.4 km (16.4 mi)
Turn right for Canoe Reach Marina campground, beyond which there are no more campgrounds on the east shore of Kinbasket Lake.

Descend from the main road. In 0.5 km (0.3 mi) arrive at the campground: a large, open, level, gravel lot.

CANOE REACH MARINA RECREATION SITE #12
Destination / Moderate
7 tables, cooking shelter, sandy playpen for kids
breakwater, cement boat ramp, mooring dock
Accessible by motorhomes and 5th-wheels

Many Forest Service roads, like this one in Kispiox Valley, are in good condition.

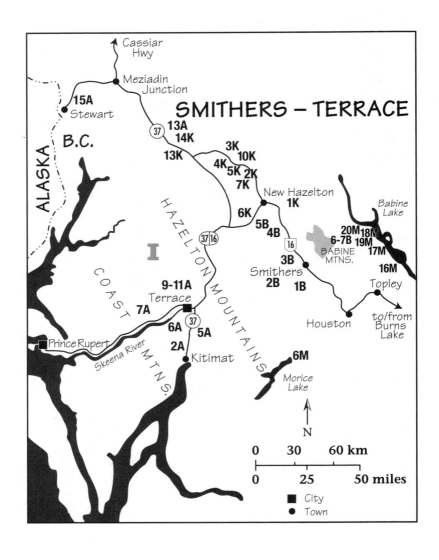

SMITHERS – TERRACE

Cassiar Hwy

Meziadin Junction

15A
Stewart

B.C.

ALASKA

37

13A
14K

13K

3K
10K
4K
5K 2K
7K

New Hazelton
1K

6K

5B
4B

37 16

COAST

HAZELTON MOUNTAINS

Babine Lake

20M 18M
6-7B 19M
17M
BABINE MTNS.
16M

16

3B
Smithers
2B   1B

Topley

9-11A
Terrace

7A

6A
37 5A

2A

Prince Rupert

Skeena River

Houston

to/from Burns Lake

MTNS.

Kitimat

6M

Morice Lake

N

0   30   60 km

0   25   50 miles

■ City
● Town

I: Smithers to Terrace

The letter indicates which FS district the campground is in. **A** stands for **Kalum FS District**. **B** stands for **Bulkley / Cassiar FS District**. **K** stands for **Kispiox FS District**. **M** stands for **Morice FS District**.

1 B	Telkwa River	7 A	Exstew River
1 K	Suskwa River	7 B	Morin Lake
2 A	Enso	7 K	Pentz Lake
2 B	Dennis Lake	9 A	Pine Lakes
2 K	Upper Kispiox	10 A	Red Sand Lake
3 B	Twin Falls	10 K	Elizabeth Lake
3 K	Sweetin River	11 A	Hart Farm
4 B	Taltzen Lake	13 A	Jigsaw Lake
4 K	Little Fish Lake	13 K	Bonus Lake
5 A	Chist Creek	14 K	Derrick Lake
5 B	Kitseguecla Lake	15 A	Clements Lake
5 K	Mitten Lake	16 M	Paul Lake
6 A	Lakelse River	17 M	Bear Island
6 B	Chapman Lake	18 M	Old Fort
6 K	Keynton (Bell) Lake	19 M	Tanglechain Lake
6 M	Morice Lake	20 M	Doris Lake

Smithers to Terrace

Excellent unofficial campsite on the Bulkley River

NEAR SMITHERS

Ask any young, mountain-minded athlete, "What are the primo towns in B.C.?" The shortlist is sure to include Smithers. It faces the Babine Mountains across the Bulkley Valley, while sitting comfortably with its back against the Hudson Bay Range. So, if you're a hiker or mountain biker, this isn't just a place to camp while travelling through. The Smithers area deserves an entire week of your precious vacation time.

Smithers has several free campgrounds nearby: (1) Telkwa River is 14.7 km (9.1 mi) southeast; (2) Dennis Lake is 29.5 km (18.3 mi) west; (3) Glacier Gulch is 9.3 km (5.8 mi) northwest; (4) Taltzen and Kitsequecla lakes are 38 km (23.6 mi) northwest.

(1) Telkwa River campground (page 300) was never attractive and has been heavily abused. It's strewn with trash and broken glass. Gang tags on the nearby bridge heighten the weirdly urban atmosphere. En route, however, are a couple pullouts acceptable for an overnight stay; they're just not big enough for motorhomes or trailers.

(2) Dennis Lake (page 302) is rated Destination, largely because of excellent hiking opportunities nearby. For non-hikers, it's a long drive for just a brief overnight stay. The potholed access road can get very muddy. And the campground is too small for motorhomes and trailers. But the scenery includes Hudson Bay Mountain, where you'll find one of the area's premier trails. Drive to the ski area, park at road's end, then ascend past the cabins to pick up the trail gently rising through meadows to Crater Lake. Scramblers can push on to the summit. The Silvern Creek trail is also close to Dennis Lake.

(3) Twin Falls (page 303) is primarily a trailhead and day-use area. The cascades plunging 150 m (492 ft) from Kathlyn Glacier on Hudson Bay Mountain are a tremendous sight. Experienced hikers can climb the steep route up Glacier Gulch. It follows a boulder-shattering meltwater torrent to the glacier toe. The unofficial campground is tiny and the parking lot busy, so don't plan on more than one night here. But the campsites are beneath huge cedars, within earshot of the falls, the setting is spectacular, and the hiking superb. For those reasons, Twin Falls is rated Destination.

(4a and 4b) Taltzen and Kitsequecla lakes (page 305) are beautiful. The ever encroaching flora is remarkably lush. Cedars crowd the shorelines. Healthy devil's club seems to float in mid-air (touch it for a painful explanation of its name). Across the lakes, distant mountains enhance the wild atmosphere. Both campgrounds are rated Weekend.

After an energetic exploration of the Bulkley Valley, you'll probably want to suds your duds, yourself, and your vehicle. In Smithers, check out Wash The Works, a spacious laundromat with clean public showers and a multi-bay car wash. It's between Queen and Manitoba streets, on Glacier Frontage Road, which parallels Hwy 16.

(1) TELKWA RIVER

If you're heading southeast on Hwy 16 from Smithers

From Main Street and Hwy 16 in Smithers, drive 2.8 km (1.7 mi) southeast on Hwy 16. Set your tripometer to 0 midway across the Bulkley River bridge.

0 km (0 mi)
Midway across the Bulkley River bridge near Smithers.

11.4 km (7.1 mi)
Enter Telkwa and pass the turnoff to Tyhee Lake Provincial Park.

12.3 km (7.6 mi)
Turn right (west) onto Hankin Avenue. Soon bear left. Midway across the Bulkley River bridge, reset your tripometer to 0.

If you're heading northwest on Hwy 16 from Houston

Drive about 49.5 km (30.7 mi) to Telkwa. At the south end of town, turn left (west) onto Hankin Avenue. Soon bear left. Midway across the Bulkley River bridge, reset your tripometer to 0.

For either approach above, now follow the directions below

0 km (0 mi)
Midway across the Bulkley River bridge in Telkwa. Proceed on paved Coalmine Road.

2 km (1.2 mi)
Pavement ends. Proceed southwest, roughly following the Telkwa River's south bank.

2.3 km (1.4 mi) and **3.5 km (2.2 mi)**
Stay straight.

6 km (3.7 mi)
Bear right.

7.2 km (4.5 mi)
Cross a creek, then bear right at the fork.

9.7 km (6 mi)
Go left at the junction onto unsigned Telkwa River FS road.

13.2 km (8.2 mi)
Continue on the main road for the official Telkwa River camp-ground. Turn here onto a narrow, overgrown spur for an **overnight pullout**—inaccessible by big RVs. It's secluded and quiet, 300 meters off the main road. The river is visible and audible. This pullout and the next are superior to the nearby official campground.

13.5 km (8.4 mi)
Continue on the main road for the official Telkwa River camp-ground. Turn right here onto a narrow, overgrown spur leading 30 meters to an **overnight pullout** beneath a cliff. Inaccessible by big RVs, it has room for only one vehicle. Though the nearby river is not visible and the bank is rugged, the site is secluded and quiet.

14.7 km (9.1 mi)
Cross a bridge. Continue 100 meters, then turn right for Telkwa River campground. It's below the bridge, next to the main road, and thoroughly trashed.

TELKWA RIVER RECREATION SITE #1
Overnight / Moderate
3 tables, 1 drive-in campsite
Too small for motorhomes and trailers

(2) DENNIS LAKE

0 km (0 mi)
Starting on King Street (one street southeast of Main), heading southwest from Hwy 16 in Smithers. Set your tripometer to 0.

0.7 km (0.4 mi)
Turn left onto Railway Avenue, following ski-area signs.

2.5 km (1.6 mi)
Cross railroad tracks.

4.7 km (2.9 mi)
Pavement ends.

6.2 km (3.8 mi)
Stay straight, continuing uphill.

7.4 km (4.6 mi)
Bear right.

11.3 km (7 mi)
Stay straight on the main road, passing the turnoff to the cross-country ski area.

16 km (10 mi)
Turn left for Dennis Lake campground. Right leads to the ski area, where the Crater Lake / Hudson Bay Mountain trail begins.

19.3 km (12 mi)
Stay straight.

21.8 km (13.5 mi)
Bear left on McDonell Lake FS road.

24.1 km (14.9 mi)
Cross a bridged creekbed.

26 km (16.1 mi)
Turn right for Silvern Lakes trailhead.

26.9 km (16.7 mi)
Cross the Silvern Creek bridge.

29.5 km (18.3 mi)
Turn left for Dennis Lake campground. It's 0.8 km (0.5 km) off the main road. The rough, descending spur is passable in a 2WD car.

DENNIS LAKE RECREATION SITE #2
Destination / Moderate
2 tables, 4 tent pads, good boat launch.
Inaccessible by motorhomes and trailers

(3) TWIN FALLS

0 km (0 mi)
At the junction of Hwy 16 and Toronto Street, in Smithers, heading northwest on Hwy 16. (There's a Taco Bell and KFC at this junction, as well as the last traffic lights before leaving town.) Set your tripometer to 0.

2.8 km (1.7 mi)
Bear left at the Y-junction onto Lake Kathlyn Road. Immediately after, stay on the main road where Proctor forks left.

4.2 km (2.6 mi)
Ascend left on unsigned Kathlyn Road, toward the mountains. Beach Road continues straight. (Already you can see Kathlyn Glacier. The trail ascends just left of it.)

5.1 km (3.2 mi)
Go left on Glacier Gulch Road.

6.8 km (4.2 mi)
Stay straight on pavement and keep ascending. Davidson Road (dirt) forks right.

6.9 km (4.3 mi)
Pavement ends. Proceed straight on the better dirt road.

9.3 km (5.8 mi)
Arrive at Twin Falls day-use area and unofficial campground.

TWIN FALLS RECREATION SITE #3
Destination / Easy
2 tables, Glacier Gulch hiking trail
Accessible by small motorhomes and trailers

Twin Falls

(4a) TALTZEN LAKE

If you're heading northwest on Hwy 16 from Smithers

0 km (0 mi)
At the junction of Hwy 16 and Toronto Street, in Smithers. (There's a Taco Bell and KFC at this junction, as well as the last traffic lights before leaving town.) Set your tripometer to 0.

21.5 km (13.3 mi)
Cross Trout Creek bridge.

23.6 km (14.6 mi)
Turn left (west) onto Kitsequecla Road. Reset your tripometer to 0.

If you're heading southeast on Hwy 16 from Moricetown

0 km (0 mi)
At the paved Moricetown Canyon overlook—worth stopping to see. Set your tripometer to 0.

5.8 km (3.6 mi)
Pass the north end of Kitsequecla Road.

7.3 km (4.5 mi)
Turn right (west) onto the south end of Kitsequecla Road. Reset your tripometer to 0.

For either approach above, now follow the directions below

0 km (0 mi)
Starting on Kitsequecla Road.

0.7 km (0.4 mi)
Turn left onto Kitsequecla Lake Road.

9.6 km (6 mi)
Stay right on the main road.

13.7 km (8.5 mi)
Stay left on the main road.

14 km (8.7 mi)
Pass Taltzen Lake.

14.4 km (8.9 mi)
Turn left and descend to reach Taltzen Lake campground in 200 meters. The lake is tiny but beautiful. See photo on page 3.

TALTZEN LAKE RECREATION SITE #4
Weekend / Easy
Elev: 700 m (2296 ft) / Lake: 10.6 ha
4 tables
Inaccessible by large motorhomes and trailers

(4b) KITSEQUECLA LAKE

Follow directions to Taltzen Lake, but instead of descending left, turn right onto the ascending spur road. Set your tripometer to 0.

0 km 0 mi
Starting northwest on the spur road directly across from the Taltzen Lake turnoff. Ascend through lush forest on this narrow, rough road.

2.7 km (1.7 mi)
Turn left for Kitsequecla Lake campground. (Rocky Ridge Chalets are right.) The final 450 meters descend a rutted, narrow road. If dry, it's passable in a 2WD car. The mountain setting is scenic, but you'll find only 2 drive-in campsites. The other 2 are walk-in tents sites, 20 meters from road's end.

KITSEQUECLA LAKE RECREATION SITE #5
Weekend / Moderate (due to rough access)
Elev: 732 m (2400 ft) / Lake: 1.7 km (1.1 mi) long, 70.6 ha
4 tables, rough boat launch, dock
Inaccessible by motorhomes and trailers

Kitsequecla Lake

BABINE LAKE ROAD

Babine Lake Road departs Hwy 16 southeast of Smithers. It heads east, around the back side of Babine Mountain Recreation Area. There, hikers can aim their boots at Mt. Hyland or Mt. Cronin. Babine Lake Road also leads to campgrounds at unattractive Chapman Lake and pretty Doris Lake. Drive 72 km (44.6 mi) from the highway and you'll reach superior Bear Island campground, on Babine Lake, just north of Granisle. The lake is huge: 46,500 hectares. Nearly 160 km (100 mi) long, it's B.C.'s longest natural lake. Its width varies from 1.6 km (1 mi) to 7.5 km (4.7 mi). But it's more impressive on a map than in reality. The low hills ringing the shore do not sustain interest.

If you're heading northwest on Hwy 16 from Telkwa

From Telkwa, at the turnoff for Tyhee Lake Provincial Park, continue northwest 7.7 km (4.8 mi). Turn right (east) onto paved Babine Lake Road. Set your tripometer to 0.

If you're heading southeast on Hwy 16 from Smithers

From Smithers, at the junction of Main Street and Hwy 16, drive southeast 6.5 km (4 mi). Turn left (east) onto paved Babine Lake Road. Set your tripometer to 0.

For either approach above, now follow the directions below

0 km (0 mi)
Starting on Babine Lake Road (labeled Eckman Road on some maps).

16.5 km (10.2 mi)
Pavement ends. Proceed on the wide, smooth, dirt road.

19 km (11.8 mi)
Bear right where Old Babine Road forks left.

20.3 km (12.6 mi)
Pass Dome Mtn. trailhead on the right.

31.6 km (19.6 mi)
Pass Little Joe Creek trailhead on the left.

39.2 km (24.3 mi)
Reach a junction. Turn left (north) onto Upper Fulton FS road for campgrounds at Chapman and Morin lakes. Continue right (northeast) for campgrounds on Doris and Babine lakes.

0 km (0 mi)
Starting north on Upper Fulton FS road.

2.2 km (1.4 mi)
Turn right and descend to reach Chapman Lake campground 100 meters.

CHAPMAN LAKE RECREATION SITE #6
Overnight / Moderate
Elev: 785 m (2575 ft) / Lake: 7.2 km (4.5 mi) long, 670 ha
2 tables in a large clearing
Inaccessible by large motorhomes and trailers

~

Continuing northwest, passing the turnoff to Chapman Lake campground.

2.8 km (1.7 mi)
Pass an **overnight pullout** on the lakeshore. It's a treed, grassy, secluded site for one vehicle only.

13.2 km (8.2 mi)
Cross a bridge over a small creek.

14 km (8.7 mi)
Turn left to reach Morin Lake campground in 200 meters. It's a confined area on a 21-hectare lake.

MORIN LAKE RECREATION SITE #7
Overnight / Moderate
2 tables, broken dock
Inaccessible by large motorhomes and trailers

Continuing northeast from the 39.2-km (24.3-mi) junction on Babine Lake Road, passing the turnoff to Chapman and Morin lakes campgrounds.

39.7 km (24.6 mi)
Bear left on the main road.

40.5 km (25.1 mi)
Cross a bridge at Chapman Lake's south end.

42.4 km (26.3 mi)
Stay straight on the main road.

47.4 km (29.4 mi)
Reach a major, signed junction. Set your tripometer to 0 whether turning or continuing. Turn left (north) for campgrounds on Tanglechain and Doris lakes. Continue straight (east) for Babine Lake and Granisle.

0 km (0 mi)
Turning left (north) at the 47.4-km (29.4-mi) junction on Babine Lake Road.

The Gift of Trees

Aside from the axe, trees receive nothing from most people.
Yet what trees offer us is abundant and profound.
Shelter. Beauty. Wisdom.

Though often silent, they are not mute.
Their tall, graceful shapes speak eloquently
  of pride, poise, and patience.
Bending in the wind, they whisper: "Give freely of yourself."
To be aware of the bearing and voice of trees is to find peace.

A tree is without pretense. Never screams for attention.
It simply becomes more of itself, in harmony with the universe.
And always, even in storm , drought or fire,
  it retains a deep serenity.

Reaching into the earth and sky, a tree secures and sustains itself.
Roots and limbs are also the tentacles of its mind,
  seeking to grasp the infinite.
With an open heart, try to sense a glisten of a tree's consciousness.
You might feel that we are not necessarily the highest form of life.

2.6 km (1.6 mi)
Go straight for Doris Lake campground and cross a bridged creek. Turn right, onto a narrow, severely potholed spur to reach Tanglechain Lake campground in 0.5 km (0.3 mi). It's passable in a 2WD car except when muddy.

TANGLECHAIN LAKE RECREATION SITE #19
Weekend / Difficult
Elev: 820 m (2690 ft) / Lake: 1.6 km (1 mi) long, 100 ha
2 tables
Inaccessible by motorhomes and 5th-wheels

3.8 km (2.4 mi)
Turn left for Doris Lake campground.

DORIS LAKE RECREATION SITE #20
Weekend / Difficult (due only to distance)
Elev: 860 m (2820 ft) / Lake: 1.7 km (1.1 mi) long, 107 ha
4 tables, 3 campsites, boat launch
Accessible by motorhomes and 5th-wheels

Continuing straight (east) from the 47.4-km (29.4-mi) junction on Babine Lake Road, passing the turnoff to Tanglechain and Doris lakes campgrounds. Set your tripometer to 0.

0 km (0 mi)
Starting on Granisle Cutoff FS road (very rough), heading east to Babine Lake.

17.5 km (10.9 mi)
Begin descending to Babine Lake.

24.4 km (15.1 mi)
Reach a T-junction with Granisle Hwy, on Babine Lake's southwest shore. Set your tripometer to 0 before turning either way. Turn right (southeast) for Bear Island campground, Granisle, and Hwy 16. Turn left (northwest) to quickly reach the camping area near road's end.

Turning left at the 24.4-km (15.1-mi) T-junction on Granisle Cutoff FS road, heading northwest on Granisle Hwy, along Babine Lake. Set your tripometer to 0.

0 km (0 mi)
Starting northwest on Granisle Hwy (unpaved at this end), along Babine Lake.

8.5 km (5.3 mi)
Pass a large clearing on the right that serves as an **unofficial camping area** on Babine Lake. It's not pretty (a mine is visible across the lake), feels exposed, and has only a small, stony beach. But it's easily accessible by motorhomes and 5th-wheels and has an excellent boat launch. If you're camping in an RV and spending your days on the water, it's an acceptable weekend campsite.

8.7 km (5.4 mi)
Reach road's end and the industrial ferry across Babine Lake. Proceed straight to enter Old Fort campground— closed in 1998. To ask about its current status, call Morice Forest Service District: (250) 845-6200.

OLD FORT RECREATION SITE #18
Weekend / Moderate
7 tables, boat launch
Accessible by large motorhomes and 5th-wheels

Turning right at the 24.4-km (15.1-mi) T-junction on Granisle Cutoff FS road, heading southeast on Granisle Hwy, along Babine Lake. Set your tripometer to 0.

0 km (0 mi)
Starting southeast on Granisle Hwy (unpaved at this end), along Babine Lake.

0.6 km (0.4 mi)
Turn left (at the bottom of a hill) for Bear Island campground.

Descend to reach the campground in 200 meters. It's a lush area, beneath big cottonwoods. The first clearing is ringed by 5 tables. Turn right to reach 3 more campsites and 6 tables.

BEAR ISLAND RECREATION SITE #17
Weekend / Moderate
Elev: 710 m (2330 ft) / Lake: 155 km (96 mi)long, 46,500 ha
11 tables, 8 campsites, small dock, boat launch
Inaccessible by large motorhomes and 5th-wheels

Continuing southeast on Granisle Hwy, along Babine Lake, passing the turnoff to Bear Island campground.

4.4 km (2.7 mi)
Pavement resumes.

5.4 km (3.3 mi)
Reach the Visitor Info Center in Granisle, opposite the school-yard. Reset your tripometer to 0.

Continuing south on Granisle Hwy, from the Visitor Info Center in Granisle. Reset your tripometer to 0.

0 km (0 mi)
At the Visitor Info Centre in **Granisle**, heading south on Granisle Hwy, above the southwest shore of Babine Lake.

10 km (6.2 mi)
Pass the turnoff for Topley Landing on the left.

19.5 km (12.1 mi)
Turn right for Paul Lake campground. Continue straight for Topley, on Hwy 16.

> **0 km (0 mi)**
> Starting west on a rough, dirt road, heading for Paul Lake.
>
> **0.7 km (0.4 mi)**
> A deep water bar (ditch) crosses the road here.
>
> **4 km (2.5 mi)**
> Continue straight across a bigger road.
>
> **7.7 km (4.8 mi)**
> Turn left.
>
> **8.1 km (5 mi)**
> Arrive at Paul Lake campground. The lake is small, secluded, ringed by scrawny trees.

PAUL LAKE RECREATION SITE #16
Weekend / Difficult
6 tables
Inaccessible by large motorhomes and trailers

Continuing south on Granisle Hwy, passing the turnoff to Paul Lake campground.

49.4 km (30.6 mi)
Reach Topley, on Hwy 16. Turn left (southeast) for Burns Lake. Turn right (west) for Houston.

GRANISLE HWY TO BABINE LAKE

Granisle Hwy departs Hwy 16 at Topley, between Burns Lake and Houston. It offers easy, paved access north to the southwest shore of gigantic Babine Lake. But there are few campgrounds along Granisle Hwy, and the scenery is unremarkable. The best reason to drive this way is to quickly reach Bear Island campground. If you go, it's possible to proceed east, past Babine Mountain Recreation Area, to Smithers.

0 km (0 mi)
Starting north on Granisle Hwy (initially called Topley Landing Road), signed for Granisle and the Lakes District.

30 km (18.6 mi)
Turn left (west) for **Paul Lake campground**; read further directions on page 313.

49.4 km (30.6 mi)
Pass the Visitor Info Centre in Granisle, opposite the schoolyard. Proceed northwest.

50.4 km (31.2 mi)
Pavement ends.

54.2 km (33.6 mi)
Turn right for **Bear Island campground**; read further directions on page 312.

54.8 km (34 mi)
Reach a junction. Stay straight (northwest) to proceed along Babine Lake and quickly reach the camping area near road's end. Turn left (west) onto Granisle Cutoff FS road (following page 311 directions in reverse from the 24.4-km point) to pass Babine Mountain Recreation Area en route to Smithers.

63.3 km (39.2 mi)
Pass a large clearing on the right that serves as an **unofficial camping area** on Babine Lake. Read page 311 for description.

63.5 km (39.4 mi)
Reach road's end and the industrial ferry across Babine Lake. Proceed straight to enter **Old Fort campground**—closed in 1998. Read page 312 for description.

NEAR NEW HAZELTON

Suskwa River and Keynton Lake campgrounds, both near New Hazelton, are small, well maintained, secluded, and in pretty settings. They're not spectacular, but even this is an advantage: they don't attract and hold crowds. If either is vacant when you arrive, you're assured of a lovely, soothing night in the bush. Free-camping in B.C. occasionally gets better than this, but not often.

Suskwa River campground is on a grassy riverbank clearing, deep in a forested River Valley, east of New Hazelton, near the Babine Range. A few giant cottonwood trees add a touch of grandeur. Summers are less buggy here than at most lakes. Though accessible by motorhomes and 5th-wheels, Suskwa is too small to comfortably accommodate them.

Suskwa River campground

Also called Bell Lake, Keynton Lake is just big enough to be worth launching a canoe on. A few campsites are in a clearing on the shore. The view is north to the Kispiox Range. Keynton is accessible by small motorhomes and trailers, but you'll need a strong engine for the steep ascents. The smooth, scenic access road is west of New Hazelton, along the Skeena River. If you enjoy the drive in, continue it on the way out. When you leave, turn right at the 22.6-km (14-mi) junction. Proceed southwest through the hills to intersect Hwy 37 just north of Kitwanga. The distance to pavement is about the same as retracing your approach.

If you're heading northwest on Hwy 16 from Smithers

For Suskwa River, set your tripometer to 0 at the paved Moricetown Canyon overlook (worth stopping to see) northwest of Smithers. Continue 25 km (15.5 mi), then turn right (north) onto Suskwa FS road. It's near the crest of a hill, just before a cement guard rail. Reset your tripometer to 0.

For Keynton Lake, drive to New Hazelton, then turn right (north) off Hwy 16. Proceed 6 km (3.7 mi) to Old Hazelton. At the junction by the store and gas station, turn right onto Kispiox Valley Road. Set your tripometer to 0 and read the directions at the bottom of page 317.

If you're heading northeast on Hwy 16, from its junction with Hwy 37

For Keynton Lake, drive to New Hazelton, then turn left (north) off Hwy 16. Proceed 6 km (3.7 mi) to Old Hazelton. At the junction by the store and gas station, turn right onto Kispiox Valley Road. Set your tripometer to 0 and read the directions at the bottom of page 317.

For Suskwa River, drive through New Hazelton. Shortly beyond, set your tripometer to 0 as you start descending near the turnoff for Ross Lake Provincial Park. Continue 8.5 km (5.3 mi) southeast, then turn left (north) onto Suskwa FS road. It's just after a cement guard rail, before another descent. Reset your tripometer to 0.

For SUSKWA RIVER, now follow the directions below

0 km (0 mi)
Starting on Suskwa FS road, heading north from Hwy 16.

1.7 km (1.1 mi)
Immediately after crossing the Bulkley River bridge, stay straight (northeast) for Suskwa River campground. A spur forks right here, leading 200 meters to an excellent **unofficial campsite** on the river—accessible by small motorhomes and trailers.

4.5 km (2.8 mi)
Continue straight at the junction. There's a public phone here.

5.2 km (3.2 mi) and **6.1 km (3.8 mi)**
Stay straight on the main road.

14.8 km (9.2 mi)
Cross the Suskwa River bridge.

14.9 km (9.2 mi)
Just past the bridge, turn left onto Itzul West FS road.

15.5 km (9.6 mi)
Pass a small **unofficial campsite** on the left, beside the river.

17 km (10.5 mi)
Turn left for Suskwa River campground, before the main road ascends steeply around a slope. Arrive in 1.1 km (0.7 mi).

SUSKWA RIVER RECREATION SITE #1
Weekend / Moderate
4 tables on a grassy riverbank clearing
Too small for motorhomes and 5th-wheels

For KEYNTON LAKE, now follow the directions below

0 km (0 mi)
Starting on Kispiox Valley Road, in Old Hazelton.

3.8 km (2.4 mi)
Pass an **overnight pullout** on the left, visible from the road.

5.1 km (3.2 mi)
Cross the Kispiox River bridge and bear left.

5.9 km (3.7 mi)
Turn left onto the dirt road, initially ascending steeply.

7.6 km (4.7 mi)
Bear left on the main road—generally level to 15 km (9.3 mi).
Roche de Boule is soon visible southwest.

20 km (12.4 mi)
Pass towering cottonwoods.

22.6 km (14 mi)
Cross a small bridge, then turn right and ascend.

24.2 km (15 mi)
Go right at the fork.

Kispiox River

25.1 km (15.6 mi)
Turn left and ascend steeply.

25.6 km (15.9 mi)
Reach the first site at Keynton Lake campground. The lake is just ahead.

KEYNTON LAKE RECREATION SITE #6
Weekend / Moderate
Elev: 396 m (1300 ft) / Lake: 1.5 km (0.9 mi) long, 60 ha
6 tables in lakeshore clearing, 2 secluded campsites
dock, good boat launch
Accessible by small motorhomes and trailers

KISPIOX VALLEY

Driving the Kispiox Valley is a backroad alternative to Hwy 37. But the scenery's no better. Heading northwest, you'll wind through low, rolling mountains, eventually intersecting Hwy 37 just south of Swan Lake. The road is fairly straight and flat for about 83 km (51.5 mi), but expect a tortuous final 20 km (12 mi). Though you'll see the Kispiox River a few times, it won't be your constant companion. Clearcuts are glaringly visible up-valley.

Continuing north up the Cassiar Highway? Kispiox Valley will add little to the journey. But if the Kispiox is your destination, you can certainly enjoy camping here. The best campground is Upper Kispiox, 41 km (24 mi) from Old Hazelton. Little Fish Lake, at 68 km (42 mi), is also pleasant. In July, the roadside near Little Fish is brilliant scarlet thanks to flourishing, head-high elderberry bushes. The other Kispiox lakes are disappointing, and the campgrounds are stingy.

If you're heading northwest on Hwy 16 from Smithers

Drive to New Hazelton, then turn right (north) off Hwy 16. Proceed 6 km (3.7 mi) to Old Hazelton. At the junction by the store and gas station, turn right onto Kispiox Valley Road. Set your tripometer to 0.

If you're heading northeast on Hwy 16 from Terrace

Drive to New Hazelton, then turn left (north) off Hwy 16. Proceed 6 km (3.7 mi) to Old Hazelton. At the junction by the store and gas station, turn right onto Kispiox Valley Road. Set your tripometer to 0.

For either approach above, now follow the directions below

0 km (0 mi)
Starting on Kispiox Valley Road, in Old Hazelton.

3.8 km (2.4 mi)
Pass an **overnight pullout** on the left, visible from the road.

5.1 km (3.2 mi)
Cross the Kispiox River bridge and bear left.

5.9 km (3.7 mi)
Bear right on the main, paved road.

14 km (8.7 mi)
In the town of Kispiox, bear right on the main road. Pavement ends, but sealcoat continues briefly.

26.3 km (16.3 mi)
For better campsites, bear right (north) on Kispiox Valley Road and stay on the east side of Kispiox River. For tiny Pentz Lake, turn left onto Poplar Park Road.

> **0 km (0 mi)**
> Starting on Poplar Park Road, heading for Pentz Lake. Immediately cross a bridge to the west side of Kispiox River.
>
> **7 km (4.3 mi)**
> Stay right for Pentz Lake. Helen Lake FS road forks left, leading to Mitten Main FS road and Mitten Lake (described on page 322).
>
> **12.3 km (7.6 mi)**
> Arrive at **Pentz Lake overnight pullout**. The day-use area parking lot has room for 2 vehicles. The ground is too uneven for a tent. Two docks invite swimmers to jump in.

Continuing north on Kispiox Valley Road, passing the turnoff to Pentz Lake.

29 km (18 mi)
Stay left on the main road.

41.2 km (25.5 mi)
Turn left for Upper Kispiox campground.

> It's 0.5 km (0.3 mi) off the main road, just above the broad, slow river. A short path leads to the riverbank. The campsites are in a grassy clearing ringed by trees.

UPPER KISPIOX RECREATION SITE #2
Weekend / Moderate
4 tables, more campsites
Accessible by motorhomes and 5th-wheels

Continuing northwest on Kispiox Valley Road, passing the turnoff to Upper Kispiox campground.

42.2 km (26.2 mi)
Stay straight where Murder Main FS road forks right.

45.8 km (28.4 mi)
Bear left where Kuldo FS road forks right.

47.5 km (29.5 mi)
Stay straight where Cancel Main FS road forks right.

54.5 km (33.8 mi)
Turn right for Elizabeth Lake campground, just before the KM 54 sign.

> Continue parallel to the reedy, lily-edged lake for 1.2 km (0.7 mi) to arrive at the quiet campground.

ELIZABETH LAKE RECREATION SITE #10
Weekend / Difficult (due only to distance)
Elev: 360 m (1180 ft) / Lake: 1.5 km (0.9 mi) long, 43 ha
3 tables, 2 lakeshore campsites, rough boat launch
Accessible by motorhomes and 5th-wheels

Continuing northwest on Kispiox Valley Road, passing the turnoff to Elizabeth Lake campground.

58.7 km (36.4 mi)
Reach a junction. Turn left (southwest) onto Mitten FS road to cross the Kispiox River bridge and continue to Hwy 37. Right (northwest) reaches **Sweetin River Recreation Site #3** in about 18 km (11.2 mi). It's a small campground on the east bank.

59.5 km (36.9 mi)
Pass an **overnight pullout** on the left. Well off the main road, it's a good basecamp for fishing the nearby Kispiox River.

61.7 km (38.3 mi)
Reach a junction with Mitten Main FS road. Set your tripometer to 0 before turning either way. Right continues to Hwy 37. Left / southeast leads 1.9 km (1.2 mi) to **Mitten Lake Recreation Site #5.** You'll find a single roadside table beside the 45-hectare lake.

Turning right (northwest) onto Mitten Main FS road, from the 61.7-km (38.3-mi) junction on Mitten FS road. Set your tripometer to 0.

0 km (0 mi)
Starting northwest on Mitten Main FS road. Stay on the main road, ignoring several forks.

6 km (3.7 mi)
Turn right for Little Fish Lake campground.

Little Fish Lake

The scenery at this small lake is pleasant, but not wondrous. The campsites are reasonably secluded among large spruce trees.

LITTLE FISH LAKE RECREATION SITE #4
Weekend / Difficult (due only to distance)
Elev: 420 m (1378 ft) / Lake: 0.6 km (0.4 mi) long, 4.4 ha
3 tables, rough boat launch
Accessible by motorhomes and 5th-wheels

Continuing northwest on Mitten Main FS road, passing the turnoff to Little Fish campground.

9.7 km (6 mi)
Bear left, uphill.

11.3 km (7 mi)
Bear right, passing a lake on your left. Proceed through regrowing clearcuts.

14.7 km (9.1 mi)
See if the lone, giant cottonwood tree is still standing.

17.6 km (10.9 mi)
Bear right and cross a bridge over Beaver Lodge Creek.

17.9 km (11.2 mi)
Stay right on the main road and cross another bridged creek.

18.7 km (11.6 mi)
Bear left. Stay on the main road at minor forks ahead.

25 km (15.5 mi)
Slow down. The road narrows and descends through sharp turns.

35 km (21.7 mi)
The road widens and improves.

41 km (25.4 mi)
Reach Hwy 37. Left leads southeast to Kitwanga and Hwy 16. Right leads northwest to Meziadin Junction.

BETWEEN KITWANGA AND TERRACE

The scientific method of measuring a highway's relative scenic merit is to count the number of cars with camera lenses poking out their windows. Between Kitwanga and Terrace, you'll see plenty—but only if you're not staring at the scenery yourself. Here it's the massive Hazelton Mountains that distract travellers, especially where the road curves around the north end of the sharp, craggy, Seven Sisters peaks. Rough spur roads lead to several trailheads. If you're a hiker, pick up a guidebook in Smithers or Terrace. There are no free campgrounds here, but there are several overnight pullouts and rest areas where you can feel relaxed about sleeping in your vehicle. And the excellent free campgrounds around Terrace and New Hazelton are not far.

If you're heading southwest on Hwy 16 from Kitwanga

0 km (0 mi)
At the junction of Hwys 37 and 16 in Kitwanga.

One of the Seven Sisters, from Hwy 16, northeast of Terrace

8.3 km (5.1 mi)
Pass an **overnight pullout** on the left—inaccessible by
motorhomes and trailers. It's just after crossing Boulder Creek
bridge. A rocky road goes beneath the bridge. Loud rapids help
muffle traffic noise. The view is excellent, southeast to the Seven
Sisters peaks.

9 km (5.6 mi)
Pass a **rest area.**

40.8 km (25.3 mi)
Pass a **rest area.**

41.9 km (26 mi)
Turn right for an **overnight pullout** down by the river.

60.8 km (37.7 mi)
Pass a **rest area.**

76.6 km (47.5 mi)
Pass the turnoff for Kleanza Creek Provincial Park on the left.
Soon cross the Kleanza Creek bridge.

85.6 km (53.1 mi)
Turn right, just after the Zymoetz River bridge, for an **overnight pullout** by the Skeena River.

87.8 km (54.4 mi)
Reach Terrace.

91.6 km (56.8 mi)
Pass the turnoff for Lakelse Lake Provincial Park on the left. For directions to the free campground on Lakelse River, read page 329.

If you're heading northeast on Hwy 16 from Terrace

0 km (0 mi)
At the turnoff for Lakelse Lake Provincial Park, on the right.

6 km (3.7 mi)
Turn left, just before the Zymoetz River bridge, for an **overnight pullout** by the Skeena River.

30.8 km (19.1 mi)
Pass a **rest area**.

49.7 km (30.8 mi)
Turn left for an **overnight pullout** down by the river.

50.8 km (31.5 mi)
Pass a **rest area**.

82.6 km (51.2 mi)
Pass a **rest area.**

83.3 km (51.6 mi)
Pass an **overnight pullout** on the right—inaccessible by motorhomes and trailers. It's just before crossing Boulder Creek bridge. A rocky road goes beneath the bridge. Loud rapids help muffle traffic noise. The view is excellent, southeast to the Seven Sisters peaks.

91.6 km (56.8 mi)
Reach the junction of Hwys 16 and 37 in Kitwanga.

NEAR TERRACE

Terrace is a camper-friendly city. Five nearby campgrounds range from good to excellent: (1) Exstew River, 37 km (23 mi) west, on the way to Prince Rupert. Even big RVs can settle in here. (2) Lakelse River, 18.2 km (11.3 mi) southwest. The secluded sites are in a magnificent grove of giant cedars and spruce. But don't try to squeeze your Winnebago between them. (3) Pine Lakes, 11.6 km (7.2 mi) north. This is a good basecamp for hikers. A trail circles the lakes, and Sleeping Beauty Mtn. trailhead is close. (4) Red Sand Lake, 26.6 km (16.5 mi) north. Perhaps the best FS campground in central B.C. It's spacious, laid out like a provincial park, has plenty of lakeshore sites and ample room for titanic RVs. The long, sandy beach is ideal for swimming, Frisbee tossing, or novel reading. But Red Sand Lake is no secret. It's extremely popular and therefore a candidate for a per-night camping fee. (5) Hart Farm, 27.6 km (17.1 mi) north, at the south end of Kitsumkalum (Kalum) Lake. The lake is way bigger than Red Sand, but the campground is much smaller and more intimate.

(1) EXSTEW RIVER

If you're heading northeast on Hwy 16 from Prince Rupert

In about 101 km (62.6 mi), look for the Exstew River bridge. Midway across, set your tripometer to 0. In another 0.6 km (0.4 mi), turn left (northwest) onto Exstew River road (unsigned). Reset your tripometer to 0. (If you reach a railroad overpass, you're too far.)

If you're heading southwest on Hwy 16 from Terrace

0 km (0 mi)
Midway across the Kitsumkalum (Kalum) River bridge, just past the sawmill and Canadian Tire store, on the west edge of Terrace.

20.2 km (12.5 mi)
Pass the turnoff for Shames Mtn. Ski Area on the right.

27.6 km (17.1 mi)
Cross a railroad overpass.

28 km (17.4 mi)
Proceed straight for Exstew campground. Turn left (south) to reach an **overnight pullout** in 0.4 km (0.25 mi). Park on level gravel to the right. You're on an old, abandoned highway here. Though close to railroad tracks and Hwy 16, it's convenient for big RVs.

31 km (19.2 mi)
Turn right (northwest) onto Exstew River road (unsigned). It's just after a yellow sign warning of logging trucks. Reset your tripometer to 0.

For either approach above, now follow the directions below

0 km (0 mi)
Starting on Exstew River road (unsigned), heading northwest from Hwy 16. Immediately cross railroad tracks.

5.8 km (3.6 mi)
Stay straight on the main road.

6.2 km (3.8 mi)
Turn left for Exstew River campground.

Exstew River

EXSTEW RIVER RECREATION SITE #7
Weekend / Easy (unless high water impedes access)
8 tables, more campsites
Accessible by motorhomes and 5th-wheels

(2) LAKELSE RIVER

From downtown Terrace, follow Lakelse Road across the Skeena River via the old, wood bridge (parallel to the railroad bridge). Just beyond the bridge, turn right (south) onto Queensway Drive. Go under the newer Hwy 16 bridge and set your tripometer to 0.

From Hwy 16, heading west into Terrace, turn left (south) onto Queensway Drive just after the junction with Hwy 37 (Lakelse Road, leading south to Kitimat). Set your tripometer to 0.

From Hwy 16, heading east through Terrace, cross two bridges over the Skeena River. After the second bridge, turn left (north) at the junction of Hwy 16 and Hwy 37 (Lakelse Road, leading south to Kitimat). Just before the old bridge over the Skeena, turn sharply left (south) onto Queensway Drive. Go under the newer Hwy 16 bridge and set your tripometer to 0.

0 km (0 mi)
Starting on Queensway Drive, heading south, initially following the Skeena River.

5.2 km (3.2 mi)
Turn right onto Old Remo Road.

6.4 km (4 mi)
Bear right, staying on pavement. Cross railroad tracks.

7.3 km (4.5 mi) and **12.5 km (7.8 mi)**
Stay right.

13.4 km (8.3 mi)
At the bottom of a small hill, turn left onto a rough, dirt road.

Giant-cedar grove at Lakelse River campground

15.2 km (9.4 mi)
Stay straight.

17 km (10.5 mi)
The road is beside the Skeena River.

18.2 km (11.3 mi)
Turn left (before the bridge) to enter Lakelse River campground.

LAKELSE RIVER RECREATION SITE #6
Destination / Easy
10 tables, secluded sites among giant trees, provincial-park quality
Inaccessible by motorhomes and 5th-wheels

(3) PINE LAKES (4) RED SAND LAKE (5) HART FARM

0 km (0 mi)
Midway across the Kitsumkalum (Kalum) River bridge, just past the sawmill and Canadian Tire store, at the west edge of Terrace, heading west on Hwy 16.

0.3 km (0.2 mi)
Turn right (north) onto unsigned West Kalum FS road, identified by a gas station on the northwest corner. Pavement ends immediately.

6.4 km (4 mi)
Stay straight on the main road.

9 km (5.6 mi)
Stay straight for Pine Lakes, Red Sand Lake and Hart Farm campgrounds. (Left leads about 9.6 km / 6 mi to Sleeping Beauty Mtn. trailhead. The final 1 km / 0.6 mi requires 4WD. The trail ends at subalpine meadows and lakes in 2.5 km / 1.6 mi, but experienced hikers can continue up to alpine ridges.)

11.6 km (7.2 mi)
Stay straight for Red Sand Lake and Hart Farm campgrounds. Turn left for Pine Lakes campground.

Pine Lakes campground comprises two small camping areas, each with a couple tables. Reach the first area in about 200 meters, on the right. The second is about 600 meters farther. There's only one Pine Lake, but the shore is serpentine, so there appears to be a couple lakes. A 6-km (3.7-mi) trail circles the lake.

Spacious beach at Red Sand Lake

PINE LAKES RECREATION SITE #9
Weekend / Easy
Elev: 213 m (700 ft) / Lake: 27.5 ha
5 tables, hiking trail
Inaccessible by motorhomes and trailers

Continuing northwest on West Kalum FS road, passing the turnoff to Pine Lakes campground.

15.7 km (9.7 mi), 21.5 km (13.3 mi) and **24.7 km (15.3 mi)**
Bear right at these forks.

26.6 km (16.5 mi)
Stay straight for Hart Farm campground. Turn right to reach provincial-park quality Red Sand Lake campground in 1 km (0.6 mi).

The sandy lake is unique in this region. The mountain views are stirring. Most campsites are near the shore. Short, easy hiking trails begin here.

RED SAND LAKE RECREATION SITE #10
Destination / Easy
Elev: 37 m (121 ft) / Lake: 38.5 ha
14 tables, 2 sites for disabled campers, cooking shelter
Accessible by motorhomes and 5th-wheels

Continuing north on West Kalum FS road, passing the turnoff to Red Sand Lake campground.

27.6 (17.1 mi)
Turn right to quickly reach Hart Farm campground on Kitsumkalum (Kalum) Lake.

HART FARM RECREATION SITE #11
Weekend / Easy
Elev: 122 m (400 ft) / Lake: 10.5 km (6.5 mi) long, 1905 ha
5 tables
Accessible by small motorhomes and trailers

BETWEEN TERRACE AND KITIMAT

Chist Creek campground is just off Hwy 37, about midway between Terrace and Kitimat. The rock face here attracts climbers. If you're a climber, or comfortable hanging out with them, give Chist a try. But most campers should head elsewhere. Chist is tiny—just two tables. Leave it for climbers. They need a convenient, free campground, close to good rock, where they won't be squeezed out by RVs.

Though less convenient than Chist, Enso campground is bigger and more accommodating. For most people, it's the best of the two options in this area. The campsites are in a stand of ancient trees, at the confluence of Wedeene River and Raley Creek, on the river's west bank. Railroad tracks are across the river, so the train is audible, but it doesn't run frequently.

CHIST CREEK

If you're heading south on Hwy 37 from Terrace

From the junction of Hwys 16 and 37, at the east edge of Terrace, drive Hwy 37 south (toward Kitimat) about 27 km (16.7 mi). Turn left (east) onto North Kitimat Mainline FS road (across from Onion Lake Ski Trails parking area).

If you're heading north on Hwy 37 from Kitimat

From the north edge of Kitimat, drive Hwy 37 north (toward Terrace) about 29 km (18 mi). Turn right (east) onto North Kitimat Mainline FS road (across from Onion Lake Ski Trails parking area).

For either approach above, now follow the directions below

Drive North Kitimat Mainline FS road about 2 km (1.2 mi), then bear left onto a smaller road. Soon reach a junction and bear left on another small road. About 1 km (0.6 mi) farther, reach yet another junction and turn right. Chist Creek campground is about 0.6 km (0.4 mi) farther, on the left.

CHIST CREEK RECREATION SITE #5
Weekend / Easy
2 tables, rock climbing area
Too small for motorhomes and trailers

ENSO

From the junction of Hwys 16 and 37, at the east edge of Terrace, drive Hwy 37 south about 56 km (34.7 mi) to Kitimat. Proceed through downtown, over the bridge, into the industrial area. Where the main road bears left, go straight to quickly intersect Enterprise Avenue. Turn right (north) onto Enterprise, which becomes Wedeene Mainline FS road. Follow it north about 14.5 km (9 mi). Enso campground is on the right, just before Raley Creek bridge.

ENSO RECREATION SITE #2
Weekend / Easy
6 tables
Accessible by small motorhomes and trailers

BETWEEN KITWANGA AND MEZIADIN JUNCTION

Considering the pupil-dilating scenery nearby (around Smithers, between Kitwanga and Terrace, and especially between Meziadin Junction and Stewart), it's surprising how mundane the drive is between Kitwanga and Meziadin Junction. The 20 km (12 mi) south of the junction, where the mountains begin to swell, might pique your interest, but that's it. Fortunately, the total distance is just 159 km (99 mi).

Heading northwest on Hwy 37 from Kitwanga, you'll drive 83 km (51.5 mi) before reaching the first free campground, at Bonus Lake. It's beside the highway, within earshot of passing vehicles. Just north of it is the turnoff for Derrick Lake, accessed via 5.7 km (3.5 mi) of rough road. Derrick won't rouse your inner photographer, but at least it's quiet. About 112 km (69.4 mi) northwest of Kitwanga is the turnoff for Jigsaw Lake campground, which is 10 km (6.2 mi) off Hwy 37, en route to Swan Lake / Upper Kispiox River Provincial Park. Your other options along Hwy 37 are the rest areas and overnight pullouts indicated in the directions below. If it's late and you just need a place to sleep, they'll suffice. Directions southeast on Hwy 37 from Meziadin Junction begin on page 339.

If you're heading northwest on Hwy 37 from Kitwanga

0 km (0 mi)
At the junction of Hwys 16 and 37 in Kitwanga.

31.3 km (19.4 mi)
Pass a **rest area** on the right. Lots of trees and the noise of Moonlit Creek make it attractive for an overnight stay.

32.7 km (20.3 mi)
Pass a big **overnight pullout** on the left, where you can park back in the trees.

69.5 km (43.1 mi)
Pass a huge **overnight pullout** on the right, where you can park back in the trees, well off the highway.

79 km (49 mi)
Proceed on Hwy 37 for Meziadin Junction. Turn right (north) onto Mitten FS road (following page 324 directions in reverse) to reach Kispiox Valley, and eventually New Hazelton on Hwy 16.

83 km (51.5 mi)
Turn left for Bonus Lake campground. It's only 100 meters off the highway. The lake is ringed by lily pads.

BONUS LAKE RECREATION SITE #13
Overnight / Easy
Elev: 350 m (1148 ft) / Lake: 1 ha
3 tables, dock
Accessible by motorhomes and 5th-wheels

Continuing northwest on Hwy 37, passing the turnoff to Bonus Lake campground.

85 km (52.7 mi)
Turn right for Derrick Lake campground.

0 km (0 mi)
Starting north on the spur road to Derrick Lake. The road is severely potholed, but it's not steep or narrow. With patience, small motorhomes can manage it. But turning a trailer around in the campground is dicey.

1.7 km (1.1 mi)
Bear left.

3 km (1.9 mi)
The road widens here, creating an **overnight pullout**.

Wander at Will

Camp Free *is full of detailed directions. Ignore them occasionally. Because when you follow a prescribed route and arrive at an intended destination, you've merely completed a trip. Only an encounter with the unexpected elevates a journey to an adventure.*

So wander. Zigzag. Spiral through B.C.'s vast network of backroads. It will lead you to surprising places, people and experiences that you'd miss by always adhering to ours or anyone else's directions.

Most of us are severely constrained by the expectations of employer, family and society. We need more time free of restrictions, to exuberantly follow our instincts rather than trudge the rut to expected results. When is that possible? More often than we realize. And certainly on a camping trip. Just veer down an unknown road.

Wandering revives youthful curiosity and a carefree spirit. It releases innate creativity. Ironically, it returns the wanderer to exactly where she or he belongs: the present moment. Right here. Right now. A place our future-oriented culture does not honor. Yet the only place anyone can truly, fully live.

5.7 km (3.5 mi)
Reach Derrick Lake campground. The first campsite is unlevel, on the right, above the lake. Proceed 200 meters for better sites with tables and views.

DERRICK LAKE RECREATION SITE #14
Overnight / Moderate
Elev: 442 m (1450 ft) / Lake: 56 ha
3 campsites, boat launch, dock
Inaccessible by large motorhomes and 5th-wheels

Continuing northwest on Hwy 37, passing the turnoff to Derrick Lake campground.

97 km (60 mi)
Pass a large **overnight pullout** on the left—convenient for big RVs—at the northeast end of Sideslip Lake.

102 km (63.2 mi)
Pass an **overnight pullout** on the left.

112 km (69.4 mi)
Turn right (north) onto Brown Bear FS road to reach Jigsaw Lake campground in about 10 km (6.2 mi) on the right. Swan Lake / Upper Kispiox River Provincial Park is about 15 minutes beyond Jigsaw.

JIGSAW LAKE RECREATION SITE #13
Weekend / Easy
Elev: 357 m (1170 ft) / Lake: 2.8 km (1.7 mi) long, 84 ha
4 tables, cartop boat launch
Accessible by small motorhomes and trailers

~

116 km (71.9 mi)
Pass a long, paved **overnight pullout** on the left.

145.2 km (90 mi)
Pass a **rest area** on the right, just before crossing the Nass River bridge.

155.7 km (96.5 mi)
Pass an **overnight pullout** with a view of mountains and glaciers.

158.2 km (98.1 mi)
Pass the turnoff to Meziadin Lake Provincial Park.

159.5 km (99 mi)
Reach **Meziadin Junction**. Hwy 37 continues right (north). Turn left (west) to drive scenically spectacular Hwy 37A to Stewart. A few minutes beyond Stewart is Hyder, Alaska. From there, a stunning road climbs beside the Salmon Glacier—fifth largest in the world.

~

If you're heading southeast on Hwy 37
from Meziadin Junction

0 km (0 mi)
At Meziadin Junction, where Hwy 37A intersects Hwy 37. Turn right to follow Hwy 37 southeast to Kitwanga and Hwy 16.

3.8 km (2.4 mi)
Pass an **overnight pullout** with a view of mountains and glaciers.

14.3 km (8.9 mi)
Pass a **rest area** on the left, just after crossing the Nass River bridge.

43.6 km (27 mi)
Pass a long, paved **overnight pullout** on the right.

47.7 km (29.6 mi)
Turn left (north) onto Brown Bear FS road to reach **Jigsaw Lake campground** in about 10 km (6.2 mi) on the right. Read details on page 338. Swan Lake / Upper Kispiox River Provincial Park is about 15 minutes beyond Jigsaw.

57.7 km (35.8 mi)
Pass an **overnight pullout** on the right.

62.6 km (38.8 mi)
Pass a large **overnight pullout** on the right—convenient for big RVs—at the northeast end of Sideslip Lake.

69.5 km (43.1 mi)
Enter Kispiox Forest District.

74.5 km (46.2 mi)
Proceed on Hwy 37 for Kitwanga. Turn left (following directions at the bottom of page 337) for **Derrick Lake campground**.

76.5 km (47.4 mi)
Turn right for **Bonus Lake campground**, described on page 336.

80.6 km (50 mi)
Proceed on Hwy 37 for Kitwanga. Turn left (north) onto Mitten FS road (following page 324 directions in reverse) to reach Kispiox Valley, and eventually New Hazelton on Hwy 16.

81.6 km (50.6 mi)
Cross a bridge over Cranberry River. Pass a **rest area** on the left. Just beyond the bridge is an **overnight pullout**.

90 km (55.8 mi)
Pass a huge **overnight pullout** on the left, where you can park back in the trees, well off the highway.

95 km (59 mi)
Cross another bridge over Cranberry River.

127 km (78.7 mi)
Pass a big **overnight pullout** on the right, where you can park back in the trees.

128.4 km (79.6 mi)
Pass a **rest area** on the left. Lots of trees and the noise of Moonlit Creek make it attractive for an overnight stay.

159.5 km (99 mi)
Reach the junction of Hwys 37 and 16 in Kitwanga.

HWY 37A TO STEWART

The scenery along Hwy 37A, between Meziadin Junction and Stewart, is the kind you see in coffee table books filled with extraordinary photographs. It's comparable to the Icefields Parkway through Banff and Jasper national parks. Here, 37 hanging glaciers are visible along a 60-km (37-mi) stretch of pavement. Where the water isn't frozen, it's gushing. Waterfalls plunge into this sheer-sided canyon like kids at a swimming-pool party. All manner of greenery thrives in the wet, coastal climate. Devils Club slurps up the moisture, growing taller than NBA players, sprouting leaves 45 cm (18 inches) wide.

The Bear Glacier

More magnificence awaits you just beyond the quaint, fiord town of Stewart. Continue around the corner into Hyder, Alaska, then follow the road north for about 40 minutes to see the Salmon Glacier—fifth largest in the world—and mountains galore. If the weather is socked-in when you arrive, wait a day or two for the clouds to lift; the scenery is definitely worth it.

Another reason to visit Hyder is to watch grizzly bears congregate at nearby Fish Creek, where they feed on salmon. Between mid-July and October, plan to spend several hours—7 to 10 in the morning, or 7 to 10 at night—waiting for the bears to appear. They almost always do. Observing them at close range in the wild is a unique and thrilling experience. US Forest Service rangers stand by to make sure people behave appropriately.

Its remote location and abrupt end at the sea ensure that Hwy 37A is never busy. So the overnight pullouts along the way are likely to be very quiet after dark. But use them with discretion and respect. Look for and obey any new signs prohibiting "overnight parking." Pull in late, drive away early, and leave no trace of your stay.

0 km (0 mi)
At Meziadin Junction, departing Hwy 37, heading west on Hwy 37A.

3 km (1.9 mi)
Pass an **overnight pullout** on the left, overlooking Meziadin Lake.

12.3 km (7.6 mi)
Cross the Surprise Creek bridge.

13 km (8.1 mi)
Pass a large **overnight pullout** on the left.

17 km (10.5 mi)
Turn right for an **overnight pullout.** It's across from three hanging glaciers.

19.2 km (11.9 mi)
Turn left for a comfortable **overnight pullout** beneath cotton-woods.

19.9 km (15 mi)
Cross the Little Entrance Creek bridge.

23.8 km (14.8 mi)
Proceed on Hwy 37A for Stewart. The paved road left (south) leads 0.6 km (0.4 mi) to Bear Glacier viewpoint and **rest area**. It should serve as a quiet **overnight pullout**.

25.4 km (15.7 mi)
Bear Glacier is visible nearby to the left.

29.7 km (18.4 mi)
Pass an **overnight pullout** on the left, just before the Cullen Creek bridge. A short road departs the highway, allowing you to park back in the trees. The roaring creek muffles highway noise. Terrific waterfalls are visible south.

33.6 km (20.8 mi)
Pass an **overnight pullout** on the right, beside a loud creek.

39.7 km (24.6 mi)
Pass a pullout with a litter barrel on the right.

44 km (27.3 mi)
Pass a round **overnight pullout** on the left, just before the highway swings right.

48 km (29.8 mi)
Pass a **rest area**.

48.4 km (30 mi)
Turn left for Clements Lake campground.

> Reach a T-junction in 100 meters. Turn left, then proceed straight. Arrive at the lake 1.2 km (0.7 mi) from the highway. Impressive waterfalls are visible across the lake. There's a lone campsite about 30 meters past the first group of tables.

CLEMENTS LAKE RECREATION SITE #5
Destination / Easy
Lake: 3 km (1.9 mi) long, 17 ha
4 tables grouped at the lakeshore, floating dock
Accessible by small motorhomes and trailers

Continuing southwest on Hwy 37A, passing the turnoff to Clements Lake campground.

59.6 km (37 mi)
Arrive in Stewart, on the north end of Portland Canal, next to the international border at Hyder, Alaska. Continue north of Hyder to see the Salmon Glacier.

Forest Service Offices

For information about camping in a particular Forest Service district, speak to the Recreation Specialist. Instead of calling the office direct, dial **Inquiry B.C.** (660-2421 from within Vancouver, 1-800-663-7867 from elsewhere in B.C.). Tell them the name of the office and the phone number. They'll connect you at no charge.

For on-line information about B.C. Forest Service regions, go to **www.for.gov.bc.ca/mof/regdis.htm**

The **hours of operation** for most Forest Service offices are Monday through Friday, 8 a.m. to 12 noon, and 1 p.m. to 4:30 p.m.

CARIBOO FOREST REGION
ph: (250) 398-4345
fax: (250) 398-4380
200 - 640 Borland Street
Williams Lake, BC V2G 4T1

Chilcotin Forest District
ph: (250) 394-4700
Stum Lake Road, Box 65
Alexis Creek, BC V0L 1A0

Horsefly Forest District
ph: (250) 620-3200
Boswell Street, Box 69
Horsefly, BC V0L 1L0

Quesnel Forest District
ph: (250) 992-4400
322 Johnston Avenue
Quesnel, BC V2J 3M5

100 Mile House Forest District
ph: (250) 395-7800
300 S. Cariboo Hwy 97
Box 129
100 Mile House, BC V0K 2E0

Williams Lake Forest District
ph: (250) 305-2001
925 North 2nd Avenue
Williams Lake, BC V2G 4P7

KAMLOOPS FOREST REGION
ph: (250) 828-4131
fax: (250) 828-4154
515 Columbia Street
Kamloops, BC V2C 2T7

Clearwater Forest District
ph: (250) 587-6700
Box 4501, RR#2
Yellowhead Hwy 5
Clearwater, BC V0E 1N0

Kamloops Forest District
ph: (250) 371-6500
1265 Dalhousie Drive
Kamloops, BC V2C 5Z5

PRINCE GEORGE FOREST REGION
ph: (250) 565-6100
fax: (250) 565-6671
5th floor, 1011 Fourth Ave.
Prince George, BC V2L 3H9

Prince George Forest District
ph: (250) 565-7100
2000 S. Ospika Blvd.
Prince George, BC V2N 4W5

Robson Valley Forest District
ph: (250) 569-3700
Bag 5000, One Cicada
(just off Hwy 16)
McBride, BC V0J 2C0

Vanderhoof Forest District
ph: (250) 567-6363
Box 190, 1522 Hwy 16 East
Vanderhoof, BC V0J 3A0

PRINCE RUPERT
FOREST REGION
ph: (250) 847-7500
fax: (250) 847-7217
Bag 5000, 3726 Alfred Ave.
Smithers, BC V0J 2N0

Bulkley / Cassiar
Forest District
ph: (250) 847-6300
Bag 6000, 3333 Tatlow Road
Smithers, BC V0J 2N0

Kalum Forest District
ph: (250) 638-5100
Room 200, 5220 Keith Ave.
Terrace, BC V8G 1L1

Kispiox Forest District
ph: (250) 842-7600
Box 215
Hazelton, BC V0J 1Y0

Lakes Forest District
ph: (250) 692-2200
Box 269
Burns Lake, BC V0J 1E0

Morice Forest District
ph: (250) 845-6200
Bag 2000, 2430 Butler Ave.
Houston, BC V0J 1Z0

North Coast Forest District
ph: (250) 624-7460
125 Market Place
Prince Rupert, BC V8J 1B9

B.C. Road Map

Modestly priced B.C. road maps are available at Tourist Info Centres in towns and cities throughout the province.

If you live out-of-province, the SuperNatural British Columbia tourism office will mail you a British Columbia Road Map and Parks Guide. Call 1-800-663-6000 from anywhere in North America, (604) 387-1742 from overseas, or (604) 663-6000 from within Vancouver.

REPORT ALL FOREST FIRES TO 1-800-663-5555

B.C. Stands for Best Camping

Camp Free authors Kathy and Craig have free-camped all their lives. While she was still a baby in diapers, Kathy's parents took her camping most weekends. Her earliest memories are of her mother cooking dinner under a tarp draped from the back of the family's pickup while her father listened to the rain. As a boy, Craig was obsessed with fly fishing. He backpacked to remote trout streams, until he realized the joy of hiking and camping is an end in itself and all that fishing gear was just slowing him down. Together, Kathy and Craig have perfected the art of free-camping. Their camping adventures have taken them throughout North America, Europe, Australia and New Zealand. They've driven all kinds of vehicles to all kinds of places in all kinds of weather. It hasn't always been idyllic.

One time, they pitched their tent at midnight on the grounds of an English country manor. They were hitchhiking. Unable to afford a hotel, they had only two choices. A fenced, tussocky paddock crowded with cattle? Or the manor lawn? They knocked at the imposing door to ask permission, but nobody appeared. So they set their travel alarm for 5:30 a.m. The next morning, they packed quickly, left unseen, and walked three kilometers to Stonehenge. They watched it emerge from the fog at sunrise, before anyone else arrived.

Asleep under the stars beside a creek near Payson, Arizona, they were startled by a gang of Hell's Angels in the middle of the night. The bikers roared in, only a few feet from the Copelands' heads, but otherwise weren't a problem. Until morning. After the bikers took off, Craig discovered they'd dumped one of their buddies. He was bleeding and out cold.

Again in Europe, they were exploring the Cairngorm Mountains of northern Scotland. This time they were driving Freida — a rusty, old, Bedford Beagle they'd bought for $93 US. As always, they wanted to camp free. A sign on a dirt road caught their eye: Forestry Personnel Only. They risked it, but couldn't find even a tiny pullout. So they started turning around, backed into a ditch and became hopelessly mired. "Guess this is where we say goodbye to Freida," Craig said. But before they could load their backpacks and start hiking, a forestry official drove up in his truck. After a light rebuke, he towed them out. Feeling lucky, the Copelands splurged that night and paid for a campsite at the national park.

On the Oregon side of the Columbia River Gorge is the Eagle Creek Trail, which the Copelands had just finished hiking. It was so late they decided to camp in their car at the trailhead, but later wished they hadn't. A light directly over their heads woke them up. Another hiker? A policeman? A thief? A murderer? They laid there wondering, zipped into their sleeping bags, stuffed into the back of their car, their hearts pounding with adrenalin. "He's going to break into the car," Kathy whispered. Craig roared like a bear. They saw the flashlight bob away into the night. It was probably a teenage burglar, but they didn't wait to find out. They raced onto the highway and, still dazed, approached the bridge over the Columbia. With Kathy still in her bag and Craig in his underwear, they presented an interesting site to the matron in the toll booth. They eventually fell asleep, parked on a residential street in North Bonneville, Washington.

Now you can understand why Kathy and Craig are thrilled to live in British Columbia. They say it offers the easiest, most enjoyable, most abundant free camping of anyplace they've ever traveled.

Home

Universe is home for earth.
Air is home for wind.
Tree is home for bird.
Meadow is home for flower.
Dirt is home for seed.
Water is home for whale.
Mind is home for idea.
Fire is home for warmth.
Tent is home for camper.
Earth is home for all.

Other Titles from Voice in the Wilderness Press

Look for these and other titles by the Copelands in outdoor shops and book stores. You can also order them by sending a cheque to Voice in the Wilderness Press, P.O. Box 71, Riondel, B.C. V0B 2B0 Canada. The prices include shipping and GST. If you order more than one book or cassette, deduct the following amount from the total cost: CDN $3 for shipments within Canada, or US $3 to the States. Allow 2-3 weeks for delivery in Canada, 3-4 weeks to the States.

Camp Free in B.C. Volume I.........CDN $17   US $15
   ISBN 0-9698016-7-x   1999, 3rd edition, 320 pages
Precise directions to over 260 official, free campgrounds accessible by two-wheel drive. Covers southern BC, from Trans-Canada Hwy 1 to the U.S. border, from Vancouver Island to the Rocky Mountains.

Bears Beware! Warning Calls You Can
   Make to Avoid an Encounter...CDN $11   US $ 9
   ISBN 0-9698016-5-3   1998 edition, audio cassette
30 minutes that could save your life. Find out why pepper spray, talking, and bells are not enough. Follow these strategies for safer hiking and camping in bear country.

Premier Hikes™
   in British Columbia.........CDN $18   US $15.50
   ISBN 0-9698016-8-8   June 1999, 208 pages,
   16 pages of colour photos
The only book you need to enjoy the most spectacular, exhilarating hikes in the province. Discerning trail reviews help you choose your trip. Detailed route descriptions keep you on the path. Includes dayhikes and backpack trips. Covers the Coast Mountains, Cascades, Selkirks, Kootenays, and Rockies.

PREMIER   **OUTSTANDING**   **WORTHWHILE**   **DON'T DO**

The Don't Waste Your Time® *hiking guidebook series rates and reviews trails to help you get the most from magnificent wilderness areas. Route descriptions are comprehensive. Includes shoulder-season trips for more hiking opportunities. Offers wisdom on mountain travel.*

Don't Waste Your Time®
in the BC Coast Mountains........CDN $17 US $15
ISBN 0-9698016-3-7   1997 edition, 288 pages
72 hikes in southwest BC, including Vancouver's
North Shore mountains, Garibaldi Provincial Park,
and the Whistler-Pemberton region.

Don't Waste Your Time®
in the Canadian Rockies........CDN $19 US $16
ISBN 0-9698016-4-5   1998 edition, 392 pages
125 hikes in Banff, Jasper, Kootenay, Yoho and Waterton
national parks, plus Mt. Robson and Mt. Assiniboine
provincial parks.

Don't Waste Your Time®
in the North Cascades...............CDN $20 US $17
ISBN 0-89997-182-2   1996 edition, 364 pages
110 hikes in southern BC and northern Washington.
Includes North Cascades National Park, Mt. Baker and
Glacier Peak wilderness areas, plus BC's Manning and
Cathedral parks.

Don't Waste Your Time®
in the West Kootenays.........CDN $19 US $16
ISBN 0-9698016-9-6   April 2000, approx. 320 pages
70 hikes in the Selkirk and Purcell ranges of southeast
B.C. Includes Valhalla, Kokanee Glacier, Goat Range,
West Arm, and St. Mary's Alpine parks.

Receive Your
Camping Pass By Mail

To camp free at B.C. Forest Service campgrounds, you must have an annual Camping Pass. A single-night Camping Pass is also available. Camping Passes are sold at sporting goods stores and government agent offices. All funds raised by Camping Pass sales go directly to campground maintenance.

To receive your Camping Pass by mail: (1) Determine the cost by reading the form on the next page. After 2001, call to confirm current prices. (2) Make your cheque payable to the Minister of Finance. (3) Complete the form on the next page and send it, along with your cheque, to **Government Agent, 250 — 455 Columbia Street, Kamloops, B.C. V2C 6K4**. Phone: (250) 828-4540. Fax: (250) 828-4542.

The annual Camping Pass allows an individual, family, or group of six, to enjoy more than 1400 Forest Service campgrounds throughout B.C., at no additional charge, for one year beginning in spring. Only about 30 of the busiest campgrounds charge a modest per-night fee to cover increased maintenance. At those, the annual Camping Pass entitles you to a 50% discount. A single-night Camping Pass allows an individual, family, or group of six, to camp one night at a Forest Service campground.

Forest Service campgrounds operate on a first-come, first-served basis. Your Camping Pass does not guarantee access to campgrounds or reserve campsites. The Forest Service asks that you limit your stay at any one campground to 14 days.

Camping Pass
Registration Form

Name _____

Street Address _____

City _____ Province / State _____

Postal / Zip Code _____ Phone _____

B.C. Forest Service Regions I'll be visiting

☐ Cariboo   ☐ Kamloops

☐ Nelson   ☐ Prince George

☐ Prince Rupert   ☐ Vancouver

My accompanying cheque for CDN $_____ covers the
total amount for the following:

☐ Annual Camping Pass — $27

☐ Seniors Annual Camping Pass — $22

☐ Single Night Camping Pass — $8

☐ Two Single-Night Camping Passes — $16

Mail this form with your cheque to
**Government Agent, 250 — 455 Columbia Street,
Kamloops, B.C. V2C 6K4.**

Camping Pass
Registration Form

Name _____

Street Address _____

City _____ Province / State _____

Postal / Zip Code _____ Phone _____

B.C. Forest Service Regions I'll be visiting

☐ Cariboo   ☐ Kamloops

☐ Nelson   ☐ Prince George

☐ Prince Rupert   ☐ Vancouver

My accompanying cheque for CDN $_____ covers the
total amount for the following:

☐ Annual Camping Pass — $27

☐ Seniors Annual Camping Pass — $22

☐ Single Night Camping Pass — $8

☐ Two Single-Night Camping Passes — $16

Mail this form with your cheque to
**Government Agent, 250 — 455 Columbia Street,
Kamloops, B.C. V2C 6K4.**

Camping Pass
Registration Form

Name

Street Address

City   Province / State

Postal / Zip Code   Phone

B.C. Forest Service Regions I'll be visiting

☐ Cariboo   ☐ Kamloops

☐ Nelson   ☐ Prince George

☐ Prince Rupert   ☐ Vancouver

My accompanying cheque for CDN $_____ covers the total amount for the following:

☐ Annual Camping Pass — $27

☐ Seniors Annual Camping Pass — $22

☐ Single Night Camping Pass — $8

☐ Two Single-Night Camping Passes — $16

Mail this form with your cheque to
**Government Agent, 250 — 455 Columbia Street,
Kamloops, B.C. V2C 6K4.**